Law, Environmental Illness and Medical Uncertainty

We've seen it before, with asbestos-related disease, leukaemia clusters and lung cancer caused by cigarettes. There tends to be a lag between the emergence of environmental risks and chemical injuries, and their recognition and therapeutic treatment by medicine and the law. *Law, Environmental Illness and Medical Uncertainty* examines how our society governs new health concerns as they emerge, and the barriers that face new and uncertain theories seeking recognition in the law.

In this book, Tarryn Phillips focuses her investigation on the struggle over the controversial condition multiple chemical sensitivities, or MCS (also known as environmental illness). Presenting nine case studies where workers sought compensation for MCS from their multinational employers, she captures a nuanced portrait of their embittered, unequal battles over the scientific, legal and insurance paradigms for understanding toxic risk, environmental illness and the regulation of industry. It draws on three years of fieldwork in Australia, including interview data with lay people and sympathetic and sceptical experts, participant observation in the courtroom and textual analysis of official reports.

The book gives a unique, ethnographic insight into the governance of risk and uncertainty within a neoliberal economy, medico-scientific controversies and courtroom dramas. It highlights how a sceptical approach towards emergent environmental concerns is encouraged within the current climate, and decision-makers face disincentives for taking a sympathetic approach. Compellingly written and easy to read, it should appeal widely to interested lay people, and students and scholars of science and technology studies, medical anthropology, sociology of health and illness, and critical legal studies.

Tarryn Phillips is an Anthropologist and Lecturer in Legal Studies at La Trobe University. Her interests lie in social justice and inequality. She researches how medicine and the law manage uncertainty, define and punish deviance and interact with their socio-cultural surroundings.

Social Justice

Series editors: Sarah Lamble, *Birkbeck College, University of London, UK*, Davina Cooper, *University of Kent, UK*, and Sarah Keenan, *Birkbeck College, University of London, UK*

Social Justice is a new, theoretically engaged, interdisciplinary series exploring the changing values, politics and institutional forms through which claims for equality, democracy and liberation are expressed, manifested and fought over in the contemporary world. The series addresses a range of contexts from transnational political fora, to nation-state and regional controversies, to small-scale social experiments. At its heart is a concern, and inter-disciplinary engagement with, the present and future politics of power, as constituted through territory, gender, sexuality, ethnicity, economics, ecology and culture.

Foregrounding struggle, imagined alternatives and the embedding of new norms, *Social Justice* critically explores how change is wrought through law and governance, everyday social and bodily practices, dissident knowledges, and movements for citizenship, belonging, and reinvented community.

Titles in this series:

Intersectionality and Beyond
Law, Power and the Politics of Location
Emily Grabham, Davina Cooper, Jane Krishnadas and Didi Herman (eds.), 2009

Regulating Sexuality
Legal Consciousness in Lesbian and Gay Lives
Rosie Harding, 2010

Rights of Passage
Sidewalks and the Regulation of Public Flow
Nicholas Blomley, 2010

Anarchism and Sexuality
Jamie Heckert and Richard Cleminson (eds.), 2011

Queer Necropolitics
Jin Haritaworn, Adi Kuntsman, Silvia Posocco (eds.), 2014

After Legal Equality
Robert Leckey (ed.), 2014

Subversive Property
Law and the Production of Spaces of Belonging
Sarah Keenan, 2015

Chronotopes of Law
Jurisdiction, Scale and Governance
Mariana Valverde, 2015

Law, Environmental Illness and Medical Uncertainty
The contested governance of health
Tarryn Phillips 2015

Forthcoming:

Power, Politics and the Emotions
Impossible Governance?
Shona Hunter

Global Justice and Desire
Queering Economy
Nikita Dhawan, Antke Engel, Christoph H. E. Holzhey and Volker Woltersdorff (eds.)

Protest, Property and the Commons
Lucy Finchett-Maddock

Regulating Sex After Aids
Queer Risks and Contagion Politics
Neil Cobb

The Sexual Constitution of Political Authority
Aleardo Zanghellini

Law Unlimited
Margaret Davies

Law, Environmental Illness and Medical Uncertainty

The contested governance of health

Tarryn Phillips

Routledge
Taylor & Francis Group

LONDON AND NEW YORK

First published 2015
by Routledge
2 Park Square, Milton Park, Abingdon, Oxfordshire OX14 4RN

and by Routledge
711 Third Avenue, New York, NY 10017

First issued in paperback 2016

Routledge is an imprint of the Taylor & Francis Group, an informa business

British Library Cataloguing in Publication Data
A catalogue record for this book is available from the British Library.

Library of Congress Cataloging-in-Publication Data
A catalog record has been requested for this book.

ISBN 13: 978-1-138-24162-6 (pbk)
ISBN 13: 978-0-415-82856-7 (hbk)

Typeset in Garamond by
by FiSH Books Ltd, Enfield

Contents

List of figures and tables   viii
Abbreviations   ix
Acknowledgements   x
Preface   xii

1   Introducing the disease of uncertainty   1

2   Knowledge and power at the medico-legal interface   22

3   Risk entrepreneurialism: the social construction of toxicity
    and disease   46

4   The medico-legal illness narratives   75

5   Medical, legal and insurance reasoning in the governance
    of uncertainty   101

6   The deviance of sympathetic experts   120

7   Non-legal governance and epistemological possibilities   140

8   Neoliberalism, scepticism and toxic knowledge   152

    Conclusion: environmental illness and the role of the law   167

Notes   178
References   181
Index   197

Figures and tables

Figures

5.1   WorkCover 'First Medical Certificate'   107
5.2   Effect of legislative changes on workers' access to common
      law proceedings   110

Tables

4.1   Submissions from the worker and defence in *Ian Harvey v.
      Vox Australia*   91
5.1   Maximum percentages prescribed under the *Workers'
      Compensation and Rehabilitation Act* 1981   108

Abbreviations

ACOEM	American College of Occupational and Environmental Medicine
ACGIH	American College of Government and Industrial Hygienists
ACTA	Australian Chemical Trauma Alliance
AMA	Australian Medical Association
CFS	Chronic fatigue syndrome (aka ME)
DDT	Dichloro-diphenyl-trichloroethane
DIMDI	Deutschen Institut für Medizinische Dokumentation und Information
EMF	Electromagnetic fields
EPA	Environmental Protection Agency
ES	Electro-sensitivity
GP	General Practitioner
ICD	International Classification of Diseases
ME	Myalgic Encephalomyelitis [medical term for CFS]
MCS	Multiple Chemical Sensitivity
MP	Member of Parliament
MUPS	Medically unexplained physical symptoms
OHS	Occupational Health and Safety
PTSD	Post-traumatic stress disorder
QC	Queen's Counsel
RCT	Randomised control trial
RSI	Repetitive strain injury
TLV	Threshold Limit Value
WHO	World Health Organization
WPI	Whole person impairment
VOC	Volatile Organic Compound

Acknowledgements

Thanks firstly go to the many participants who offered their thoughts, memories, carefully compiled documents and friendship over the three years I conducted field work. I promised them confidentiality and the use of pseudonyms, however, I now regret that I cannot name them individually and thank them for their time, diligence and generosity. My sincere thanks go to the editors of the Social Justice series, Davina Cooper and Sarah Lamble for their exacting critique, incisive suggestions and patient support. This work is infinitely better because of the directions in which they suggested I take it. Thank you also to Rebekah Jenkins and Colin Perrin at Routledge for their friendly assistance.

Parts of Chapter Four are reprinted with kind permission from the publisher Elsevier, for the article 'Repressive authenticity in the quest for legitimacy: Surveillance and the contested illness lawsuit' in *Social Science and Medicine* (Vol 75, pp. 1762–1768) Copyright © 2012. Thanks to permission from the publisher, John Wiley and Sons, excerpts of Chapters 6 and 7 are reprinted from the article, 'Debating the legitimacy of a contested environmental illness: A case study of multiple chemical sensitivities (MCS)' (Vol 32, no. 7, pp. 1026–1040) Copyright © 2010. Parts of Chapters 6 and 7 are also reprinted with kind permission from the American Anthropology Association for the article, '"I never wanted to be a quack!": The professional deviance of plaintiff experts in contested illness lawsuits: The case of multiple chemical sensitivities (MCS)' in *Medical Anthropology Quarterly* (vol 24, no. 2, pp. 182–198) Copyright © 2010.

A very special mention to Beverley McNamara for giving me so much time and helpful advice as an anthropologist, a mentor, a friend and, at times when I needed it, a mum. I am also grateful to Martin Forsey and Sandy Toussaint for their thought-provoking recommendations with regards to my research. Thanks also to Joanna Moore for her help on the manuscript; she is an exceptional editor and a dear old friend. Philippa Chandler also offered comments on an earlier draft, came with me to Berlin, and shared many cups of coffee along the way. I am also grateful to my UWA and La Trobe friends and colleagues who have provided camaraderie, support and lively conversation over the past few years; an especially big thank you goes to Catie Gressier, Nicola Henry, Ray Madden, Nick Smith, Sue Davies, Evan Willis and Michael O'Keefe in this regard. Friends Raili Simojoki, Briar Stevens, Arthur Floret, Poh Lin Lee, Lise Cooper, Sara James, Jasmine-Kim Westendorf and Peter Woelert were also an important listening ear and source of insight and friendship over the last few years, and Jade Jontef was tireless, efficient and lovely in her research assistance. To Mum and Dad, for sharing their worldly curiosity and interest in medicine and the law; you've taught me so much. To Raajni and Navin, both born during this project, for keeping things in perspective, and always making me smile. And finally, my greatest debt of thanks go to Eddie Narain, my best friend, for *everything*. For his rare, thorough and constant engagement with my ideas, his critiques, patience, tolerance, time, love and, most of all, for his recommendation that I use pseudonyms like Dr Rupert Bupert and Professor Hymie Van Blymie. I am deeply grateful to all of these people for their support.

Preface

Jeff Carlson first heard of Multiple Chemical Sensitivities in 1990 when a woman approached him in desperation. She had seen a number of solicitors, none of whom had agreed to represent her, and seeking help from Jeff's small law firm was her last resort. Her husband suffered from sensitivity to a wide range of chemicals in everyday life, such as perfumes and household cleaning products. She believed his condition had developed after seventeen years of employment in the mineral sands industry, where he had used heavy industrial chemicals in a poorly ventilated workshop. He had been sent to a psychiatrist and prescribed shock treatment to the brain. Eventually, after experiencing severe mental deterioration and memory loss, he committed suicide. After a three year legal battle, Jeff succeeded in negotiating compensation for the widow, although the money did little to alleviate the loss she had suffered.

For nearly two decades thereafter, Jeff was approached by an increasing number of chemically sensitive people seeking compensation for often debilitating ill health. He developed a professional relationship with a number of medical experts who were concerned about an emerging phenomenon – the chemically sensitive worker. Jeff often worked for these clients on a no-win, no-fee basis. He succeeded in receiving compensation for a small number of them – in out-of-court settlements – yet the cases tended to be long, embittered and unsuccessful. The defendant insurance companies always engaged a number of local and international medical experts who rejected the workers' claims. Judicial officers tended to reason that there was insufficient evidence to suggest that the worker was exposed to chemicals at a toxic level. The workers' were usually declared depressed, paranoid or mentally unstable.

After fighting all the way to the Supreme Court of Western Australia for a spray painter with alleged lead and solvent poisoning, Jeff received the final decision in 2007. Two out of the three judges maintained that there was an inconclusive link between the chemicals the worker had been exposed to and his alleged symptoms. Since this case, which cost Jeff's firm approximately quarter of a million dollars, Jeff has closed down his business, no longer agrees to act on behalf of chemically injured litigants, and has lost his faith in the legal system. While working for Jeff as a clerical assistant during this case, I became intrigued by the MCS lawsuit, which later became the topic of my doctoral research. Over the next three years, I met many experts on the condition, one of whom was Professor Brian Sturt.

Brian is a clinical toxicologist who treats and assesses people for toxicological conditions. He sees the results of poisoning on a daily basis and is a widely renowned expert on chemical injuries. Over the course of his career he has seen an increasing number of people who present with sensitivities to everyday chemicals. He has noticed that these patients are often embroiled in litigation, and tend to harbour much anger towards their employer. In his experience, they usually do not return abnormal test results. Brian believes MCS is predominantly psychosomatic and he reassures his patients they are not poisoned. He is uncertain, however, whether it is caused by a psychological aversion to chemical odours, a compensation neurosis, a belief system perpetuated by supportive doctors, or perhaps a mixture of all three.

Insurance companies often engage Brian as an expert witness in chemical sensitivity compensation litigations. He has provided an opinion about most of the chemically sensitive workers that Jeff Carlson has represented, consistently rejecting that the workers suffer from a toxic injury. Brian is frustrated with solicitors like Jeff, who he believes perpetuate unfounded fears about chemicals and exacerbate the mental instability of the chemically sensitive. There are, however, those health providers who have an entirely different view of MCS, like Hannah Miller.

Hannah works at a small suburban psychology practice, where she treats and assesses people for a broad range of neurological problems. She was first introduced to MCS in the 1990s, when Jeff Carlson requested that she assess his client, who, in her opinion, developed neuro-toxic brain damage after working with an industrial chemical cleaning agent. Hannah has subsequently developed an international reputation for her expertise regarding chemical sensitivities. She believes workers with the condition are suffering from a genuine, physiological condition that can affect multiple organ systems, disable their everyday activities, damage their social relationships and even cause birth defects in their children.

Hannah has provided reports for almost all of Jeff's chemically sensitive clients. She and the sceptic, Brian Sturt, often discredit each other's expertise and diagnoses in medico-legal reports. Though Hannah receives kudos amongst the alternative community of people with environmental illness, scientists and medical experts internationally who believe MCS is toxogenic, or caused by chemicals, the mainstream medical community in Australia disagrees.

However, there has been support from the community for people with MCS, often harnessed by the media. Clinton Bracks, investigative journalist, was first introduced to MCS as he was sitting in his chief of staff's office. A hand-written letter sat on the desk, and, curious as ever, Clinton strained to read it. It was a desperate plea for help from a resident living beside a mine site in regional Western Australia named Kylanta. She was concerned about smoke that was billowing from the company's chimneystack and flowing to neighbouring townships. Residents and workers were falling ill and nearby livestock were allegedly dying. Clinton asked his chief of staff what he was going to do about the letter, and the chief said he would probably discard it. Accompanied by a photographer, Clinton visited the woman hours later and a personal interest story about her experience was printed on the front page of the newspaper the following day. For the next few years, Clinton worked on nothing else but investigative articles regarding Kylanta's activities. He introduced the concept of MCS into his articles gradually and systematically, until it became a frequent discussion point in newspaper articles and letters to the editor. He won a global journalism award for his environmental reporting on the affair.

Yet Kylanta's management consistently threatened Clinton's editor with legal action and, eventually, he was kindly asked to find another story to follow. He resigned, and the newspaper now rarely publishes negative material about Kylanta's operations and a massive expansion of Kylanta's operations has since been approved by the State Government.

Finally, Roger Harvey worked for Kylanta for over a decade but is now on a disability pension. He suffers from MCS and multiple sclerosis, and he feels the fumes from Kylanta's chimneystack are to blame for both conditions. With a group of similarly affected workers, he underwent a five year legal battle with Kylanta. Eventually the company conceded to a compensation payout, though never admitted liability. Roger feels the redress he received was inadequate as it did little to pay for his mortgage and children's education. Now that coverage of the issue has all but dried up, Roger feels let down by the medico-legal process, abandoned by the community and angry about the way his life has turned out.

These characters, along with many others introduced in the following chapters, are playing out an extraordinary and complex drama that is much more significant than a few workers' relatively small claims for compensation. The medico-legal dispute over MCS ties in with a broader debate about the legitimacy of environmental illnesses, the toxicity of our current lifestyle and how effectively our community deals with emergent and contested conditions.

Chapter 1

Introducing the disease
of uncertainty

In 1900, a London doctor's post-mortem of a local asbestos-factory worker found that asbestos fibres in the worker's lungs were probably responsible for causing his death (Merewether and Price 1930). However, because of its valuable strength and fire-proofing qualities, the manufacture and use of asbestos continued to grow throughout the next few decades, as did the number of early deaths of many of those exposed to the substance. While there was burgeoning concern about the dangers of asbestos from some sections of the medical and lay community, and some efforts at regulation, legal actions brought against asbestos companies tended to be lost by the workers or resolved in secret out-of-court settlements. It was not until the 1970s that landmark legal decisions favoured plaintiffs, asbestos companies were publicly found liable of knowingly placing workers at risk, and governments started to regulate asbestos manufacture and use more heavily, although regulatory approaches continue to vary around the globe.

Sufferers of asbestos-related conditions such as pulmonary fibrosis and mesothelioma are now widely accepted as having legitimate diseases in most parts of the world. Their conditions are now largely diagnosable, there are medical experts and law firms who specialize in such cases and there is strong legal precedent behind plaintiffs seeking compensation. However, the above history highlights that this was not always the case. Those who fell ill from asbestos in the first half of the twentieth century often faced medical dismissal, political disinterest and bitter, unsuccessful legal battles (Galanter 1994; Waldman 2011). We saw a similar story with lung cancer caused by cigarettes, where smokers and their sympathizers fought for decades – often against the legal establishment, insurance sector and medico-scientific sceptics – to have tobacco companies found liable for knowingly selling them addictive and harmful products. These cases demonstrate that there is often a lag between the emergence of a condition and its widespread recognition and effective response by medicine and the law.

The scientific controversy

In this book I examine how our society governs new illnesses as they arise. To do so, I focus on a condition that is currently unrecognized, medically unexplained and in a period of legal limbo: the controversial condition multiple chemical sensitivity, or MCS. Since the emergence of MCS in the late 1980s, the chemically sensitive and their supporters have been lobbying to convince doctors, scientists and the courts to recognize their condition. The manifestation of MCS is much less dramatic and measurable than the early deaths caused by asbestos and cigarette smoke. Its cause remains contested and the condition may never receive widespread legitimacy, or be considered as deserved or compensable as these other conditions. However, there are similarities between the way people with MCS are currently treated in the medico-legal field, and the way in which sufferers of asbestos-related disease and smokers experienced the period of uncertainty and contestation over the cause of their condition. MCS is thus a useful contemporary case study to examine what happens at the coalface when an uncertain, emergent condition arises.

MCS was first labelled in 1987 by an American occupational physician, Professor Mark Cullen, who identified that a number of his patients had started to develop an extraordinary sensitivity to everyday chemicals.[1] After long-term exposure to low levels of workplace toxins, Cullen's patients had started to react to a range of chemicals on a daily basis. Simply walking past perfume stores, recently painted walls and newly laid carpets would lead the workers to experience headaches, fainting, chronic fatigue, and behavioural changes. Cullen tentatively called the condition 'MCS', although it has since been variously renamed as 'environmental illness', 'idiopathic environmental intolerance', 'twentieth century disease' and 'chemical AIDS'. These titles reflect the diverse and often contradictory perspectives about the cause and legitimacy of the condition. (In this book, I predominantly use the term MCS, since it is the term most commonly used in the literature and in governmental documents – (Bartha *et al.* 1999). When I use the term 'environmental illness' I am referring more broadly to the range of contested conditions that allegedly have environmental causes.)

Although accurate data is difficult to collect, it is estimated that between two and six per cent of the population in industrialized countries suffer from a loss of tolerance to low-level, everyday chemical exposures (Caress and Steinemann 2003). For the chemically sensitive, exposure to chemicals affects their bodies in a very real and debilitating way and can impede them from maintaining employment, socializing with friends and family, and leading normal lives (see Dumit 2006; Kroll-Smith and Floyd 1997; Lipson 2004). However, the clinical medical profession is generally sceptical that toxins are responsible for MCS. The symptoms experienced after exposure are not outwardly visible or evidenced. The toxins alleged to be in the chemically reactive body are generally not apparent in pathological test results. The levels of air contaminants that are claimed to be causing the symptoms tend not to pose a significant problem for the rest of the population, and are usually insignificant according to international health and safety standards (although the accuracy of these standards is contested – Karmel 2008). So if the condition *is* toxogenic (chemically caused), physiological, and organic (organ function is affected), it would contradict the long-held biomedical assumption that if diseases exist, they should be evident and measurable in the body.

One view amongst sceptical medical researchers is that the chemically sensitive have a pre-existing condition of mental instability coupled with an anxiety about chemical substances. This means that whenever they detect an acrid odour, the smell triggers a psychosomatic reaction in the sufferer (e.g. Hausteiner *et al.* 2006; Staudenmayer 1999; Van Den Bergh *et al.* 2001). The sceptical experts I spoke to have suggested that a pop-cultural paranoia about chemicals is to blame, perhaps socially perpetuated through hype about 'bubble boys' and Hollywood films about corporate chemical conspiracies (see Winters *et al.* 2003). Others question whether MCS is iatrogenic, which means the illness is generated by doctors who hand down erroneous diagnoses and fuel their patients' belief in bogus conditions (Staudenmayer 1999).

Even some of the strongest sceptics hasten to add that the chemically sensitive are not malingerers and that the condition is no less legitimate for being psychosomatic (e.g. Staudenmayer 1999). Yet the chemically sensitive are not usually placated by this; for them, a psychosomatic diagnosis implies that they are 'crazy', or the condition is 'all in their head' (Dumit 2006; Ware 1992). A psychosomatic diagnosis also means they are deemed more culpable for their condition, can be disallowed insurance and compensation, refused medical assistance and even denied sympathy by friends and family. Legitimacy, then, means different things to different people in the MCS debate, but for the chemically sensitive it is inextricably linked to proof of a physiological basis.

The status of MCS in developing contexts is unknown. Almost all of the epidemiological and scientific research in English on MCS and its prevalence focuses on higher-income countries of the world, such as Canada, the US, Western European countries, Australia, New Zealand and Japan. There is little or no research on the condition in Africa, most parts of Asia, or South America. The chemically sensitive from these parts of the world – if they exist – are more or less silent on chatrooms, blogs and websites. There are several possible explanations for this global discrepancy. One explanation is that MCS may not be a significant health concern in these demographics. According to sceptics like Showalter (1997), hysteria is particularly contagious in populations in which news of potential risks and paranoia can be spread easily through self-help books, internet usage, newspapers, magazines and television talk-shows. According to this theory, populations in less affluent countries, if they are more focused on meeting immediate needs, may have less time and money to consume these media and the 'contagious ideas' they contain. Another possibility is that the symptoms of chemical sensitivity do exist in poorer parts of the world, but local research on MCS is scant and information on the diagnosis is lacking for both health providers and patients. This would tie in with a global trend in which only a fraction of the international budget for health expenditure and research funding is dedicated to problems that face lower-income countries (McCoy *et al.* 2009); moreover, funding priorities in these areas tend to be on more immediate – and fatal – concerns such as malaria and HIV AIDS.[2]

The controversy over MCS has some similarities to the publicity surrounding chronic fatigue syndrome, or CFS. CFS is characterized by a similar array of symptoms to MCS, including fatigue, myalgia (muscle pain) headaches, dizziness, gastro-intestinal problems and nausea. Both CFS and MCS are emergent, in the sense that despite volumes of research, very little about them is settled medically, legally, or popularly (Dumit 2006: 578). Indeed, along with other controversial conditions, such as Gulf War syndrome and fibromyalgia, MCS and CFS are increasingly recognized as a grouping of medically unexplained physical symptoms (Engel, Adkins and Cowan 2002). This phrase is a default way of categorizing people who currently defy medical explanation. When these unexplained symptoms are in existence, as the medical interactions in this book will emphasize, the provider–patient interaction can be a hostile battleground, since the patient's explanation for their condition and the expert's understanding of disease can be very discordant (Engel, Adkins and Cowan 2002).

Importantly, however, there is a minority of medical practitioners and scientists around the world who are sympathetic to the claims of the chemically sensitive. Often called clinical ecologists, these experts believe the condition is a genuine, organic condition that is triggered by toxic exposure (Ashford and Miller 1998; Colborne, Myers and Dumanoski 1996; Donohoe and Cullen 2007; Pall 2007; Winder 2002). According to them, chemically sensitive people suffer from a disorder that predominantly affects the nervous system – in particular the brain – although the exact causal mechanisms are still unclear (Donohoe 2005). It is suggested that certain individuals might have a genetic predisposition to react to chemicals at a lower threshold than the rest of the population (Ashford and Miller 1998: xiv). This explanation is reminiscent of the theory about the health impact of cigarettes: out of all long-term smokers only a percentage will contract lung cancer, which suggests that although there are other environmental variables at play, some have a genetic lower threshold for the substance. Despite cigarettes affecting people differentially, smoking is ultimately deemed harmful and manufacturers are considered negligent if they do not disclose information concerning the hazards of their product. Applying this theory to the MCS context, sympathetic experts believe that the condition's relation to chemicals should be better researched and more widely publicized, and the chemical industry held more accountable (see for example Ashford and Miller 1998).

However, despite this alternative view about the aetiology and nature of MCS, there is largely a default consensus in the orthodox medico-scientific community that the condition – and its advocates – should be treated with caution. Clinical ecology is a subfield of medicine that is often disowned by professional associations and even labelled 'quackery' by some (Huber 1991; see also Jasanoff 1995: 131–134). In fact, the position statements released by medical associations about MCS in the Anglo-American world have been sceptical and dismissive ever since the publication of Cullen's paper. Two American medical associations warn physicians 'not to treat patients "as if" the disease existed' (Kroll-Smith and Floyd 1997: 28). The American College of Occupational and Environmental Medicine released their position on the condition in 1999, which argued against the title MCS because it incorrectly implies the condition is toxogenic and related to the nervous system, where in its view, no such certainty exists (see ACOEM 1999). The ACOEM qualified that patients should be treated compassionately and not as malingerers, yet the association 'continues to support the position that the relationship of MCS to environmental contaminants remains unproven'. This document is noncommittal while simultaneously implying that a physiological causation is unlikely. It also hasn't been updated since 1999, which in itself emphasizes how the conflict surrounding MCS remains unresolved after all these years.

Yet the plot thickens globally. There has been somewhat of an agreement regarding the *physiological* nature of MCS in some parts of the world. In 2005, the Danish Environmental Protection Agency published a report that concluded there was sufficient evidence to suggest that MCS was a result of environmental contaminants and sought to establish measures that would prevent further sensitivities (Danish Environmental Protection Agency 2005). Further, following Germany's lead, the Austrian Government added the category 'Multiple Chemical Sensitivity: Allergy, not otherwise specified' to code T78.4 in the WHO register of diseases, the ICD-10 (Australian Department of Health and Ageing 2010). By including MCS, Austrian authorities further stated that the condition is physiological and specifically *not* psychological. The ICD-10 is intended as a classificatory guide to assist medical practitioners in their diagnosis. It is important to note, however, that the category of 'allergy not otherwise specified' includes 'ideosyncrasy not otherwise specified' and the meaning of the MCS inclusion remains ambiguous and contested in countries such as the UK, US and Australia. Further, as I will explain later, this re-categorization in Germany has not manifested in greater on-the-ground support for German sufferers of MCS.

A number of sympathetic experts in my research believed acceptance of the toxogenic nature of MCS was increasing amongst their colleagues, though it was certainly not the dominant position. The official acceptance of the condition in Germany and Denmark makes the controversy in the Anglo-American world all the more intriguing. It highlights that the local treatment of an emergent illness is an artefact of social life in that milieu, which is reinforced in the present study about the Western Australian experience with MCS.

Non-scientific sources of controversy

The medico-scientific contestation over the organic nature of MCS is not the only source of debate over the condition. MCS claims are controversially linked to toxic exposure events, which implicates the powerful chemical industry. History demonstrates that there is often a corporate and governmental reluctance to accept responsibility in an environmental health outbreak. Politically powerful entities across the globe have vehemently contested the cause and legitimacy of chemical injuries, including those of Vietnam War veterans exposed to the herbicide and defoliant Agent Orange (Schuck 1987), communities who discover childhood leukaemia clusters (Brown and Mikkelson 1997) and veterans who conducted nuclear tests in the Pacific Ocean (Trundle 2011). Vested interests, for example, played a dramatic role in the treatment of victims of the Bhopal disaster. In this case, on a December night in 1984, a toxic leak of methyl isocyanate escaped from the American company Union Carbide's factory in Bhopal, India. Within days, it was estimated that between 2,500 and 10,000 people had died from inhaling the toxins (Shrivastava 1987). Without having counted the victims, half of whom had not yet been medically examined, the Supreme Court of India eventually made a ruling that Union Carbide pay only US$470 million, and be granted immunity from criminal prosecution (Das 2000: 282). Although Carbide shares had plummeted immediately after the disaster, the market 'corrected itself' after the settlement was reached, and the company's profits doubled (Fortun 2001: 117). The settlement figure was adequate for the company to continue to be an extremely profitable enterprise. The extent of legitimacy granted to the sufferers is therefore arguable.

Of course, unlike the variable, somewhat invisible effects of MCS, the Bhopal case involved poisoning at irrefutably toxic levels, resulting in thousands of deaths. Yet even in such a clear cut, critical mass of chemical injury victims, there was strong corporate resistance to medico-legal recognition of the suffering experienced by the Bhopal victims. Similarly, if MCS were to achieve widespread recognition by the medical profession and in the courts as an organic disease caused by toxic exposure, some of the parties liable to lose are governments, multi-national employers, insurance companies and the entire chemical industry (Ashford and Miller 1998; Radetsky and Phillips 1997; Dumit 2006). These parties – and the way in which they are protected by broader political arrangements – can be strongly influential in the scientific debate over an emergent illness, as the following stories illustrate.

Adding to the controversial nature of MCS is that it has emerged as an environmental illness in an era when environmental concerns are both popular and divisive. Many suggest that the social trend towards environmental concerns owes a lot to pioneering ecologist Rachel Carson (Ashford and Miller 1998). Carson's book, *Silent Spring* (1962) highlighted the damage caused by industrial pesticides to the complex biodiversity of the American countryside, a radical book for its time. Carson suggested some dramatic reform to industry and lifestyle was required if the Earth was to survive. Increasingly throughout the following decades sustainable living became a worldwide concern: international summits were held, policy changes were made, the first green political parties were formed and there were widely publicized bottom-up environmental campaigns against ecological crises (Pakulski and Crook 1998).

The environmental *health* movement has 'cross-fertilized' with general environmentalism and shares many of its ideologies (Klawiter 2005). This is a global alliance between advocates for breast cancer, Gulf War syndrome and leukaemia, among other conditions that are believed by some to be environmentally caused. The movement includes sufferers, lay activists, academics and scientific professionals who are united in their belief that these conditions result from the ecological damage of industry. This alliance provides grassroots support for people with these conditions who are seen by some activists as victims of a chemical-obsessed and materialist society (see for example Ashford and Miller 1998). The increased resonance of environmental health concerns is reflected in the success of the hit film *Erin Brockovich*, starring Hollywood starlet Julia Roberts. The 2000 Soderbergh movie is based on the true story of a single mother who investigated a cluster of people falling ill near the Californian Gas and Electric Company. The corporation attempted to cover up the affair, but Brockovich successfully led a compensation lawsuit against it. A similar plot runs throughout *A Civil Action* (Harr 1996), a novel made into a major motion picture about a controversial water contamination lawsuit surrounding a childhood leukaemia cluster in Woburn, Massachusetts. These David versus Goliath narratives, coupled with more widespread sympathetic media coverage about ecological concerns, are linked to a burgeoning public consciousness about the potential effects of industrial exposure.

Some argue that this awareness is testament to a cultural shift that is partly inspired by activists in the environmental health movement (Brown 2007; Klawiter 2005). However, many sceptics consider paranoia about chemicals and conspiracies about big business responsible for fuelling erroneous belief in MCS. Interestingly, we see a similar division – between the ecologically concerned on the one hand and sceptics of social hysteria on the other – in other environmental disputes such as the debates over climate change and logging in old-growth forests (Satterfield 2002). As I go on to illustrate, popular interest can generate disbelief in environmental illness just as much as it rallies support.

Environmental politics thus cloud and confuse the debate over an emergent condition. Competing discourses swirled in the debate over sick building syndrome in the US, where relatively privileged workers alleged to become sensitive to toxic exposures arising out of office décor, furniture, and office supplies (Murphy 2006). Many stakeholders – including workers, corporate managers, ecologists, engineers, toxicologists, environmental protection agencies and feminist and labour activists – offered conflicting explanations for the condition. The politics surrounding the condition shaped and constrained when, how and to what extent the office exposures (and the resultant symptoms) became perceptible to sufferers, supporters and sceptics (Murphy 2006). Similarly, in the MCS debate, the divisive nature of environmental health concerns refracts the way MCS is understood and experienced by the chemically sensitive, and treated by the broader community.

A final axis of controversy is that MCS often arises in workplaces. When workers and employers collide in compensation battles over an emergent condition, the stakes rise in the conflict over its cause, as demonstrated by the history of repetitive strain injury (RSI). Emergent in the same decade as MCS, RSI refers to musculoskeletal pain occurring after repetitive use of the limbs, and is sometimes referred to as over-use syndrome. A large number of workers – particularly typists – sought compensation for the condition in Australia in the 1980s, causing it to be deemed a distinctly Australian 'occupational epidemic' (Reid and Reynolds 1990; Willis 1994). Like MCS, sceptical experts believed RSI to be an emergent socio-somatic condition caused by medicalized hype about changing work practices (see Awerbuch 1985). According to these physicians, sufferers with pre-existing stress and anxiety psychologically generated symptoms from social paranoia regarding repetitive work. Bizarre new illnesses have often arisen simultaneously with the advent of new technology: for example, after the invention of the railway in 1830 (when there *were* numerous horrific injuries arising from crashes), a more spurious label of 'railway spine' was used to explain a range of medical presentations including shock and meningitis (Trimble 1981). Insurers in particular are sceptical of this social tendency to ascribe a medical label to what is largely 'post-traumatic neurosis', and tend to believe medical specialists and entrepreneurial plaintiff lawyers profit from and encourage musculoskeletal diagnoses (Ericson and Doyle 2004). In other words, these commentators believe it is a case of 'compensationitis'. However, sympathetic experts argue that, while the label of RSI might have been new, musculoskeletal injury from repetitive work had been afflicting musicians, for example, for centuries (Fry 1985).[3] Others highlighted that changing work practices, such as modified keyboards, could conceivably create more injurious repetitive movement.

During the period of uncertainty over RSI, many afflicted workers were treated with scrutiny and disdain from employers, physicians, the media and the broader community (Reid, Ewan and Lowy 1991). Since a disproportionate number of sufferers were ethnically and racially diverse women, racist and sexist medico-legal stereotyping abounded (Willis 1994). The debate also played out in the courts, where bitter battles over compensation both reflected and exacerbated the controversy. In a landmark lawsuit, in which a typist alleged to have contracted RSI after working for the Australian Taxation Office, the jury found against the claimant and she was forced to pay the costs of the litigation (Reid and Reynolds 1990: 174). Yet, decades later, RSI has been officially recognized as a plausible physiological injury by the medical and legal communities in Australia. Occupational Health and Safety (OHS) regulations with regard to repetitive work practices have been implemented throughout the country (see Comcare 2000). RSI has been largely legitimized, both at the legislative level and in the social arena. Nowadays, most people would accept the possibility of musculoskeletal injury from repetitive work. Importantly, however, it remains difficult to have individual cases of RSI accepted in a court of law, since the impacts are hidden, medical detection technology in this area is limited and specific causation is complicated to prove.

While occupational conditions can become political hot topics, they can also be depoliticized and lowered as a priority. In the US, although asbestos litigation is an established billion dollar enterprise, the legal system failed to provide 'nearly enough compensation to nearly enough victims' (Gaskins 1989; cited in Durkin and Felstiner 1994). In her comparative anthropological investigation of asbestos-related disease in India, South Africa and the UK, Linda Waldman highlighted how dominant medical and legal understandings of risk and disease shape and constrain governmental responses to asbestos. The workers' compensation system in the UK privileges some asbestos-related diagnoses as more severe and deserving than others, which means workers' groups and the labour movement are still fighting for more generous and open compensation measures. In India, due to the fact that asbestos sales benefit the newly industrializing economy, the production and consumption of asbestos is relatively unregulated. Given this politico-economic impetus, diseases associated with asbestos receive little acknowledgement in India. By contrast, in South Africa, where activism is strong and the science over asbestos has become a political issue related to race and poverty, sufferers and activists have gained more recognition for their alternative, experiential knowledges in the political sphere, and have received compensation for a wider range of asbestos-related conditions

(Waldman 2011). These disparate local histories of asbestos-related conditions and RSI emphasize that the legitimization of an occupational illness like MCS – if it is to be recognized at all – is likely to be lengthy, non-linear and differential throughout the globe.

In essence, the uncertainty over the cause of MCS is exacerbated by its medically unexplained, chemical, environmental, occupational and political nature. Furthermore, the conflict over knowledge about chemical sensitivity outlined in this book has striking parallels with the epistemological battle over more recent technology-related illnesses. A drama about the safety of mobile phones and wireless technology is currently playing out in scientific journals, town hall meetings and courtrooms. A growing number of people claim to suffer from electro-sensitivity or ES. The cause, they believe, is electromagnetic fields – or EMF – a form of low frequency radiation that emanates from mobile and cordless phones, wireless modems, communication towers, power lines and even fluorescent lights, televisions and computer screens. Surveys conducted in Sweden (Hillert *et al.* 2002) and the UK (Eltiti *et al.* 2007) estimate that between 1.5 per cent and 5 per cent of the population claim to be sensitive to EMF. The alleged health impacts, which can range from a mild discomfort to an extremely debilitating condition for sufferers, include insomnia, fatigue, headaches, tinnitus, skin irritations and abdominal pain. And yet, like MCS, the mainstream medical and scientific communities around the globe do not recognize ES as a physical condition caused by exposure. In 2005, the WHO stated that there is currently no scientific basis linking ES symptoms to EMF exposure.[4] The familiar orthodox stance is that ES is caused by a nocebo effect, where physical symptoms are triggered by negative expectations about a health reaction, often fuelled by media sensationalism. Consequently, the prevention of low-level EMF from mobile phones and wireless technology is not a health priority in Australia. Like MCS, though, there are different approaches worldwide. Sweden has recognized ES as a valid disability and sufferers are eligible for state financial assistance (Johansson 2006). In 2007, the environment ministry in Germany warned its citizens to stop using WiFi wherever possible because of its potential risk to health (Lean 2007), and leading researchers on mobile phone health in the UK made similar warnings (Fleming 2007).

Wind Turbine Syndrome is another notable environmental illness in the middle of a heated controversy in the last decade. People living beside wind farms claim to suffer from a range of symptoms including tinnitus and sleep deprivation from sub-audible noise emissions emanating from wind turbines (Farboud *et al.* 2013). Similar to ES and MCS, questions arise about whether low-level emissions can cause physiological effects, and whether some individuals are more susceptible to hypersensitivity than others. This too is an inherently political debate, since vocal activists lobbying against wind farms have contradictory interests to environmentalists and the renewable energy sector.

One thing is certain; in these heated controversies, doctors, legal decision-makers, town-planners and policy-makers face a difficult challenge in responding to these burgeoning concerns. While MCS continues to be shrouded in uncertainty, it offers an opportunity to observe, in real time, how our society weighs up the economic benefits and potential human costs associated with technological advancement. We can learn important lessons from the MCS experience.

Contribution and engagement

Since medico-scientific orthodoxy says their experience of illness is implausible, people with contested environmental conditions seek a paradigm shift in the way medical science understands their bodies' relationship to the environment. Previous social science scholarship has highlighted some of the avenues through which the environmentally ill are doing so. In Steve Kroll-Smith and Hugh Floyd's (1997) sociological investigation into MCS, they profile chemically sensitive people who – like the informants introduced in this study – have studied medical science extensively, created their own libraries and consulted with supportive toxicological experts to explain their condition. Interestingly, their theories of disease are expressed in technical biomedical terms. A retired computer program analyst, who disagrees with the diagnosis of allergy that is often applied to the chemically sensitive, noted:

> The term "allergy" generally refers to a genetic disorder that involves acute...reactions mediated by an antibody called immunoglobin E. I don't have this. My problem is an acquired one that comes from toxic overexposure and produces delayed reactions which can come in response to very tiny amounts of airborne contaminants...food additives and some foods (the list of which is always changing).
>
> (cited in Kroll-Smith and Floyd 1997: 128)

Thus, the chemically sensitive are not merely resorting to traditional folk knowledge or alternative medical ideas to understand their condition, but rather are co-opting biomedical language of the enlightenment in novel ways (Kroll-Smith and Floyd 1997: 34). In appropriating this technical register, they are conversing with the medico-scientific community in its own language, thereby increasing the commensurability (or translatability) of their theories.

Furthermore, since those with MCS are alienated from mainstream biomedical support, emergent illness participants in Joseph Dumit's (2006) online research developed strategies to fight their dismissal by insurance companies and government bureaucracies. In the US, as in Australia, in order to be diagnosed and eligible for insurance, people need to fit into codes and categories of illness. When they fall outside of these categories, they are overlooked and defeated by 'information and symbols, categories and bureaucracies' (Dumit 2006: 579). Dumit found that, because MCS and CFS were 'illnesses you have to fight to get', people with these conditions consequently shared 'facts' with each other about manoeuvring the medical, legal and bureaucratic fields. They formed alliances and mobilized tactical information to assist fellow chemically sensitive people in their quest for legitimacy (Dumit 2006).

Thus, support groups have formed, email lists have been developed and internet chat-rooms are buzzing. And, in some locations, environmental health activism has been transformative for contested illness such as MCS. Given their experiences, scholar-activist Phil Brown (1992; 2007) and author Jonathan Harr (1996), among others (e.g. McCormick 2009; Zavestoski *et al.* 2004b) are optimistic that community activism can provide a challenge to mainstream epidemiology which can, in turn, change what is considered scientifically credible regarding environmental risk. Local movements such as the breast cancer activism that emerged in San Francisco in the 1970s have, over time, facilitated a more sympathetic approach towards environmental conditions (Klawiter 2005). In other contexts, the environmentally ill have been able to bypass medical orthodoxy by re-framing their struggle as a non-scientific issue. In some parts of the US, environmental illness movements have aligned with the political battle of disability activists. People with disabilities largely seek improved access to public places and better awareness of their special needs, while MCS disability activists specifically strive for public spaces to be made chemical and fragrance free. In fighting for disability status, the chemically sensitive have to some extent been able to side-step the need for mainstream medico-scientific acceptance (Floyd 1999; see also Canadian Human Rights Commission 2007). Indeed, in some jurisdictions, MCS has been legally recognized as a valid disability (Kroll-Smith and Floyd 1997: 163–172). Once the chemically sensitive have proven they suffer from a disability, being able to isolate the exact causal mechanisms (which they are required to do in the medical realm) is of reduced importance. From their research, Kroll-Smith and Floyd were optimistic that 'the legalization of the chemically reactive body is occurring well ahead of its medicalisation' (172).

So there are movement dynamics and anti-establishment strategies that are being engaged – to varying levels of success – in the quest for a paradigm shift in the understanding and treatment of MCS. However, this book highlights that medico-scientific scepticism about the condition's cause and a lack of legal recognition remain crucial barriers to official support and everyday assistance for most chemically sensitive people. This is particularly evident in Western Australia, where the environmental health movement and the fight to achieve disability status for people with MCS have gained relatively little momentum or, at least, visibility. As a consequence, the dispute over MCS legitimacy has principally played out on the legal stage, when workers have sought compensation for their condition in the medico-legal system and the courts.

I became interested in MCS when, as a clerical assistant in a small plaintiff law firm, I witnessed the lengthy, embittered battles of chemically sensitive clients against politically powerful employers and insurers, a generally disbelieving medical institution, a largely disinterested legal profession and a dismissive judiciary. When I later started my doctoral research in anthropology, I recalled the medico-legal field as a hub of activity during the quest for emergent illness legitimacy. Vested interests clashed, the most sceptical experts collided with the most sympathetic, activists for MCS recognition conflicted with industry representatives and significant decisions were pronounced about the condition's cause. It was where the epistemological conflict over the existence of chemical sensitivities seemed most pronounced and most adversarial.

Here, my own epistemological starting point with regard to MCS requires reflexivity. Sceptics complain that sufferers and sympathizers of contested environmental illnesses commonly exploit the adage of 'the canary in the coal mine' and make (sometimes dubious) comparisons with asbestos-related disease. There is, of course, cultural resonance and political traction in identifying with such an obvious example of mis-managed risk (De Graff and Bröer 2012). And yet, I believe that continuing to make this comparison is crucial because it leaves open epistemological possibilities where they otherwise tend to be closed off. The asbestos story is an acute illustration that there can be immense barriers that obstruct the recognition of new occupational, chemical diseases at the medico-legal interface, which delays when they become a visible problem that is deemed to warrant action by decision-makers.

Moreover, this research illustrates that the dominant approach to emergent conditions in the fields of medical science, the law, the insurance industry and in the political sector is scepticism. Positivist scepticism (or not accepting the validity of a novel medical explanation without an acceptable level of proof) is usually seen as neutral, measured, rational and scientific. Sympathy (or considering the possibility that a theory is valid while it is still uncertain) is often deemed biased, emotional, unscientific and rash. It is largely unquestioned logic that treating and compensating uncertain conditions that may be psychosomatic *as though* they are caused by external risks is politically, economically and medically troublesome. It can lead to social hysteria (Showalter 1997); a spike in diagnoses and compensation claims, which, in turn, can lead to crippling losses for insurance companies (Ericson and Doyle 2004); and unwarranted, foolish restrictions on industrial production (Lofstedt *et al.* 2011). However, the lag in the official response to asbestos-related disease problematizes the logic of waiting-for-further-proof in times of uncertainty. It underscores that while sceptical decision-makers wait for a moment of truth, for precedent, for an undeniable crisis, for a critical mass of sufferers, a public health crisis can steadily grow.

Despite not foreclosing the possibility that MCS *might* be chemically caused, it is not my endeavour to adjudicate whose perspective is more valid in this dispute, whether MCS is toxogenic or not. Indeed, I later suggest that the very fact that the debate over the legitimacy of emergent diseases is so contingent upon a physiological/psychological binary needs to be questioned and rethought. For now, though, what is undeniable is that, while they cannot be *reduced* to the label of 'sufferer', the chemically sensitive *are* suffering. Aside from their often debilitating ill-health, all of the workers who appear in this research have been left angered and hurt by their medical and legal experiences. Their stories highlight extremely undesirable consequences that arise out of the current medico-legal process for resolving debates over novel, uncertain conditions. This is reinforced by a recent quantitative Australian study which highlights that people who undergo claims for injury compensation tend to have worse long-term health outcomes than those whose injuries fall outside of compensation schemes (Grant *et al.* 2014). Stress, anxiety and depression are relatively common for people seeking compensation, which in all leads to a worse quality of life for claimants in the long term. It is thus worthwhile to ethnographically highlight shortcomings in the legal apparatus and how it might be reformed to deal with emergent conditions in a just, timely and therapeutic way, irrespective of what causes them.

So, with this book, my scholarly contribution is both empirical and theoretical. Empirically, I aim to provide thick ethnographic description about what happens when proponents of a novel scientific theory – intersecting with a social movement – seek legitimacy at the medico-legal interface. Examining both medicine and the law 'in action', my research illustrates how competing truths about bodies and environmental risk are negotiated, governed, accepted or rejected in the courtroom and clinic, how the community and political actors engage with and refract this epistemological conflict, and the impact that the medico-legal controversy has on those involved.

Theoretically, this book responds to two crucial questions. First, I address the challenges that face new knowledge seeking recognition in the medico-legal field. In essence, I argue that there are two layers of epistemological constraint. On the first layer, there are historically entrenched assumptions in the medico-scientific, legal and insurance sectors that constrain if and when a new condition reaches the threshold of proof and earns the status of legitimate and deserved. While each of these fields have different ways of measuring the body and assessing probability – and all of them have elements that could potentially fast-track the recognition of a new disease – they tend to encourage and reinforce each other's default conservatism. At a broader level, I demonstrate a second powerful layer of constraint. A neoliberal pattern of risk-management – whereby emergent theories involving corporate risk tend to be dealt with slowly and sceptically – strongly influences what knowledge is recognized and when at the medico-legal interface.

The second question I explore is the extent to which the law – and the workers' compensation apparatus more specifically – is a catalyst for social and epistemological change with regard to emergent conditions. Ultimately, I demonstrate that legal processes are embedded within a broader constellation of politico-economic interests and thus the scope of what can be achieved through legal action is limited. While a lack of legal recognition is currently debilitating for the chemically sensitive, substantive improvement to their lives – and to the process for governing upcoming emergent conditions – is unlikely to be realized through the law without more fundamental changes to the neoliberal order.

MCS and the workers compensation system in Australia

Up until the mid-nineteenth century, workers in the Anglo-American world were unable to claim compensation from their employer for accident or injury: the ethos was that workers should simply be grateful for gainful employment and their employer owed them no duty of care (Epstein 1982). After several landmark decisions in favour of plaintiffs in the US and the UK, precedent allowed injured workers to sue their employers under the tort of negligence, but they needed to prove their employer was at fault to be compensated for the injury. Growing dissatisfaction from across the political spectrum with this tort-based system led to a no-fault insurance scheme becoming the preferred system of governing workers' injuries in industrialized countries. Under a no-fault scheme, injured workers can claim replacement of wages and medical benefits (up to a certain limit) without having to prove their employer's negligence. However, workers also make a trade-off: by engaging a claim for compensation under the scheme, in some circumstances they relinquish their right to sue their employer for negligence (which, by contrast, is an avenue that offers greater financial redress since compensation is not capped, and the payout can include general pain and suffering as well as punitive damages).[5]

In Western Australia, for example, when workers have the support of a qualified medical practitioner, they are able to enter a claim for a work-caused condition via the government agency *WorkCover*, which is a no-fault insurance scheme legislated and governed at a state level. If the employer rejects that the injury is work-related and seeks medical evidence to the contrary – as did all of the employers in my case studies – the dispute enters legal proceedings, which start with a process of conciliation and arbitration before resorting to trial. If in this process the worker is found to have a work-caused disability deserving of compensation, the employer – usually underwritten by an insurer – will be ordered to pay the damages. Workers alleging to have more severe injuries caused by their employer's negligence can make more substantial claims for recovery under common law, but they must be deemed eligible for these proceedings by a judicial officer. As Chapter 5 will demonstrate, legislative changes have made this channel increasingly difficult for workers to access.

Of the eight chemically sensitive *litigants* I studied (the ninth participant with MCS never followed legal action through), three tradesmen were paid out-of-court settlements, an air hostess abandoned her lawsuit, an engineer escaped to his farm after receiving a payout in his New South Wales legal action, a retired teacher in Western Australia and a student in Victoria were still in dispute at the time of writing up the research, and a spray-painter took his case all the way to the Supreme Court of Western Australia before losing his quest to prove disability and, thus, access to common law. Though their experiences inevitably varied, in all, none feel like they achieved adequate resolution within the medico-legal system.

I focus on the narrative of two lawsuits in particular, which need brief introductions here. The first story is a conflict between Kylanta International, a multi-national mining company, and workers and residents who were alleged to have contracted MCS from emissions from a Kylanta plant. A group of Kylanta workers, who were unable to maintain employment after contracting MCS, took out a workers' compensation claim against their employer, and the ensuing, highly publicized battle lasted for five years. The State's Department of Health eventually commissioned two parliamentary inquiries and a medical panel to investigate the affair. Eventually, on the eve of a trial, Kylanta settled all except one of the workers claims for disability under a shroud of confidentiality, without officially admitting liability for their conditions.

I watched and participated in the second case study as it unfolded. This was a more private struggle between one man and his employer. After working for a number of years as a trade-assistant and spray-painter (using lead-based paint and toxic solvents) for a multi-national company called Vox, Ian Harvey's mental health and behaviour changed dramatically. Vox denied liability and, indeed, rejected that Ian suffered from any significant health complaint at all. Over the next nine years, Ian lost his quest to prove work-caused disability (and access common law) in the review directorate and continued to lose his appeals to the Compensation Magistrate's Court and Supreme Court of Western Australia. During the process, Ian's finances were severely depleted, his marriage was strained almost to breaking point, and he developed extreme feelings of anger towards the medical and legal systems that consistently found against him.

Ian's case is vastly different from the Kylanta affair. It involves only one person with chemical sensitivity, as opposed to a cluster of them, and his allegations of toxic exposure are less verifiable than billowing emissions from a chimneystack. His medico-legal experiences, however, have striking similarities to those of the Kylanta workers. Having watched Ian and his family undergo this process provides me with an insight into the daily inter-actions that constitute the battle for legitimacy in the medico-legal field.

These two case studies occurred either in or around Perth, Western Australia, which is a noteworthy place from which to examine the treatment of MCS. Located on the south-west coast of the island nation of Australia, Perth is one of the world's most isolated capital cities. Western Australia has historically been known as a conservative state within Australian politics, and in the late 1990s and early 2000s the state enjoyed a mining boom due to its rich wealth of primary resources. The state's subsequent economic prosperity is often credited to the mining industry, which has meant that mining-related companies (such as Vox and Kylanta) are culturally impor-tant and politically protected sources of the state's income.

There has been another high-profile MCS litigation that has caught public attention in Western Australia, against a now-defunct national airline, Ansett Australia (and British Airways, the manufacturer of their BAe 146 airplanes). As in the Kylanta case, numerous workers have sued their employers for allegedly exposing them to chemicals resulting in MCS. Although a number of out-of-court settlements have been reached in each context and parlia-mentary inquiries have been conducted into both affairs, the companies largely continue to deny liability and there has been little meaningful government intervention into the industries that are alleged to have caused the condition (see Vakas 2007).

Just as accurate data on the extent of the chemically sensitive population in Australia is unavailable, the number of litigants that have sought, or are seeking, compensation for their condition is unknown. Anecdotal evidence, however, suggests that the percentage of lawsuits that fall in favour of the chemically sensitive is small. The medical and legal experts I spoke to who deal with such cases on a regular basis say that legal successes for litigants with chemical disorders are rare. In Western Australia, there have been no such cases to my knowledge that have reached trial and succeeded. In New South Wales, there have been a small number of successes for workers with occupational chemical injuries, but most have been settled out of court and none of the wins have been landmark, highly publicized affairs. Australia has demonstrated little impetus towards officially recognizing the condition.

Methodology and chapter outline

To examine the medico-legal treatment of MCS ethnographically, I researched nine peoples' disputes over chemical sensitivity that were playing or had played out in Australia between 2006 and 2009, with a partic-ular focus on Western Australia. For Ian's case, which was ongoing during my research, I conducted participant observation at three court hearings over three years, and at informal events throughout his legal proceedings (for example, at meetings between Ian, his family and friends and legal team). For all of the case studies, I carried out textual analysis of the documents related to the disputes that I had access to (amount and access varied in each case), including medico-legal reports, legal correspondence, court transcripts, judicial reasons for decision, parliamentary documents and media arising out of the disputes. I also conducted interviews with 29 key players involved in the conflicts (some of them living internationally). These included MCS litigants, their friends and family, involved community members, legal practitioners and medical experts of both sceptical and sympathetic persuasion. From the outset, I made a promise to informants that I would attempt to keep their identity concealed as far as possible, so I have used pseudonyms for them and re-named the companies they worked for. I have also only discussed the details of their jobs or their company's operations in a general manner and shifted the dates of events to prevent identification through media coverage as much as possible.

Several trends and limitations in the research require reflection. I sought equal representation from all parties in the MCS dispute, as I wanted to present a balanced account of the competing truth-claims in the debate. However, those willing to participate tended to be sympathetic to a chemical explanation for MCS, with only three exceptions: a sceptical toxicologist, a disbelieving infectious disease specialist and an equivocal district court registrar. There is, consequently, a much smaller representation of employers, insurers and defence experts in the interview data collected. While I could glean their perspective in court observation, parliamentary inquiry transcripts, media exposure and medical reports, their silence or unwillingness to be interviewed is indicative of their role in – or perception of – the conflict. Experts who believe MCS is predominantly psychosomatic tend to see the problem as one of individual instability and/or social hysteria, a stance that does not render medical and legal critique necessary. Research that views the perspective of contested illness sufferers as equally valid is presumably something that these individuals consider problematic, or, at least, a low priority. Further, sceptical experts can sometimes face attack from special interest groups (Deyo and Psaty 1997). The medical historian Elaine Showalter (1997), for example, who argued that conditions such as chronic fatigue and Gulf War syndromes were contemporary manifestations of hysteria – received death threats (Larkin 1998). Awareness of this vitriol may make sceptics reluctant to be involved in an all-inclusive project.

The demographic of the interviewees is also noteworthy for its lack of diversity. Apart from one MCS litigant, whose first language is Italian, all of the participants were of Anglo-Saxon background. This is consistent with the relative lack of cultural diversity within Perth more generally.

There have been recent calls for more gender sensitivity in the design and analysis of empirical health research, so that differentiated health outcomes between men and women are better understood and addressed (Schofield 2012). In the present study, there are more males than females in the sample of both experts and lay interviewees. The gender imbalance amongst the workers with MCS (three women in contrast to six men) is explicable because the two main case studies happened in the mining industry, wherein the workforce is markedly more male than female. However, this disparity is not characteristic of the chemically sensitive population on the whole. Literature reviews suggest that an estimated 60 to 80 per cent of chemically sensitive people are women (Sears 2007).[6] Indeed, some theorists have used a feminist lens to study the delegitimation of chemical sensitivities such as sick-building syndrome and MCS, highlighting the link to earlier, chauvinist, socio-medical discourses about women and hysteria (Gibson 1997; see also Murphy 2006). Very few studies have specifically focused on the experiences of men with MCS (see Nadeau and Lippel 2014). There is, moreover, a need for more analysis of how work-related injuries (particularly contested ones) hinder the perceived ability of men to fulfil gendered expectations related to work ethic, strength, and providing for the family (one notable contribution, though, is Waldman 2011). While gender is not a focus in the present study – since there were no discernible differences between male and female participants' responses about MCS – it is nonetheless an important site for future analysis.

Any study of occupational illness must also take into account the existence and impact of socio-economic disparities. Pearce and Tombs (1998; 2000), for example, call for a Marxist analysis in the study of the chemical industry, highlighting how global capitalism enables corporate elites to continue relatively unimpeded in carrying out toxic negligence. Moreover, class does play a role in the present study: the difference between the wealth and status of corporate CEOs, insurance solicitors, and toxicology professors – versus (mainly) injured trades people who may never work again – is vast, and such a gap in resources inevitably plays a part in their medico-legal struggles. However, as in many studies of MCS, litigants hail from many walks of life. In my study, there was an engineer, a pilot and a former communications officer (now an academic) who contracted chemical sensitivity. In the research of Kroll-Smith and Floyd (1997), the chemically sensitive included an orchestra conductor, computer program analyst and university professors. While economic disparity and cultural status is relevant at times in the struggle over MCS legitimacy, at others the barriers to its recognition are more multifaceted.

In the next chapter, I discuss how a scientific paradigm (in this case for understanding disease) comes to be agreed upon, entrenched as commonsense, and linked to power, money and conflict. New theories can lead to controversy, be rejected by the scientific community, or overthrow current knowledge. The chapter outlines other battles over new scientific theories that have been fought out and resolved in courtroom dramas. I thus introduce four themes that influence the law-science response to uncertain epistemologies – juridical power; the salience of risk; neoliberalism; and governmentality.

Chapter 3 introduces how workers and multinational corporations utilize strategies in the struggle over the definition of environmental risk and illness. Despite the ways in which the chemically sensitive exploit social networks, capitalize on media support, harness medical advocacy and take advantage of accessible legal avenues, the recognition and compensation available to them through the medico-legal apparatus is ultimately restricted, and often short-lived.

Chapter 4 draws on narratives recounted by chemical sensitivity litigants about their lived experience as they face uncertainty and seek legitimacy in the workers' compensation scheme. The powerful barriers of adversarialism, burdens of proof, economic disadvantage and methods of surveillance are keenly felt by the workers, which causes much acrimony, anger, self-doubt and even paranoia. Their stories both illustrate how the medico-legal process is weighted against the recognition of new environmental illnesses, and vividly emphasizes that the process is therapeutically counter-productive for litigants.

Chapter 5 scrutinizes the social processes of medicine, the law, and the insurance sector, and how they are set up to manage uncertain conditions. Although each of these bodies of expertise contain concepts and clauses which, in theory, would allow a recognition of MCS as a valid condition, experts are socialized to privilege observable, objectively evidenced 'facts', which confine medico-legal outcomes to a narrow set of possibilities.

Chapter 6 focuses on the professional community as a source of governmentality that shapes and constrains the role of medical and legal experts who take an unorthodox position on emergent conditions. I elucidate how external and psychological forces place pressure on experts to conform, which disenfranchises those who seek paradigmatic change and makes epistemological transformation in the medico-legal field unlikely.

Chapter 7 analyses how litigation constrains scientific debate and consensus over new forms of knowledge. The adversarial legal system fosters suspicion between scientists, polarizes their opinions, prevents dialogue between them, and exacerbates the controversy over MCS. By contrast, I highlight the potential for productive dialogue about new forms of knowledge that are opened up by different, non-legal modes of governance.

In Chapter 8, I discuss the predominant model for managing risks in this society, and the impact this has on the legal process when emergent concerns arise. I highlight a pattern whereby risky individuals (for example, people accused of terrorism and ethnically diverse youth loitering in public places) are subject to a precautionary, punitive legal response and are segregated pre-emptively. This is in distinct contrast to the slow and unwieldy legal system for governing risky corporations, which is particularly evident in the ongoing asbestos saga. It places in stark relief the ways in which a neoliberal political impetus also drives epistemological outcomes over new forms of knowledge.

Finally, the conclusion reflects upon the transformative potential of law in sites of scientific uncertainty. Ultimately, while workers' compensation avenues initially seem to offer workers a tool through which to claim remedy for injury, fight for industrial change, and shift the scientific paradigm for understanding environmental risk, powerful constraints tend to delay and limit the possibility of meaningful recognition and sustained social change through the medico-legal field.

Chapter 2

Knowledge and power at the medico-legal interface

At the heart of environmental illness lawsuits is a battle over environmental contaminants, what they do – or do not do – to our bodies, and what should be done about these potential risks. One side is proposing a controversial explanation for an emergent illness, while the other is dismissing these claims on the basis of current scientific understandings. In this chapter, I engage with previous scholarly conversations that address how mainstream knowledge comes to be agreed upon, entrenched as common-sense, and linked to power, money and conflict in the medico-scientific and legal fields. First, I examine the process of scientific inquiry and how the scientific community internally resolves conflict to arrive at consensus and close off debate about its basic assumptions. Second, I investigate the conditions that have produced scientific revolutions in the past, and the constraints that provide barriers to paradigm change. The third section illustrates that when scientific controversies play out on the legal stage, the law has the potential to grant legitimacy to revolutionary theories. Given this potential, the fourth section outlines how new forms of knowledge have been governed in a range of different legal contexts, from native title claims to feminist engagement with the courts. I sketch out four themes – juridical power; the salience of risk; neoliberalism; and governmentality – that significantly shape how knowledge is managed at the medico-legal interface.

In later chapters, I emphasize how local struggles and grassroots social movements can offer powerful resistance and epistemological challenges to the status quo. First, however, it is important to outline the mechanisms through which medical science and the law tend to dictate what is true, and in doing so often help to demarcate identities, morality and the distribution of resources.

The production of scientific knowledge and consensus

In the early twentieth century, positivists understood scientific inquiry to be a logical, linear process of extracting truths about nature, in which scientists experimented with theories that would only be deemed true if they could be empirically tested and verified (see Friedman 1999). However, later science and technology theorists emphasized the human variables that effect scientific inquiry. One of the first challenges to the positivist perspective came from Popper (1963), who theorized that innovation occurs in the scientific field through a process of conjecture, where a hypothesis is put forward by a scientist, and attempted refutation, in which other scientists seek to disprove the theory. If the theory withstands this process, it will gradually be accepted and appropriated. Popper's theory painted the scientific community – and humans generally – as able to learn from past mistakes through trial and error and therefore progress our knowledge.

Thomas Kuhn (1962), however, disagreed. He examined the history of scientific thought with a particular focus on pivotal shifts that occurred in the fields of physics, astronomy and chemistry. Kuhn concluded that for the most part, scientists are inherently reluctant to accept changes to the fundamentals of their education, which he defined as a paradigm, or a 'network of theory through which [the scientific community] deals with the world' (Kuhn 1962: 7). In order for a paradigm to be efficient, scientists need to have reached a consensus about the fundamentals, which means dismissing further debate about core beliefs. Science students are socialized to believe in the unassailable truth of these fundamentals, which means they develop a deep faith in their paradigm (Kuhn 1962: 77). Of course, novel elements do arise, but these are tested and resolved through 'puzzle-solving', which allows the basics of the paradigm to be repeatedly confirmed. Controversially, Kuhn claimed that as a consequence of their profound commitment to the current worldview, most scientists are unable to see the logic in alternative viewpoints or theories. They cannot make a rational assessment of a crucially different theory because it is *incommensurable*, or irreconcilable, with their worldview. The fact that Kuhn referred to only one paradigm within a field is a point of contention amongst later philosophers, who have argued that the scientific community is more multivocal than Kuhn implied (e.g. Lakatos 1976). However, Kuhn's notion of the paradigm fruitfully highlighted that experts tend to be guided by a set of assumptions, which delimit the possibilities of scientific debate, and determine if, how and when new theories may take hold, or even be considered.

Looking beyond the theoretical commitments of individual scientists, Latour and Woolgar (1979) demonstrate that conflict influences how the scientific community accrues knowledge. These sociologists conducted participant observation in a laboratory to witness 'science in action'. They observed and analysed work sequences in the laboratory, the building and maintenance of professional networks and the techniques by which scientific arguments were developed. According to them, the behaviour of scientists could not merely be explained by a mutual, altruistic concern with 'nature' and how it works. Rather, the activity that they observed was polemical, or characterized by hostile disputes and strategic alliances between practitioners. Scientists necessarily sought investment in their careers, which could only be secured if they accumulated credentials (in the form of data, equipment, publications and recognition). This led them to compete with other practitioners for limited resources in a fiercely competitive environment. As a result, decisions about which theories to test and verify – and which researchers and laboratories to support, invest in or align with – were made according to economic and business imperatives.

This behind-the-scenes insight sheds further light on how 'facts' are produced. Latour and Woolgar argue that concepts that are defined by scientists in epistemological terms – proof, fact, validity – are more accurately explained by the notion of agonistic social conflict (1979: 393). They conclude that scientific 'hard facts' are actually fictional accounts that emerge out of the politics of the laboratory as 'stabilised objects' (390). In this process of stabilization, the socio-historical processes that necessarily produce these facts are rhetorically removed, which allows the knowledge to be presented as, and believed to be, objective and true. In other words, the human messiness involved in the research process is overwritten and forgotten, in order to produce a rather seamless, natural-seeming and linear account of scientific discovery. This enables the credibility attached to scientific knowledge to remain intact.

So, when scientific conflict eventually reaches 'closure', it is often through non-scientific means. Collins (1975; 2004) examined more than 25 years of disagreement between the central players in a debate over gravitational wave science. He noted that scientists who worked in this highly divisive field tended to be allied to a particular theoretical leaning, which influenced their choice of experiments and thus, to some extent, predetermined their findings (1975). For Collins, when closure on the gravity wave controversy was ostensibly achieved, it was not due to new, irrefutable evidence or wide-ranging consensus. Rather, those scientists with the most credibility strategically pronounced the controversy closed, even though disagreement persisted. As a result, the victorious group of scientists in gravity wave physics were the writers of its history, and those who lost the debate often left the field disillusioned, and expressing frustration that their claims had not actually been legitimately disproven (Collins 2004).

Further, the final consensus on a particular strand of inquiry can have very tangible impacts for those involved in the preceding conflict. Latour and Woolgar demonstrate that money, equipment, data, publications and reputation all produce one another in a cycle of conversion, such that success can beget success for scientists, and failure can become a vicious cycle. In this respect, the sociologists advance Bourdieu's (1975) work on the socio-economic conditions that produce authority in the scientific field. However, they explicitly depart from Bourdieu, since they argue that he applied economic models to scientific activity without sufficiently accounting for how value is ascribed to scientific content (1979: 341). For them, the agonistic social conflict described above is the means by which value is placed in or taken from epistemological claims.

At this juncture it is important to define how medicine fits into this picture. Biomedicine is a term used to describe the application of the natural sciences (biology, chemistry, physiology) to clinical medicine. In this book, I use the term 'medico-scientific community' in an inclusive way, referring to those experts who research medical conditions, treat patients, or assess occupational or environmental risks to health; be it in the laboratory, the clinic, or in the workplace environment. As I will go on to explain, there are many roles expected of health practitioners, including that of healers as well as gatekeepers to compensation, insurance, and disability pensions. Some scholars argue that a clinical 'medical' understanding of the patient's body is more holistic – with a greater focus on the patient's experiences and a bigger value placed on care – than the more reductionistic laboratory sciences (e.g. Jasanoff 1995: 125). While these differences are sometimes relevant in this research, allied health practitioners are also scientists, in the sense that they engage with, challenge and utilize scientific knowledge in the clinic and the laboratory. All of the experts in this research explicitly referred to their commitment to scientific methodologies, and felt pressure to conform to mainstream scientific beliefs. They are all consequently referred to as members of the medico-scientific community, even though some (such as occupational therapists) are considered more peripheral to biomedicine than others (such as clinical toxicologists or psychiatrists).

Traditionally, social scientists conceptualized 'disease' as the object of scientific enquiry, whereas 'illness' included the individual's experience and the popular social beliefs around sickness (Eisenberg 1977; Kleinman 1983; 1980). This characterization indirectly implied that disease – and the medical scientists who studied it – were unaffected by social influences. Later researchers emphasized the role of non-biological determinants in the definition, treatment and professional understanding of disease (Aronowitz 1998; Rosenberg 1992). Similar to other branches of science, an historically entrenched set of beliefs underlie medical doctrine, which shapes the lens through which the scientific community understands disease (Romanucci-Ross and Moerman 1991). Politics also plague medical research laboratories, which influence the medical facts that are eventually immortalized in publications, as well as the pharmaceutical treatments that enter the market (Fisher 2008).

While I borrow insights from the above literature, I am also wary of overemphasizing the social construction of scientific truths, especially those about disease. As Lupton (1995: 5) states:

> Throughout the lifespan, the body is taken up and transformed by social relations, but within certain limits imposed by biology. There is,

therefore, a symbiotic relationship between the body and society which defies determinism of either a biological or social constructionist nature.

We cannot downplay the very visceral biological impact that disease has on people's bodies, and the very tangible therapeutic benefit offered by treatments that are innovated by the medico-scientific community. Moreover, as illustrated in the following chapters, people with contested conditions desperately seek the authority provided by scientific proof of disease, want the legitimacy provided by a medical label and yearn for a cure. It is therefore important that critical scholars do not undermine the value of scientific knowledge when it holds so much worth for our participants. Further, only emphasizing the social variables of a new disease can be misconstrued as a denial of any physiological basis, and can thus be used to justify its medical and legal dismissal (Bammer and Martin 1992). Finally, interview data demonstrated that most practitioners are acutely aware of politico-economic influences in their field, and seek to conduct good science in spite of them. (Importantly, however, what constitutes 'good science' is a matter of interpretation and was a source of conflict between sympathetic and sceptical scientists in this work.)

Social constructionist theories are nonetheless fruitful because they highlight how accepted scientific truths that are often taken for granted as commonsense have in fact been reified through conflict and consensus. And consensual reality is crucial to the perception, labelling and response to disease. An emergent condition will not earn a physiological label in the ICD – the diagnostic bible – unless there is widespread agreement within the medical community that it should. In turn, doctor–patient interactions are strongly contingent on clinical practice guidelines, which are developed through consensus meetings (Ankeny 2003). Ultimately, medico-scientific agreement forms a sort of closure about the status of each disease: what causes it, how it should manifest and the best treatment regime. So, as the characters in this book demonstrate, diseases are understood through a paradigm of mainstream knowledge and consensus, which means alternative explanations for disease that fall outside of these parameters are likely to be dismissed.

And yet, at pivotal moments in history, fundamentally novel theories have successfully challenged mainstream scientific knowledge that was once taken for granted as truth. The section below consequently outlines the various scenarios that can happen when an unconventional scientific theory is proposed.

The potential for paradigm shift

According to Kuhn (1962), paradigm shifts occur when anomalies start to emerge which cannot be explained by the current worldview, and a scientist (or group of scientists) presents an alternative theory, thus becoming an agent of change. When Galileo Galilei famously theorized that the Earth revolves around the Sun rather than the other way around, he put in motion a process that discredited prior beliefs about geocentrism, and entirely changed the way European society thought about the world. During a revolutionary period in science, proponents of new paradigms are often initially penalized for their deviance; socially, politically, and financially. Although Galileo was eventually immortalized as a scientific hero, during his lifetime he was opposed by fellow astronomers for disagreeing with their theories, tried for heresy by the Roman Inquisition for going against the edict of the scriptures, and ultimately put under house arrest for the remainder of his life (MacLachlan 1997). However, paradigm shifts are eventually successful when further refutation proves unfruitful and other scientists begin to convert to the new way of thinking. Eventually, a critical mass subscribe to the new theory and, in time, when the period of 'intellectual violence' has subsided, this new paradigm becomes the dominant unquestioned conceptual framework for understanding the world, into which new science students are indoctrinated (Kuhn 1962).

An example of revolution in the history of medical science is the switch from the miasma theory to germ theory that occurred in the nineteenth century. Miasma theory was a historically entrenched assumption that disease was spontaneously generated by 'bad air'. This belief was largely considered unassailable until 1854, when John Snow, a sceptic of the theory sought an alternative explanation for the cause of a cholera outbreak in London. By charting the instances of cholera against a map of the town, he was able to prove the disease was linked to a water pump that contained poor quality water, even though he faced initial resistance from physicians and town planners (Hempel 2007). Snow's epidemiology – the first of its kind – paved the way for later scientists such as Louis Pasteur, who further strengthened scientific understandings of the causal relation-ship between microorganisms and disease, ultimately leading to many crucial medical advancements (Hempel 2007).

So the scientific community's conversion to a new paradigm does not occur as a sudden overthrow, but rather as a gradual, generational shift. When more and more members convert to a new paradigm, those who 'cling to older views' are gradually pushed out of the profession, which begins to ignore their work (Kuhn 1962: 18–19). The status of the know-ledge the old guard once held – the value once inherent in their education and training – is reduced when the 'truths' of their science are refuted.

Yet, not to be forgotten are the many attempts at scientific innovation and paradigm change that have been unsuccessful. Latour and Woolgar (1979) witnessed 'small gold-rushes' in their laboratory, where initial experiments created excitement and possibility in a particular set of propositions, which prompted numerous practitioners to invest in the new field of inquiry. However, when many of these theories were 'bankrupted' by hard data findings, negative results forced these scientists to re-evaluate their career progression, and some career prospects and reputations were damaged in the process (1979: 329). Similarly, as in the appearance and disappearance of 'Railway Spine' introduced in Chapter 1, certain disease labels and lines of medical inquiry have been overturned, replaced or discredited.

In all of these accounts of scientific activity, it is clear that the cultural value of one's knowledge in the scientific community is proportionate to social status and economic benefits. This is the case for all scientists in a controversy: those who champion a new theory that they believe will be revolutionary; those who reject theories that might disqualify their prior work; and those who align in a timely fashion with theories that are coming into vogue. However, a shortfall of the literature above is that it tends to caricature scientists as though they are *only* motivated by the accumulation of capital. A recent example of a paradigm shift in the medical community complicates this suggestion. In the 1990s, the Australian gastroenterologist, Barry Marshall, alongside his mentor, Robin Warren, hypothesized that gastric ulcers were caused by bacteria. Since prevailing scientific wisdom held that stomach ulcers were caused by stress or lifestyle factors the duo were consequently faced with scepticism from their colleagues, rejections for publication and a lack of economic investment from funding bodies. Marshall famously experimented by infecting himself with the virus, which enabled him to cure it with anti-parasitic medication and thus prove his claims. For their discovery, Marshall and Warren received the 2005 Nobel Prize for Physiology or Medicine. This confirms that the scientific community sometimes (retrospectively) awards those who are perceived as altruistic heroes who fought for inconvenient truths against the establishment. However, Marshall's ambition to find a cure for gastric ulcers also required moral conviction, supreme confidence in his own theory, and resilience to continue in the face of scepticism from his colleagues (see Marshall 2005). Morality, emotions and personality traits also drive individual scientists' reactions when they are faced with an anomaly, or a new theory to explain it.

Of course, changes to the scientific field are also enabled and hindered by the broader political economy. Funding structures can discourage scientists from taking professional risks, and certainly from advocating for paradigm shifts. As university budgets have dramatically reduced, scientists around the globe are increasingly reliant on attracting external funding (Laudel 2006). Research projects are evaluated and funded according to particular criteria, which in turn affects which strains of scientific inquiry are supported and advanced. Some analysts have questioned the inherently conservative nature of funding systems that distribute money on the basis of peer-review (Travis and Collins 1991). Reviewers can be reluctant to support unorthodox, novel and high-risk research, which encourages scientists to be 'mainstream' and risk-averse in their applications (Laudel 2006). Laudel's 2006 study in Germany and Australia found that most scientists are forced to adapt and modify their research to suit funding conditions. This means that many scientists abandon avenues of research that have difficulty attracting funding, irrespective of the scientific integrity of their ideas (Chubin and Hackett 1990). By contrast, there is often a dramatic growth in funding – and therefore research – on topics that are currently in vogue. Somewhat predictably, we saw a rapid increase in research in the field of climate change science after it became a political hot topic, and a funding favourite. In the medical context, research funding tends to be unevenly distributed to diseases that are the subject of successful lobbying, and funding politics can limit research into stigmatized diseases and diseases that predominantly affect disadvantaged populations (Best 2012).

Turning to the local research infrastructure particularly, Australian universities tend to be funded according to research outputs, which are calculated in rather crude measures of quantity, rather than quality (Butler 2003). Since universities then allocate money to departments and individuals according to similar measures, this has meant that, like most academics, scientists have unsurprisingly responded by publishing more often, particularly in lower-impact journals that have a higher acceptance rate for publications (Butler 2003). Further, this heightened productivity necessarily includes rehashing past material rather than taking the time (and the risk) to publish new and inventive research results (Woelert 2013).

In all, the literature above demonstrates that – while shifts in paradigm are possible and change agents sometimes appear – the socially mediated nature of knowledge, the internal politics within a given paradigm and the risk-averse nature of research funding play a crucial role in constraining epistemological possibilities in the medico-scientific field. And yet, debates are not always resolved internally by the scientific community. Below, I examine how scientific battles are fought and resolved on the legal stage, and how courtroom dramas can influence scientific truths.

Scientific controversy and legal closure

Law and science each offer different, but historically related, ways of fact-finding, assessing truth-claims and resolving conflict (Jasanoff 1995). Thus, when they turn to each other for answers, it gives us an opportunity to examine how they 'work out their differences' (Lynch *et al.* 2010: 14). The courtroom is a public forum in which new scientific theories can be tested in the public eye, and their perceived reliability can be weakened or strengthened through judicial decisions. Indeed, Jasanoff (1995: 20–21) argues that lawsuits involving scientific controversies are a form of 'civic education', since they inform how society understands epistemological, social and moral dilemmas that accompany technological change.

An interesting case study of this law–science nexus is the history of DNA criminal profiling in the courts.[1] After its development in the mid-1980s,

DNA profiling was rapidly taken up by prosecutors as a tool to prove the guilt of a suspect by matching their profile with biological samples found at a crime scene (Lynch *et al.* 2010). Although it may now seem to constitute a 'paradigm shift' in forensic science, the DNA technique was once the subject of much scepticism in the scientific community.[2] It was, for example, developed out of profiling techniques that have since been called subjective and 'prescientific' (Lynch *et al.* 2010: 8). In fact, forensic science has traditionally been looked down upon by the natural sciences as somewhat dubious, given that it is answerable to the politico-legal sector and its peer-review quality control is less rigorous (Saks and Koehler 2005). Critics of the DNA technique, who published in top-tier journals such as *Science* (Lewontin and Hartl 1991), pointed out the possibility of error when calculating match probability, since there may be similarities in DNA between suspects that share the same race, age and stature. Moreover, some concerning cases of false convictions and wrongful imprisonment from DNA databases highlight the potential for human errors in the laboratory – problems with the collection, administration and analysis of DNA samples.

Yet, Lynch and colleagues (2010) traced how the uncertainty of the science behind DNA profiling was finally resolved, and how the technique came to be perceived as near-certain evidence in the courts. A description of their findings is useful here because there are intriguing parallels – and some stark and telling contrasts – between DNA lawsuits and the legal treatment of environmental illness.

When DNA was first used as forensic evidence, prosecution teams of experts gave extraordinary estimates of the reliability of DNA matches, which meant that defence lawyers were ill-equipped to cross-examine on this issue. The technique did eventually become vulnerable to legal attack: defence lawyers sceptical of the DNA bandwagon were eventually able to gather scientists with enough 'firepower' to counter the prosecution's experts and question the admissibility of DNA evidence (Lynch *et al.* 2010). After this first successful challenge, a number of admissibility challenges followed in the early- and mid-1990s, with the most visible attack on the technique's credibility being the O.J. Simpson double-murder trial, which was televised to US audiences.[3]

However, by the late 1990s, the vast majority of judicial rulings in the US, Europe and Australia were decided in favour of DNA admissibility. One of the main reasons for this, which also becomes relevant in this study, is that ambiguities in scientific knowledge can be glossed over in legal disputes due to stipulations surrounding the presentation of evidence (see Chapter 7). In the context of DNA, probability tended to be quantified in terms of the usually very small likelihood that a person *other* than the accused would match the crime stain: for example, as a 'one in three million chance'. This makes the evidence seem almost certain. However, if it were instead qualified in terms of the potential for error – i.e. 'there are conceivably ten other people in this country besides the suspect who could match the sample' – the inherent uncertainty would be laid bare (Lynch *et al.* 2010: 178, 250). If it were stipulated that DNA matches must be presented with all their incumbent ambiguity, the science behind them would seem far less certain and impressive. This omission enabled increasing decisions in favour of the prosecution.

The fact that DNA evidence was successfully challenged initially, then largely admitted, led to the perception that it had 'passed the test', and now has an aura of irrefutability about it. Rather than being one tool amongst many for the prosecution, the technique has become the most glamorous piece of evidence – and sometimes the crux of the case against the accused (Lynch *et al.* 2010). Moreover, the legal 'resolution' has also had ripple effects in the scientific community. The dispute was rhetorically declared resolved by scientific proponents of DNA typing – most famously in a *Nature* piece conveniently titled 'DNA Fingerprinting Dispute Laid to Rest' (Lander and Budowle 1994). Even the most vocal opponents of the technique in the scientific community reticently agreed that the dispute was over, although they believed that state power and politics drove the outcome (Lynch *et al.* 2010: 227). Importantly, just like the scientific disputes described by Collins, Latour and Woolgar above, closure was *not* achieved through a 'crucial test, definitive legal judgment or moment of truth' (Lynch *et al.* 2010: 228), but rather through non-scientific means.

Arguably, the theory behind DNA profiling is less contentious than physiological explanations for MCS, and more aligned with mainstream scientific understandings of the body. However, the important point here is that DNA profiling was once a controversial theory, arising from a nominal field of science, and shrouded in heated scientific debate. And yet, very soon after its proposal, it was appropriated by powerful state actors as evidence in a court of law, increasingly validated by judicial decision-makers, and eventually closed off to further debate in the scientific community. Its trajectory in the legal system highlights the law's potential to certify uncertain scientific knowledge. It therefore provides a useful measure against the current legal response to environmental illness, a comparison that I return to in subsequent chapters. First, it is necessary to introduce the forces that frame how new forms of knowledge are governed in different institutional contexts.

Governance and knowledge

There are four themes that appeared time and again in my research as forces that produced certain kinds of reasoning and social activity and disallowed others. In other words, they determined how the debate over MCS was governed. Governance is a concept I use broadly to describe the shaping of thoughts and behaviour. Using insights from other contexts in medicine and the law, this section introduces four themes – juridical power, the ever-presence of risk, neoliberalism and governmentality – and the influence they can hold in controversies over new knowledge.

Juridical power

The first, more traditional mode of power conceptualized by social scientists is the top-down authority of the state – the power of the law and institutions. It operates when those in positions of authority dictate what is 'true' about our world and what is false. In turn, 'specific effects of power become attached to the true' (Gordon 1980: 132). In other words, power can beget the right to determine what is true, and that which is declared 'true' tends to further endow the powerful.

The medical and legal institutions are both historically imbued with authority by the state. When medical science and law began to emerge as specialized areas of knowledge and practice in modern Europe, the hospitals, asylums, courts and prisons in which they operated became important tools in social planning and administration (Foucault 1973). A healthy, functioning and compliant citizenry was deemed pivotal to the success of the rapidly industrializing society. The brief of the emerging medical and legal professions was thus to solve social problems, particularly by reforming those who violated social norms – the sick, the insane, the criminal – such that they could again become contributing members of society. Moreover, as representatives of the state, medical and legal professionals were endowed with the authority to define which truth-claims were valid – and thus which people were legitimate and deserving recipients of assistance – and which were not. Through these institutional processes, the state began its monopoly over defining identities and administering justice (Bourdieu 1994).

Native title law in Australia is an interesting example of how the legal institution remains powerful in this regard. When European colonizers first landed in Australia, they termed the land *terra nullius*, meaning 'land belonging to no-one', which enabled them to declare British sovereignty. This officially negated the presence of Aboriginal and Torres Strait Islander groups whose ancestors had lived on the land for up to 50,000 years. Buoyed by the civil rights movement of the 1960s, Indigenous groups sought to have Aboriginal laws and customs relating to land-custodianship legally recognized, and accrued a groundswell of support from the broader Australian population. After years of unfavourable decisions in lower courts, the 1992 High Court bench eventually upheld the *Mabo* decision, a landmark ruling that declared the concept of *terra nullius* void and for the first time recognized the legitimacy of Indigenous sovereignty at the time of European settlement. The highly controversial decision went against the State of Queensland and became the subject of much criticism from conservative corners for being politically biased and an act of judicial activism (see Lumb 1993). The Labour government of the time formalized the native title doctrine by setting-up a specialist tribunal designed to preside over subsequent land claims. It was, in essence, a paradigm shift in the official framework for understanding Australian legal history.

And yet, the Native Title Tribunal defines Aboriginal identity in its own, juridical terms. The outcome of land claims are determined based on the extent to which Indigenous groups can prove continuing cultural ties and kinship connections to the land in question, extending from prior to British arrival to the present day. The burden of proof lies on the claimants to provide sufficient evidence that they maintain elements of a traditional lifestyle. So, in order to be successful, plaintiffs must represent themselves in a way that meets the expectations of indigeneity defined by the legal system and the broader society (Merlan 1995; Weiner 2003; Short 2008). As anthropologist Veronica Strang (2004: 11) explains:

> It is evident that all of these representational discourses, whether positive or negative, share the idea of aboriginality as a prior state of being, a pre-modern ideal [...] All of these tropes are impressed upon Aboriginal people. In effect, Aboriginal people are surrounded by a hall of distorting mirrors. Most of the images presented to them about themselves are based on the beliefs, hopes and desires of the larger and more powerful society.

Ultimately, while people have agency to resist this portrait of them, the legal apparatus has significant power to declare how a *true* Aboriginal person should look and behave to be officially recognized by the state as deserving of land rights. Moreover, the decisions handed down by judges directly equate to the (re)distribution of resources, which reinforces the immense value inherent within legal categories.

It is important before continuing to problematize the law and the state. In the highly centralized political systems of industrialized societies, it is tempting to see 'the law' as a fixed body, insulated from and capable of controlling its social context (Moore 1973). Yet, as in cultural communities across the globe, the law includes a changeable set of norms, governing practices, professional bodies and processes that can involve regulation, legislation, litigation, bureaucratic administration, enforcement and punishment (Moore 1973; Balint 2012). Moreover, those who execute these legal processes are diverse and often divided. Furthermore, the 'state' is a complex body which cannot be simplified as fixed, monolithic and unified. Instead, the modern industrialized state is made up of a *bureaucratic field* of varied and often conflicting interests (Bourdieu 1994). Tess Lea (2008) in her study of the governance of Aboriginal health in Australia – aptly titled *Bureaucrats and Bleeding Hearts* – highlights the emotions and social dynamics involved in the way policies are formulated, debated within and rolled out by government departments. The same can be said of the process for legislating and reforming the legal system. Yet, zooming out from the complex minutiae of everyday interactions in government departments and legal processes– when one takes an aerial view – there is a strong, historically repeated pattern to the way institutions tend to respond (or delay response) to emergent forms of knowledge. For social movements and individual litigants that come up against this paradigm and seek to shift it, the state and the legal system can seem like a monolithic and consistent barrier. It is in this context that I use 'the law' and the 'state' as necessary short terms to describe what are nonetheless complex organisms.

Medicine is also a multifaceted institution that is historically invested with the power to shape knowledge. Since the professionalization of medicine in enlightenment Europe, the medical community has been given relative autonomy by the state, which has enabled its dominance over the specialized field of diagnosis and treatment (Daniel 1990; Freidson 1986). It consequently has a monopoly over the distinction between what is *normal* and what is *pathological* (Canguilhem 1989). Unlike the patient's knowledge, which is considered subjective and able to be misled, the doctor's 'clinical gaze' has an attached aura of truth and objectivity. Further, as is evident in this book, the medico-scientific community remains the authority on what are *normal pathologies* – those that can be objectively measured, easily identified and treated – and what are abnormal or unwarranted pathologies, which are considered more socially problematic. This distinction can be usefully explained through the notion of the 'sick role.' Functionalist Talcott Parsons (1951: 428–447) developed the concept of the sick role to encompass a sort of contract: a person who is labelled legitimately ill by the appropriate experts will be absolved of blame; receive recognition for their illness; access medical support; and be temporarily exempt from various duties such as full-time employment. These benefits are referred to as 'secondary gains', which those with illness are entitled to if they, in turn, cooperate with the authorities involved and actively try to recover. In contrast to the legitimacy of the sick-role, an unfavourable diagnostic label can lead to delegitimation, which involves the removal of political authority and acceptance. Delegitimation is a process whereby a person's claims to an experience of illness are deemed invalid – it is a 'disaffirmation' of the subjective reality of the sufferer (Kleinman 1995: 136; see also Ware 1992). It highlights how diagnosis trumps the experiential knowledge of illness felt by contested illness claimants. Being denied the sick role in turn means they are refused its secondary gains, and are sometimes even considered ineligible for sympathy from friends and family (Clarke and James 2003; Dumit 2006). Medical diagnosis consequently has tremendous social currency.

Importantly, however, medical and legal sovereignty do not go unchallenged. While the legal profession broadly holds a monopoly over many aspects of fact-finding, contract-writing and dispute resolution, Australians have always maintained a dose of mistrust towards lawyers, epitomized by jokes about sharks and ambulance chasers.[4] Moreover, the traditional media (and now social media) commonly criticizes the judiciary for their lenience in sentencing, and is quick to distrust the criminal justice system when a parolee reoffends. There have also been several challenges to medical dominance in recent decades. As discussed later, society has become increasingly sceptical of the fallibility of science and its potential risks (Wynne 1996). This has produced more discerning lay consumers of medical information, and even 'patient-experts' (Pols 2013). Complementary and alternative medical practices have gradually increased in profile and challenged the monopoly over diagnosis once held by medicine (Willis and Coulter 2004). Nonetheless, this may be a 'glass half full' perspective on medical dominance, since the medical profession still remains the final authority on many aspects of health and illness (e.g. Willis and White 2004), just as legal expertise continues to be engaged for determining things of social import.[5]

The lawsuits that unfold in this book highlight how medico-scientific and legal authority can both collude and collide. Even though the medical profession has the license to define disease and injury, legal battles occur when there is a lack of consensus between experts over diagnosis. Judicial decision-makers consequently play a crucial role in affirming the legitimacy of a new disease, or dismissing its validity (and, in doing so, removing credibility from the medico-scientific experts who support it). The workers' compensation apparatus is consequently a unique site from which to examine how these forms of juridical power intersect.

The salience of risk

A second mode of power that is crucial at the medico-legal interface is the increasing cultural salience of the concept of *risk*, and the rise of *risk management* as a way of dealing with uncertainty. To explain this, I first define the 'risk society' before exploring how it shapes the role of medical and legal professionals.

Although society has always been subject to a level of risk, sociologists Beck (1992; 1994; 1996) and Giddens (1990) argue that in the latter quarter of the twentieth century, the social body became increasingly reflexive about the risks associated with modern 'progress'. Industrial disasters and concerns about global warming have led to heightened social concern about man-made threats to safety. The principle concern of Beck's (1992; 1994; 1995) work is how scientific and technological advancements have come to be perceived as risky, with the potential to produce disastrous consequences. Social and environmental movements have mobilized mistrust of science, and lobbied against scientifically approved development (Brown 1992; 2007; Couch and Kroll-Smith 2000). (And yet, a paradoxical feature of risk culture is that science and technology are also consulted in times of uncertainty, to calculate and mitigate risks and to help manage disasters – Ericson and Doyle 2004).

Some scholars have suggested that this weariness of 'risk' has influenced medico-scientific and legal practice in the last few decades, and even given rise to a new regime of governance (Rose 1996a). In the previous regime described by Foucault, the imperative of the medical and legal professions was to cure individuals and society of undesirable or dangerous elements. Now, it is to assess the risk of that dangerousness eventuating and to manage those risks accordingly. Medical practitioners, lawyers and judges are today considered part of a community of caregivers and case workers – social workers, police, child protection services, housing officials and so on – who are all involved in the identification and mitigation of risks and risky individuals (Rose 1996a). Neo-Foucauldians such as Nikolas Rose argue that this cultural shift has adjusted the role of medico-scientific and legal practitioners who, along with being conceptualized by society as healers and purveyors of justice, are now also expected to insure society against risk, and are blamed if these risks go unheeded.

An important distinction lies between uncertainty and risk. One of the rhetorical functions of medicine and the law is to solve social problems and, in doing so, to improve and maintain order, safety, healthiness and efficiency. However, uncertainty is a constant in the daily functioning of medicine and the law. Medical experts always experience a degree of uncertainty when they diagnose (Fox 1959; 2000) and judges must adjudicate over the unknown in their decisions regarding negligence or guilt, compensation or sentencing (Frank 1974). Yet, uncertainty is unquantifiable and presents a challenge to the consistency and reliability of institutional processes. Reframing uncertainty as a *risk* allows it to be calculated in terms of probability and potential severity. Risk *management* thus 'achieves certainty through a different kind of logic: that of precaution, vigilance and pre-emption' (Ericson and Doyle 2004: 7) Thus, sophisticated risk-assessment technologies have been engineered to quantify risk, to allow for rational analysis and to measure it against 'pre-determined objectives'. As Smallman (2000: 67) notes, 'such supposed rationality, coupled [with] technically sophisticated risk assessment methods which parallel cost benefit analysis sits well with bureaucrats and legislators...[it] seems to offer a feeling of security'.

While many businesses explicitly implement programs to assess and mitigate risks, risk-management logic is also engaged at a more implicit level in other organizations. For example, the medico-legal system has in-built procedures to manage risks; there are rules that guide practitioners to capture, remove and avoid ambiguities as far as possible. There are conventions that guide medico-scientific research into disease and criminality; professional codes that determine the ways in which experts diagnose in the face of unexplained symptoms and behaviour; evidentiary laws that constrain the evidence that is admissible in a court of law; and burdens of proof that designate a default decision when uncertainty is unsurmountable.

The rise of a risk society leads to a heightened perceived need for *insurance* as a method of managing risks. Fear mongering is a logical part of the insurer's advertising campaign – they 'market (in)security' (Ericson, Doyle and Barry 2003: 4) – which reinforces the cultural preoccupation with risk. Ericson, Doyle and Barry (2003) conducted an extensive sociological study including interviews with both insurance experts and everyday consumers of insurance products. They argue that insurance has become a form of governance in and of itself, with its own form of regulatory power. For example, industry associations regulate insurance practices and lobby for legislative reform, just as insurance contracts regulate the insured (Ericson and Doyle 2004: 3). Moreover, other institutions such as medicine and the law increasingly rely upon the private insurance industry for the actuarial assessment of risks and the indemnification of losses. For example, in Australia, businesses are mandatorily required to maintain active workers' compensation insurance that prevents them (and their employees) from financial hardship in the event of workplace injury. The state thus relies upon the private insurance industry to share the cost of risk – to underwrite the health of its citizens and the economic stability of businesses – which reinforces the politico-economic strength of the insurance sector. Consequently, insurance companies have a powerful voice in defining what constitutes risk and injury.

And yet, for both insurers and the insured, uncertainty is never far away. Risks are vast and varied; they include those to the safety of the individual, the broader community, the environment and the economy. Diminishing the likelihood of one of these risks may heighten the probability of another, which means trade-offs are often necessary. Scientific controversies show how expert decision-makers can disagree on how to weigh-up these risks, and *which trade-offs to allow*. This can be usefully illustrated through the precautionary principle. Embodied in the old adage, 'better safe than sorry', the precautionary principle dictates that when there is a perceived threat of harm to humans or the environment – in the absence of scientific certainty – we must nonetheless act in a preventative way that avoids risk. Furthermore, the principle commands that the burden of proof should fall to the proponents of the activity in question to prove its harmlessness, rather than forcing the public to prove cause and effect beyond doubt (Raffensperger and Tickner 1999). This principle has often been used to push for regulation and bans on chemical, industrial or agricultural technology that is allegedly harmful to human health or the environment. However, critics have pointed out that the concept of precaution is interpretive (see Sunstein 2005).[6] An example is the debate over the much-reviled pesticide, dichlorodiphenyl-trichloroethane (DDT). Ecological experts and lay environmentalists argued for the adoption of the precautionary principle to ban DDT, since it has been linked to ill-health effects for birdlife and is potentially carcinogenic. However, DDT is also used to control the mosquito problem to prevent malaria, which kills millions of people, particularly in sub-Saharan Africa (Goklany 2001). In other words, DDT may be saving millions of lives. So what constitutes 'being safe' and 'being sorry' is a subjective determination that depends on one's priorities in terms of risks and their consequences.

In the following chapters, I demonstrate how a particular pattern of risk-management influences decision-making with regards to environmental harms and contested illness; not only by the corporations accused of contamination, but also the insurers who underwrite them, and the medical and legal decision-makers who preside over the debates about their activities. To explain the prioritization that underlies many of the decisions, the pervasive influence of neoliberalism needs an introduction.

Neoliberalism

Neoliberalism is a term used to refer to a global political development that holds economic growth as its central value. It is an ideology that gained traction in the latter half of the twentieth century and, though it was highly politicized by the Reagan and Thatcher governments in the 1980s, continues to inform policy and shape social life in the twenty-first century (Peck and Tickell 2002). In his seminal work on the governance of social security, Loic Wacquant (2009) usefully outlines four, interlinked, trends that constitute neoliberalism. Its liberal tropes of market freedom and individual responsibility – discussed below – are historically traceable (e.g. Ireland 2010). However, I deliberately use the term *neo*liberalism, because these concepts have arguably become more advanced (see Rose 2009) and have taken on 'neo' aspects in the contemporary capitalist economy (see Rose 1996a; Scheppele 2010).

The first feature of neoliberal governance is reduced economic regulation. This ideology sees the competitive market as the most effective economic model for society. There are two consequences that arise from this trend: first, the corporate sector is given more freedom and authority. A central theme of this volume is how the relative autonomy given to corporate employers limits the state's gaze over its activities. Second, under the rhetoric of 'improved efficiency', public services (such as education and health) are progressively privatized, or at least managed increasingly as profit-making entities. This has been particularly visible in the healthcare sector, where governance of public hospitals increasingly involves outsourcing and contracting, and the quality of health provision is measured through 'efficiency dividends' and 'competition' (e.g. Gadiel and Sammut 2012).

The second trend attributed to neoliberalism is the 'devolution, retraction and recomposition' of the welfare state (Wacquant 2009: 307). Governments promoting laissez faire economics have increasingly 'rolled-back' social-democratic policies once rhetorically designed to ensure full employment and safeguard social welfare. Indeed, Wacquant (2009: 307) argues that in the American context, social security has been reformulated as a disciplinary mechanism. Lower class recipients of welfare find themselves in a 'quasi-contractual' relationship with the state, where they are expected to adhere to behavioural obligations as a prerequisite for public assistance. In Australia, similar contracts called 'work-for-the-dole' programs, which dictate reciprocal obligations for welfare recipients, have been criticized for being punitive towards the disadvantaged (see Bessant 2000).

Crucially, the shift from welfarism to liberalism also changes the ideology underpinning insurance. When the prevailing political ethos is one of welfarism, the goal of insurance is to raise enough money through premiums to cover the cost of services (Ericson and Doyle 2004: 108). Insurance is then 'underpinned by a sense of responsibility for collective solidarity', which means risk is 'spread across broad pools for the public good' (2004: 108). By contrast, under the neoliberal framework, there is a 'deterrence-based market approach' to insurance. Since companies must compete within a free market economy, their focus becomes reducing premium inflation by minimizing their losses, and 'cracking down on claims' (2004: 108). The result is that insurance payments, like social security in the US, are increasingly conditional. As demonstrated in Chapter 5, economic imperatives drive legislative reforms that place further caveats on workers' access to insurance schemes. In workers' compensation 'reforms' in the US, the economic rationale of 'efficiency' is used to justify cutbacks to compensation benefits for workers (McCluskey 1997). While these measures are usually framed as neutral, necessary reforms 'for the good of all,' they are actually informed by politically biased, moral judgments about who does and does not deserve a share of public monies. Such economic rationalism was similarly appropriated when the House of Lords withdrew the compensation available to British sufferers of pleural plaques, a common precursor to asbestos-related disease, on the basis that the suffering involved did not warrant the cost (Waldman 2011).

A third, related constituent of neoliberalism is the cultural trope of individual responsibility. Under a capitalist discourse that rewards entrepreneurialism and competition, all individuals and parties are considered formally 'equal' and autonomous, with access to the same opportunities and choices. This understanding of the world largely rejects the existence of deep-rooted inequalities and diminishes any impetus for the state to provide a 'leg-up' for socio-economically disadvantaged groups (Thornton 1990).[7] It therefore justifies the minimization of protectionist policies and the deregulation of the market. In a medical context, this has meant that the provision of free public healthcare has declined, while the responsibility for one's health and the management of illness has been placed squarely upon the shoulders of individuals and their family carers (Rose 2007).

These first three elements of neoliberalism logically follow on from one another, since they all involve a transferral of authority and responsibility away from the state. However, Wacquant identifies a fourth, initially contra-dictory-seeming, neoliberal phenomenon: an 'expansive, intrusive and proactive penal apparatus' (2009: 307). He argues that although the state has withdrawn its presence in many realms of social life, it has *increased* intervention and paternalism on issues of law and order. The reduction of economic and social protection for the disadvantaged, in conjunction with the precariousness of employment opportunities for non-skilled workers, greatly increases inequalities. This typically heightens dysfunction amongst disadvantaged urban communities, which leads to ghettoization. And yet, the same governments that retract welfare simultaneously foster a 'moral behaviouralism' which successfully casts certain behaviours often born out of dysfunction – such as welfare dependency and substance abuse – as deviant and in need of punishment. This in turn gives the grounds for a heavy penal response and retrospectively justifies the state having with-drawn assistance in the first place.

This therefore points to a deep hypocrisy in the way neoliberal ideol-ogy gets applied in practice, and a fundamental inequality in how it can effect social relations. While governments have expanded intervention, surveillance and penal apparatuses to monitor and punish the 'deviant' behaviour of risky individuals, in the meantime, private businesses are given increased freedom, their expansion encouraged, and barriers to their operations are removed by the state. A concomitant trend is that businesses (particularly multinational ones that transgress sovereign borders) are less accountable for health and environmental impacts, and can more easily evade liability for any damage they may cause (Monshipouri *et al.* 2003). Though perhaps somewhat reductionistic, David Garland expresses the paradox simply: 'Control is now being re-emphasized in every area of social life – with the singular and startling exception of the economy, from whose deregulated domain most of today's risks routinely emerge' (2002: 165).

Neoliberalism is thus a framework for understanding the political econ-omy, a tool for analysing how political institutions and economic policies shape and are shaped by social change. Yet theories about neoliberalism have also come under significant criticism. Narratives regarding the ills of neoliberalism are 'mobilised overwhelmingly by left-wing academics and political activists' (Larner 2006). They have strong moral overtones, since they tend to see more traditional concepts of the social, the collective, and welfarism, as utopian, while demonizing the contemporary focus on indi-vidualism and the market economy (Muehlebach 2012). Furthermore, while neoliberalism is often referred to as a coherent, globalizing ideology, neoliberalization has occurred at different rates, been differentially contested, and had varied effects around the globe (Larner 2000).

Undiscerning complaints about 'neoliberalism' without a nuanced illustration of how it actually works (and how new it actually is) are problematic. In this study, I examine the specific effects of market policies on the workers' compensation scheme in Australia, and what this does to the social process of recognizing emergent diseases. Neoliberal inequalities can be witnessed in the empirical data of this study. The preoccupation with economic freedom and individual responsibility has visibly disadvantaged workers concerned about risk and illness, while simultaneously enabling employers and their insurers to, at times, avoid accountability and transparency. The trends above are therefore a necessary explanatory tool.

An important feature of neoliberal governance is that it does not merely manifest as power imposed from above. As illustrated through the concept of governmentality below, it shapes our behaviour and decision-making when we seek to maintain, or earn, legitimacy within this status quo.

Governmentality

Emphasized by Foucault in the latter part of his career, governmentality refers to the mechanisms through which power becomes internalized and embodied by individuals. Instead of being purely top-down and centralized, this is a form of *capillary* power that permeates all parts of the social body. In his lecture entitled 'Governmentality' (1991), Foucault explains how the concept relates to juridical power: as the state increased its power through the pre-eminence of governmental institutions such as the prison and medical clinic, the categories established in this process began to shape how individuals conducted themselves and judged each other. This mode of governance has come to discipline the population through a process of *normalization*, where being normal required being compliant, law-abiding and healthy; in other words, consistently being good citizens. Individuals embody and reproduce institutional power when they conform to these categories, while policing the behaviour of others such that they too normalize themselves.

It works via the mechanism of surveillance, which Foucault (1977) first illustrated through the metaphor of the panopticon. This is a prison security arrangement visualized by English legal philosopher Jeremy Bentham, which enables an omniscient view of prisoner behaviour. Although prisoners cannot know if they are being watched at any one time, the perception that they *could* be enforces self-control at all times. Foucault describes the effect as:

> An inspecting gaze which each individual under its weight will end by interiorizing to the point that he is his own overseer, each individual thus exercising this surveillance over, and against, himself. A superb

formula: power exercised continuously and for what turns out to be minimal cost.

(Foucault 1980: 155)

This interiorized 'gaze' has helped in shifting responsibility from the state onto individuals in the contemporary health system. People are increasingly expected to regulate themselves as good medical subjects – to maintain a healthy lifestyle and, if ill, comply with medical advice and seek to return themselves to 'normal'. Moreover, as in Wacquant's study of welfare, this neoliberal trend is maintained and justified through a sort of 'moral behaviouralism'. 'Getting better' is an implicitly moral process, since it demonstrates loyalty towards the group's standards (Clarke and James 2003; Tishelman and Sachs 1998). In this way, the value that was placed on the healthy, compliant worker during the industrial revolution – the importance of returning to work wherever possible and demonstrating a good 'protestant work ethic' – is a moral imperative still imposed on injured workers in the health system today (Niemeyer 1991).

Normalization is also required for legal recognition. As in the previous example of native title law, while top-down definitions prescribe what constitutes Aboriginality and how this should be manifest, this applies pressure on Aboriginal claimants to conform to a legally prescribed identity. Wolfe (1999) describes this phenomenon as 'repressive authenticity', where authenticity denotes a version of reality that is perceived as being more correct than others. Being authentic can require land claimants to repress elements of Aboriginality that may seem non-traditional or abnormal to a decision-maker. In turn, by normalizing themselves to fit this description, they reinforce the veracity of this representation. This governmentality leads to the hegemonic power of law, whereby subordinated groups may gradually accept the unfavourable status quo and internalize the worldview of the more dominant group – and their own subordinate position – as natural and inevitable.

However, it is also important to be mindful of the various critiques of the concept of governmentality. Foucault (1977) conceived of self-surveillance as such a powerful way of governing society that it would eventually replace the need for existing institutions, such as the prison. For him, juridical power would eventually be redundant as society gradually learnt to selfgovern. However, a number of theorists have disagreed that top-down authority is on the decline. Critical criminologist Carol Smart (1989), for example, investigated the role that law plays in women's lives. Smart highlights the law's continued ability to dictate the extent of women's rights and constrain the possibilities of the feminist project. While she acknowledges that women do normalize themselves and govern each other at times, she argued that the legal institution has maintained (and sometimes expanded) its authoritative presence. This power is socially reinforced because people continue to 'resort' to law as a means for attaining justice and solving their problems, rather than engaging with alternative (non-legal) strategies. Smart thus took issue with Foucault's emphasis on normalization, since she saw the continuing relevance of the other sort of power: that which is handed down as a right, and gate-kept by the politico-legal elite. In her words: 'we not only continue to talk about power as a commodity, we also act as if it were' (Smart 1989: 7).

Like Smart's participants, the sufferers of MCS in this book similarly turn to the legal apparatus as a remedy – a place to have their experience of suffering validated and compensated. Similar to the feminist movement, the environmental health movement also places hope in legal decision-makers to prove the veracity of their claims, and to provide them with the rights and resources they seek, thus reinforcing the power of law in their lives. However, as with land claimants, those with environmental illness are also pressured to behave injured in a way that conforms to medico-scientific and legal norms (see Chapter 4). Additionally, experts who believe in unortho-dox theories about MCS standardize the way they present their disciplinary knowledge in an attempt to have their expertise validated in professional settings (see Chapter 6). Thus, I demonstrate that normalizing forces have a significant effect on the boundaries and possibilities of scientific debate, even before it is presented to the bench.

Wacquant provides another critique of governmentality in his analysis of America's punishment of the poor. He argues that juridical power has expanded its disciplinary influence *over some and not others*. In Foucault's conceptualization, surveillance was imposed upon the entire citizenry, and all sections of society were forced to normalize themselves as good citizens lest they face punishment. However, Wacquant persuasively illustrates how surveillance methods can be used to observe and discipline the 'deviant' behaviour of the poor, while the elite can largely continue their behaviour relatively unobserved. He uses the example of corporate crime, and the weak and ineffectual way in which the law responded to, for example, the Wall Street scandals and corporate corruption of the 1980s and 1990s (2009: 297). While the disadvantaged must normalize themselves or face a harsh penal response, the economic elite are often left relatively unregulated and, thus, less subject to the coercive power of governmentality.

If normalizing power were indiscriminate across the population, then the behaviour of employers would be under significant surveillance, which would lead to meaningful regulation of workplace conditions. The present study places in stark relief the law's limited power to make corporate activ-ity transparent and accountable in disputes over new and alleged occupational injuries.

Conclusion

This chapter has demonstrated how medical science and the law have developed privileged ways of knowing. While mainstream knowledge is produced through social conflict, it becomes reified as truth when it is rhetorically closed off to further debate. Although paradigm shifts *can* occur, social interests and politico-economic pressures restrict the extent to which unorthodox scientific theories can be explored. And yet, as illustrated by the DNA example, when scientific debates play out on the legal stage, the law has the potential to remove uncertainty over controversial theories and grant them legitimacy. The law is consequently an avenue for having new propositions tested and validated.

Yet, some forms of uncertain knowledge (such as the DNA profiling technique) are taken up rapidly and receive a sympathetic politico-legal reception overall, where others (such as the unorthodox explanations for MCS outlined in this book) face lengthy battles against the establishment, and may ultimately be rejected. While the theories behind DNA and MCS are undoubtedly at different points along a spectrum of scientific legitimacy and are heard in different courts, their comparison is nonetheless enlightening. They show that power dynamics alter the legal response to epistemological conflict.

Hence, I have introduced above my conceptual architecture for understanding how knowledge and power intersect at the medico-legal interface. Traditionally, the state has invested authority in the medical and legal institutions, which imbues both with a form of top-down power that can define and take away people's identities, worthiness and wealth. To an extent, the neoliberal framework has reformulated institutional sovereignty, since it has shifted authority *away* from the state and its medical and legal representatives in some contexts. Conceptualizing everyone as 'equal' and diminishing the state's protectionist role has had the dual effect of investing the economy (and *its* representatives) with more unregulated freedom, and placing more responsibility at the foot of individuals to ensure their own welfare. Yet, paradoxically, as noted by Wacquant (2009) the state's authority has become more expansive, interventionist, and punitive in other institutional contexts. Individuals – both lay people and experts – take on these neoliberal ideologies and reinforce their power when they conform to the norms expected of them in the workplace, courts or medical clinic. We are all consequently neoliberal subjects, but some can be disproportionately disadvantaged by neoliberal governance.

Advancing the scholarship above, this book examines how the medico-legal apparatus – at once a reflection and a reinforcement of the neoliberal framework – governs epistemological conflict. Previous literature on neoliberalism, scientific controversies and the law insufficiently addresses why decision-making varies between sympathetic and sceptical experts in controversies over risk (see Chapter 6), and why – when judges err on the side of 'caution' – this tends to lead to a very different outcome in personal injury law than in criminal law (see Chapter 8). This study emphasizes that, when we take an aerial view of medico-legal history, the logic of neoliberalism tends to shape the patterns by which decision-makers resolve uncertainty about injury and liability, criminality and guilt. This helps to explain why the law so often lags in its recognition of and response to new knowledge about emergent illness.

Chapter 3

Risk entrepreneurialism

The social construction of toxicity and disease

Aside from the politics of knowledge within the medico-scientific and legal fields, a complex web of interests within the community also influences how a scientific controversy unfolds and eventually reaches closure. I now turn to the Kylanta case study, in which a group of workers claimed to suffer from MCS and sought compensation from their multinational employer, who denied the claims. The ensuing struggle revolved around three scientific questions with uncertain answers: whether the Kylanta mine site emitted risky levels of environmental contaminants; whether the workers' alleged suffering constituted a physiological and disabling condition; and whether the two were causally linked. This chapter chronicles how the workers and the company each tried to influence medico-scientific understanding, manipulate public understanding of the science, and sway politico-legal outcomes in their favour.

There are two strands of sociological commentary that explore environmental health controversies but differ in outlook. The first, most notably advanced by scholar-activist Phil Brown and colleagues (Brown 2007; 1992; Hess 2005; Kroll-Smith *et al.* 2000; McCormick 2009; Zavestoski *et al.* 2004a; 2004b), examines how local community groups and global cooperatives have mobilized themselves in attempts to prove the causal link between environmental contaminants and burgeoning diseases such as breast cancer, Gulf War syndrome and MCS. Given the experiential basis of their claims, they are often perceived to arrive at 'erroneous lay conclusions' (Brown 1992: 278), which justifies their dismissal by decision-makers. However, this first thread of work emphasizes how lay movements can develop a subversive form of science to chart the effects of environmental contamination, which can potentially overthrow mainstream medical scepticism and, eventually, prove the scientific credibility of their experience.

The second sociological trend is to focus on the prevailing influence of industry and insurers to counter environmental concern and dissuade regulators from taking precautionary action. Significant chemical disasters in the latter half of the twentieth century, such as Bhopal and Chernobyl, placed in stark relief the *extent* to which industrial progress posed a risk to human health. In conjunction with the financial impact on the companies involved, there was an immensely negative media and public backlash surrounding these events. A number of regulatory changes were imposed upon corporations, not only by law enforcers but also by their insurers. These included that workers and nearby residents had a 'right to know' about hazards and toxicological risks; labour and community groups must be included in risk management and emergency response; and environmental and biological monitoring must be compulsorily implemented (Pearce and Tombs 2000). Furthermore, environmental groups, medical associations and trade unions called into question the human cost of economic growth, and fought for 'corporate social responsibility' in business. It was hoped that corporations would voluntarily adhere to this ethical code because if they did not, they would no longer be able to retain consumer loyalty, and would face economic consequences (Dhir 2006; Monshipouri *et al.* 2003). Yet some commentators believe concepts such as 'community consultation' and 'rights to know' tend to be used by industry and governments as a legitimating technique – a bureaucratic box to tick before going ahead with development as planned – rather than as a place where citizens can meaningfully play a part in shaping their society (Flear and Vakulenko 2010; Pearce and Tombs 2000).

So another scholarly tradition emphasizes how industry can exploit these circumstances and manipulate scientific knowledge, consumer loyalty and government intervention. This can occur through a manipulation of, first, the levels of chemical exposure permitted in industry (Ziem and Castleman 2000); second, how and when workplace safety measures are instituted (Brodeur 1974; Pearce and Tombs 2000), and, third, the production of evidence that refutes the dangers of environmental contaminants (Beder 1998a; Michaels and Monforton 2005).This perspective presents a more pessimistic view that emphasizes the barriers that prevent grassroots movements from effecting epistemological change.

The following discussion shows that the power to define risk and categorize emergent disease is not simply top-down, institutional and juridical; rather, it is diffuse, contested and refracted amongst experts, business owners, insurers, the media, various sections of the community and government representatives. However, it also underscores the disproportionate influence held by the corporate sector to influence scientific debate and constrain regulatory activity in the face of scientific uncertainty.

The emergence of community concern

When a group of workers were first diagnosed with MCS near Forrestville in Western Australia, it was the first time that most locals had heard of the condition. The multinational mining corporation Kylanta has several plants in regional Western Australia. The Forrestville plant is positioned near three small townships, the closest of which is several kilometres away. A tall chimneystack installed at the plant in 1994 emitted a range of volatile organic compounds, or VOCs, which, according to a large number of workers and neighbouring residents, caused bad odours. Kylanta experts and health inspectors reassured that the emissions from the stack were harmless to humans on the ground because the toxins were dispersed into the air.

The workers I spoke to explained that they were relatively content working at Kylanta until 1994. After the chimneystack was installed, however, they started to notice patterns where an 'invisible wall' of gas would accumulate in 'weird, weird ways.' Hayley, for example, was in a particularly fit state of health when she first started working for Kylanta since she was training for a long distance swim. However, after working at the plant for a number of months, she would 'nearly collapse' upon walking up a flight of stairs. Another worker at the plant, Evan, started to frequently wake up in the mornings with profuse bleeding from his nose. He also suffered from an infection in the chest:

> ...basically from that chest infection, my life changed forever. That was it. I couldn't handle deodorants, fumes, I couldn't read the paper anymore. I'd get in a coughing fit from reading the paper [...] The guy that I was travelling with [to work] had bought himself a new ute, and the smell of the new car was making me sick. And I'd get in coughing fits to the point where I'd throw up, because I couldn't stop reacting to the car.

Before the chimneystack was installed, the Forrestville site received on average 40 complaints per year. Afterwards, Kylanta received up to 1,000 complaints annually. As more and more people began to complain of health effects, the town coined the term, 'The Forrestville Flu.'

While many suffered from mild complaints that would disappear upon leaving the area, one sympathetic medical practitioner estimated that more than 100 workers and nearby residents were diagnosed with chemical-related conditions. Some workers experienced long-term impairments alleged to result from chimneystack emissions. Roger described the lifestyle change that occurred due to his continuing condition:

> [My now wife] was an honest girl and I married her and our lives were looking rosy. We worked hard, she helped me, I helped her and things looked good. Then end of '96 when I started getting sick that really... that was bad [...] What I was and what I am today...it's taken my lifestyle away. And now, who would've thought? I'm...I turned 46 in March. I'd be struggling and I've got my wife working [as a cleaner]... that's not my way. You know, we were married 25 years and I couldn't go out and buy my wife a present.

When the workers informed their employer about their symptoms, Kylanta management rejected that the chimneystack was the cause of the health complaints. If the workers claimed to be sensitive to chemicals in the particular part of the plant in which they worked, their managers denied the conditions were hazardous but agreed they must be susceptible to an adverse reaction and found them a job elsewhere in the mining operations.[1]

Just months after the chimneystack had been installed, the workers with MCS engaged plaintiff solicitor Jeff Carlson, who applied to the Supreme Court of Western Australia for an injunction requiring the company to shut down the chimneystack. With the imminent threat of the injunction, Kylanta management stopped operating the chimneystack in November 1995, a hiatus that lasted for just over six months. The majority of the workforce did not experience any chemically related health problems during this period and Kylanta notably retrofitted millions of dollars worth of anti-pollution equipment intended to reduce the emissions from the stack. When it started up again, however, the health complaints reappeared, and the company again denied liability.

Kylanta International is a self-insured company, which means that it was the party liable to pay in the event that the workers were found to have a work-caused condition. This is consistent with a worldwide trend, in which multinational corporations organize self-insurance (Pearce and Tombs 2000). This can be an economically strategic decision because insurance companies often impose their own safety regulations and inspections on businesses and disagree with companies about what insurance covers. During times when the effected employees were temporarily unable to work, Kylanta would sometimes agree to pay the workers' wages out of a special fund; however, this fund was separate to workers' compensation and therefore no admission of liability could be implied. Kylanta most often refused to pay the workers' medical expenses and rejected claims for any disability payouts that were filed in relation to the fumes from the chimneystack.

The handful of affected workers finally filed a legal action for compensation and a total and permanent disability payout from the plant. During the dispute, the company and its workers each engaged techniques to shape broader understandings of environmental risk and chemical injuries.

The powerful strategies of Kylanta international

Throughout the conflict with its workers, Kylanta managers were entrepreneurial consumers and producers of scientific information. Their strategies included reinforcing industry guidelines, promoting psycho-social causal explanations, emphasizing uncertainty, and engaging their own version of environmentalism.

Reinforcing industry guidelines

In all the monitoring of contaminants that Kylanta conducted, the detected emissions were reportedly always well below international OHS guidelines. Irrespective of the number of health complaints the company received, members of Kylanta management reassured their workforce that there could be no significant health impacts if emissions measured no higher than industry regulations. One member of management explained their good intentions at the inquiry:

> If there was clear evidence linking Kylanta's emissions to health effects, we would find the source and eliminate it. However, despite extensive testing, no chemical or particle has been found in the refinery emissions at a level that would explain these reported health effects. We have involved the community, government agencies, universities, health professionals and consultants to examine the issue. Nobody has been able to find a link between emissions and the health effects that people are reporting.

The exposure levels typically relied upon in industry are termed threshold limit values, or TLVs, which are industry guidelines for working with air contaminants. They are intended to delineate the difference between 'insignificant' and 'significant' exposure for workers to be exposed to on a daily basis (Karmel 2008). The concept of regulating 'maximum allowable concentrations' of contaminants in the workplace was developed in 1942 by the American College of Government Industrial Hygienists, or ACGIH (Subcommittee Report 1942; see Ziem and Castleman 2000: 121). One of the key hygienists of the ACGIH qualified at the time that 'compliance with the figures listed would [not] guarantee protection against ill-health' (Cook 1945). A decade later, however, the committee had changed the name of these calculations to 'TLVs' and discursively changed the definition to health hazard thresholds, providing more of a guarantee of safety than initially intended (Ziem and Castleman 2000). The committee also explicitly stated that one of its principal intentions was to curtail the burden these regulations would have on industry (122). Consequently, industry – which has a vested interest in minimizing any cost to reduce emissions – has played a significant role in the process of determining these limits. Recommendations from industry consultants have historically been given significant weight during negotiations, and, further, they have been able to delay and sometimes prevent precautionary action (Castleman and Ziem 1988). The medical accuracy of these guidelines is thus controversial and most attempts to regulate toxic substances are challenged by industry, and environmental, labour and consumer groups for either being too severe or too lenient (Halton 1988; Karmel 2008: 3).

Companies must comply with TLVs in Western Australia by regulation, but it is acknowledged that these standards have limitations as a unit of measurement. In the preface to WorkSafe Australia's 'Exposure Standards for Atmospheric Contaminants in the Occupational Environment' (1995) – the Australian version of the ACGIH recommendations – it is stipulated that TLVs are only valid according to 'current knowledge' and that they cannot guarantee that 'a very small proportion of workers who are exposed to concentrations around or below the exposure standard may suffer mild and transitory discomfort' and that 'an even smaller number may exhibit symptoms of illness' (1995: 5).

[The guide also notes that TLVs are void in the event of chemical mixture, just as they are if the employees are working in excessive heat, work for longer than eight hours a day, or are exposed to more than inhalation; for example, chemicals on the skin (1995: 5). This relates to one of the major sources of argument in relation to MCS. While sceptical experts see the debate over whether or not low-level exposures cause ill-effects, sympathetic experts are arguing that in fact continued exposure to toxins over time constitutes a more substantial chemical dose. According to the sympathetic experts I spoke to, as well as scientists writing on the topic, science is not adequately advanced to understand synergism between chemicals (in other words the concept that two chemicals may have a multiplicative, rather than merely additive, effect on one another), as well as the insidious and cumulative way in which toxins may penetrate the body (see for example, Brown, Kroll-Smith and Gunter 2000: 10). According to them, these concepts are at the forefront of medical science. However, for sceptics, medical science is adept in differentiating between a toxic dose of chemicals on the one hand and a harmless, low-level exposure on the other, and there isn't any in this case.]

Nonetheless, in most toxic torts and in each of my case studies, the defendant company 'takes refuge in' these limits to deny liability for their workers' conditions (see also Karmel 2008). When a worker claims they are getting ill from the company's emissions, the company can use these established measures to deny the possibility of health impacts rather than question the accuracy of the established measures – or 'current knowledge' – in the first place. TLVs provide a deceptive safeguard for industry that makes them exempt from having to critically examine the standards and averts the need for constant medical monitoring (a need that was initially identified by the ACGIH in the 1940s – see Ziem and Castleman 2000). This problem aligns with a broader critique of legislative regulation of industry. The value of legislating and enforcing industrial guidelines is that it prescribes a set of standards that the community can expect. However, as Smallman notes (2000: 74), its strength is also its main weakness:

...organisations can claim to have done enough to, meet legal requirements and that they can 'stop' at that point. In other words they impose no moral duty or business stimulus to go beyond what the law requires.

In the case of Kylanta, the company denied that the chimneystack emissions were harmful to human health, while acknowledging that a fine caustic mist emanating from the chimneystack would sometimes pit car windscreens and affect the paint of vehicles parked near the operations. Workers recall it was company policy to pay for the replacement of car windscreens for any worker who needed it. Later, one of the managers was asked in a parliamentary inquiry, 'if caustic mist pits glass and car bodies, surely it would affect the respiratory system? [...] Could that not be a significant part of the culprit [in causing the ill-health effects]?' The manager replied, 'It could be part of the issue, but, as we said earlier, we have not been able to measure the caustic in levels that would suggest there is an issue'.

The uncertainty and disagreement regarding exposure level standards favours defence companies such as Kylanta. Since they are 'unable to measure the [chemicals] at levels that suggest there is an issue,' they are not technically required to make changes to their operations and cannot be held legally accountable for neglecting foreseeable risks. TLVs have an aura of scientific credibility, which the company reinforces when it embraces the regulatory framework as a measure of environmental risk.

Emphasizing psycho-social causal mechanisms

Kylanta also engaged in the medico-scientific debate about the causal mechanisms of MCS. One of the explanatory models for the condition in medical literature is that psychological conditioning to odours is responsible for the symptoms of chemical sensitivity (Van Den Bergh et al. 2001; Van Diest et al. 2006; Winters et al. 2003). This view holds that the chemically sensitive are relating particular odours to a *sense* of ill-health, and then psychologically expanding that reaction to many odours. An infectious disease specialist expressed it simply:

> You are very, very unlucky as far as I'm concerned if you're Kylanta and [...] you're making some kind of acidy smell or sulphur smell and people have an illness, because they'll blame you.

Contradictory medical research, however, has suggested that *physiological* mechanisms involving the olfactory and limbic systems are at work (Ashford and Miller 1998; Bell, Miller and Schwartz 1992; Bell et al. 1993). These systems create a connection between one's sense of smell and the parts of the brain that deal with emotion, behaviour and memory.

Kylanta managers contributed to this medico-scientific debate by emphasizing the importance of odour and cultural conditioning. The company's manager of OHS was asked during the parliamentary inquiry why the Forrestville plant had so many chemical-related health complaints in contrast to the mining company's other plants in Western Australia. He replied:

> It is possibly a cultural aspect of the workforce. Each site has a particular culture. There are different concerns at every [Kylanta plant] and some common concerns; however, odour is not a common concern.

In their press releases and public responses to community concern, the company frequently favoured the term 'odour' in contrast to 'emissions'. One member of Kylanta management typifies this exchange of terms:

> The issues involving the Forrestville plant have been upsetting for all involved...How did those problems arise? All [mining sites like Kylanta's] have an identifiable odour [...] unacceptable odour and noise from the chimneystack during 1994 and 1995 provoked the breakdown in relations between the refinery and its neighbours.

Another explained:

> It is the potential odour that really bothers people. And it does bother people...Kylanta has commenced an aggressive emissions reduction program, focusing in particular on odorous emissions that may conceivably cause discomfort and nuisance to employees and neighbours.

With the attention on odour, Kylanta managers reframed the impact of the plant's emissions as a 'bother', 'discomfort' or 'nuisance', which belittled the severity of the suffering that workers and residents complained of. Moreover, the emphasis on psycho-social mechanisms behind MCS locates the problem as inherent to the group of sufferers. This individualization shifts the attention away from the broader question of whether workplace emissions are harmful, and further frames the MCS issue as an unjustified inconvenience that might harm the economic health of the company. A risk assessment report provided by a consultant to the company stated:

> The focus therefore is to get the employees and the affected community unconcerned, so reducing the risk of costly programs for the company, which may be required to ensure that the chimneystack project continues and is cost-effective.

Another MCS explanatory model favoured by Kylanta was that the condition was invented and perpetuated through iatrogenesis, whereby the medical profession constructs erroneous diagnoses to generate more business. This is a common gripe from insurance companies, who argue that there are fads in disability insurance claims caused by iatrogenic effect (Ericson and Doyle 2004: 100). As Aronowitz (1998: 19) notes with regard to chronic fatigue:

> [Antagonists believe that] the 'epidemic in diagnosis' requires not only patient abuse of the sick role, but also doctors' willingness to be accomplices.

There were three local health practitioners in particular who expressed extreme concern about the chimneystack and its link to ill-health in the community: a GP, an occupational physician and a psychologist. Each of them, after being approached for treatment by a number of the workers and community members, developed the opinion that their patients were genuinely ill and their conditions were toxogenic. Thereafter, these practitioners wrote submissions to the state health department, vocalized their concerns to local and national newspapers and later were invited to participate in government deliberations regarding the health impacts from Kylanta operations. Due to their burgeoning reputation for treating the environmentally ill, these doctors were accused of iatrogenesis. In a medico-legal report about the worker Ian, a psychiatrist noted that although Ian is not physically ill, neither does he have a 'hypochondriacal disorder' because he has 'three doctors supporting his belief that he has been adversely affected by chemicals.' A defence clinical toxicologist who treated the Kylanta workers offered a similar observation:

> Certainly in this town, the patients who I'm asked to give an opinion on seem to come through a very narrow channel. Now they do seem to have seen a certain number of people and they do seem to have ended up with the same label regardless of what the real diagnosis is.

Kylanta management capitalized upon this causal explanation for the condition. The company's compensation delegate cast aspersions over the workers' MCS diagnoses in the parliamentary inquiry:

> All are or have been in the care of the same medical general practitioner [...] who has provided the following diagnoses ... [*The delegate goes on to demonstrate that the workers have all received similar labels*]

Thus, the corporation supported and reinforced scientific explanations for the workers' suffering that rejected environmental cause and organic mechanisms, thereby disqualifying the scientific possibility that the company was liable.

Waiting for consensus/manufacturing uncertainty

During the dispute with its workers, Kylanta magnified the lack of consensus within the expert community about MCS in two important ways. First, it emphasized scientific uncertainty and areas of expert disagreement wherever possible. For example, the company's compensation delegate noted:

> In all [of the workers'] cases, we have received conflicting medical diagnoses from various medical doctors and specialists.

Moreover, after one of the most senior managers 'unreservedly apologized' for, and expressed 'deep regret' about, some of the company's actions during the conflict with its workers, the following interaction took place:

THE CHAIRPERSON OF THE INQUIRY: Can we say then that Kylanta accepts responsibility for the health impacts that [the workers] continue to suffer?

KYLANTA MANAGER: Kylanta has accepted that there was an issue that needed to be addressed through a range of measures. We do not understand the mechanisms [...] I do not think I could give you a response that is any more informed than that [...]

Such a statement emphasizes the ambiguities in science about the cause of MCS, as well as about the harmfulness of Kylanta emissions. Industry groups have been known to magnify and even manufacture scientific uncertainties about toxicity when they are blamed for ill-health (Michaels and Monforton 2005: S40; see also Michaels 2005). Moreover, the Kylanta case shows a concomitant strategy of defence companies: to further reinforce the requirement to *wait* for a definitive scientific consensus. This is illustrated in the following excerpt, in which three Kylanta managers were interviewed by the inquiry committee:

THE CHAIRPERSON: Clearly you are saying to us that the health impacts that are being reported, which is the reason that we are sitting here today, are in a sense a mystery in that the [medical] science does not explain what is going on.

KYLANTA MANAGER 1: That is true.

THE CHAIRPERSON: Would any of you or all of you be prepared to make some speculative answer as to what the cause could be, rather than a scientific answer? What is your gut feeling about what is going on here?

KYLANTA MANAGER 2: I prefer not to speculate. I would rather continue to look for the science and get an understanding of that.
KYLANTA MANAGER I: I agree with [him].
KYLANTA MANAGER 3: Same here.

The Kylanta managers defer to the authority of scientific agreement on the issue, which is currently evasive due to the vehement disunity over MCS. Simultaneously, by 'continuing to look for the science' – in other words, by waiting for a consensus – they delay any justification for precautionary action in the meantime.

Environmental spin

The final technique engaged by the company was in public relations efforts that promoted Kylanta as a proponent of good science. The company organized a targeted advertising campaign during the height of the worker dispute, published in a community newspaper distributed in areas near the Forrestville plant. In this campaign Kylanta painted itself as an environmentally sustainable and socially responsible operation. The theme to this chain of advertisements was 'Things that make Kylanta great.' One particular full-page spread has the headline 'Koala's dine out on Kylanta Trees'. The focus is on a geographic area that was once a Kylanta mine and has since been regenerated through the company's 'extensive rehabilitation program', now housing thousands of waterbirds. According to the advertisement, the wetlands nurture a species of eucalypt that is now being fed to koalas at a Perth wildlife park. The accompanying nature photography includes close-ups of koalas and panoramas with native wetland birdlife. The summary at the bottom of the advertisement states 'Kylanta spends over $8 million a year on community partnerships in WA including scholarships, leadership awards and training programs.'

Although Kylanta is a multinational corporation, the advertisement strategically engages local and nationalistic discourses. In environmental campaigns, images of native animals and landscapes invoke public empathy towards victims of ecological damage as well as appeal to a sense of nationalistic pride and belonging (Einarsson 1993). The Kylanta advertisement with images of flora and fauna – iconic, Australian, and in the case of the koala, charismatic and threatened – epitomizes this technique.

Indeed, similar campaigns have been utilized by industry in other epistemological disputes regarding industrial risk. The concept of *greenwash* refers to public relations campaigns that configure potentially ecologically unsound activities in a new and positive light. After environmental concern heightened internationally in the late 1980s, and regulatory agencies 'got tougher', many corporations whose activities were directly jeopardized by the increased environmental focus reacted by attempting to allay public anxiety about ecological crises and persuade politicians against strict regulation (Beder 1998a). Powerful corporations began to protect themselves from scrutiny by manipulating public knowledge about ecological risk (Beder 1998a; 1998b; Ehrlich and Ehrlich 1996; Greer and Bruno 1996). According to Stauber and Rampton (1995), greenwash techniques are taught and encouraged within the public relations industry. Although these authors take extreme examples of hoodwinking – such as public relations efforts that imply 'toxic sludge is good for you!' – their perspective highlights the significance of *spin* in the environmental dispute. Admittedly, greenwash theorists sometimes have a totalizing view of multinational corporations and their power; they imply that the public are manipulated by – and largely unaware of the role played by – public relations. Yet lay participants in this study were very critical consumers of environmental spin, and developed their own communication strategies in response, as the second half of this chapter shows.

Kylanta's campaign did, however, capitalize on existing rifts within the local community over the chimneystack controversy. On the one side, there were concerned workers and community members who were calling for radical adjustments to Kylanta's operations. On the other, there were those who emphasized Kylanta's contribution to the community as it provided jobs, assisted local business and sponsored community activities. One union manager claimed in the parliamentary inquiry:

> The union and, I suspect, a number of people in the community hope that there will be an opportunity in the future for the [Forrestville Kylanta mining operations] to expand to provide further job opportunities for people in the community. Obviously that will also provide a spin-off to local businesses. It would be unfortunate, to say the least, if those opportunities were delayed or lost due to unfounded allegations or perceptions that are not supported by scientific fact.

[This discourse relates to a common theme regarding local branches of multinational corporations. Since industrializing countries often have a need to attract international investment, they can be dependent on multinational corporations to boost their economies, which gives the companies significant local support and political leverage (Monshipouri *et al.* 2003). The Forrestville community, and the Western Australian government more generally – though not 'developing' on a global scale – nonetheless have a significant reliance on multinational corporate investment. Because companies such as Kylanta are free to take their business elsewhere in a competitive global market, there is a strong incentive to protect them from inconvenient bureaucratic red tape, to keep their business and encourage their expansion.]

In addition to their bargaining power, corporations can capitalize on the tension existing between radical environmentalists and more conservative members of the community. A Kylanta manager noted defensively, for example:

> ...surveys and conversations with people in the community show that the majority want the [plant] here, they want the jobs and they want the income that flows to the state and to the community from the [plant].

Kylanta thus reinforced the division between those workers calling for structural reform versus those who prioritized Kylanta's economic contribution, which would be jeopardized in the event of radical change. It is, again, typical of environmental controversies that companies forge an alliance with pragmatists, which increases their social legitimacy and disempowers dissenters (Beder 1998a; 1998b; Stauber and Rampton 1995). One worker with MCS, Roger, poignantly summed up his experience of the community division:

> And you know the thing was, yes, we were sick. Well, you could see we were sick, but people – the community – the majority of it would say [we're] going for a payout. 'Kylanta is alright, Kylanta creates 600 jobs. We can't get rid of Kylanta' and Kylanta was saying 'we'll close up, we'll go elsewhere.' And that was scaring people. So, people weren't believing us.

As Kylanta promoted itself as a proponent of environmentalism, a socially responsible corporation, and a large contributor to the local economy, it raised its authority to deny toxicity and make credible claims about the company's commitment to worker safety. In turn, its bolstered image undermined community support for the workers with MCS and shrouded in doubt the truthfulness of their experiential knowledge.

Scientific defiance: the workers' resistance

When the workers and residents in Forrestville first started to feel and articulate a connection between their symptoms and the Kylanta chimneystack, they met with enormous scepticism. Yet, similar to lay social collectives around the globe, the Kylanta workers were extremely resourceful in disseminating an alternative interpretation of science to compete with biomedical dismissal. In turn, this helped to counter the aforementioned corporate denial of environmental risk, and, to some extent, democratize the scientific debate. Below I highlight three strategies they used to raise their credibility: honing their own scientific expertise; politically undermining corporate science; and disseminating alternative causal explanations through the media.

Developing lay expertise in science

A common observation in controversies over emergent diseases is that sufferers and concerned community members often progress from lay people to 'lay experts' in their quest to understand their experience and improve support structures (Epstein 1995; Pols 2013). Lay expertise has been particularly visible in environmental health controversies. For example, after receiving little government or professional support over their leukaemia concerns, the Woburn community developed a form of 'popular epidemiology' to highlight the prevalence of cancer and document its link to contaminated groundwater (Brown 1992; Harr 1996). They formed alliances with supportive scientists, which, in conjunction with their experiential knowledge of environmental harm, allowed the community to produce an alternative and plausible scientific explanation.

Since lay science can be flawed according to professional standards, some experts question how effective lay expertise can be (see Prior 2003), particularly with the proliferation of lay diagnosis using online information technologies. However, lay involvement in scientific debate can also promote 'good science' (Brown 1992: 277). For example, community action can identify cases of 'bad science' conducted by corporate or political authorities; and point out that 'normal science' has drawbacks, such as its slowness to accept new concepts of toxic causality (277). Furthermore, popular epidemiology yields valuable data that would be unavailable to scientists, and which may be lost if not solicited by governments (277).

In the Kylanta case, two blue-collar workers in particular sought to confront the mainstream scientific paradigm that dismissed their claims. The first was Jim Hirschovicz, who had started working as a tradesman for the Forrestville Kylanta plant in 1982 when the operations were first established. When the controversy over the chimneystack flared more than a decade later, Jim was appointed to a quasi-management role as a consultant to the company about the workers' safety concerns. Ironically, after some time in this position, Jim contracted MCS himself, and thus had an emotional and financial vested interest in negotiating better work conditions and a settlement for the affected workers.

To the chagrin of Kylanta management, Jim used his special position to obtain internal documents, and later supplied incriminating evidence to the media and parliamentary inquiry.[2] For example, Jim had been told that there was a geographical report commissioned to evaluate the suitability of the Forrestville site for Kylanta's operations before the plant was built. After having asked his superiors to see a copy of the report, he was repeatedly told that they either did not have it, or could not find it. One day, Jim looked more closely at the book that was used to prop up the computer monitor on his desk and, serendipitously, found the report he'd been looking for. Upon analysis, the report announced the Forrestville site unfit for a plant since in certain weather patterns, emissions would certainly be carried to neighbouring townships.

Jim also discovered internal memos containing incriminating proof that the managers knew about the chimneystack's toxicity before and during its instalment. One memo read, 'Yes, the stuff put out [by] the stack is harmful, very toxic indeed...' This memo goes on to say 'the ground level concentrations are well within Occupational Exposure Standards' and 'the smell is most likely a smell only.' However, it concludes that '...the plant has not operated to correct conditions yet. If they get the plant running well then the design engineers say there won't even be a smell. Nice dream let's hope it scores in reality'.

Moreover, Jim's research into Kylanta documents uncovered instances where the company commissioned suspect science. One document revealed a collegial relationship between Kylanta management and an 'independent' health inspector engaged by the company called Dr Portsmouth, who was asked to report on the health impacts of the chimneystack. Jim found a letter from Dr Portsmouth to one of Kylanta's managers before he undertook his assessment, which read:

> I note your requirement to answer **"there is no long term health effects associated with the operation of the chimneystack plant"** and will present a summary document regarding this in the near future. [*Emphasis in original.*]

Two weeks later, Dr Portsmouth's final report stated:

> Long term health effects arising from [the chimneystack] substances at these levels, specifically will not be a problem.

It was later remarked by one member of the parliamentary inquiry committee that this situation seemed, 'rather like providing a report to order, if you like.'

An interesting feature of Jim's transformation to expert is that he became acutely aware that lay knowledge is often dismissed on the basis that it is subjective and prone to overstatements. He explicitly mentioned that he made a deliberate effort to restrict his evidence to confirmed facts, never participated in hearsay and always provided conservative estimates regarding toxicity and health effects. This strategy increased the perception that he was measured, rigorous and objective, all of which are prerequisites for credibility in the scientific and legal fields. Importantly, it also prevented defamation suits against him.

Peter Hawkins was another person who developed expertise as a result of his experience with Kylanta. When I met him, Peter's appearance was striking: a well-built carpenter wearing a blue singlet and short football shorts, with a 'mullet' haircut and large tattoos on his arms. Yet Peter is a renowned self-taught expert in environmental toxicology and public health, despite only having high-school level chemistry. When the town became concerned about the emissions from the chimneystack, he started to research more about the VOCs being emitted. He educated himself in meteorological science and geography to understand how weather patterns would carry emissions from the chimneystack to residents' houses. He trawled through scientific research in its infancy to investigate how long-term, low-level exposures might affect people's health. He then sought access to Kylanta's data on emissions monitoring in order to compare the figures he calculated and those printed in the company's public statements. His submissions became of particular interest in the parliamentary inquiries, where he informed the committee of a number of discrepancies in Kylanta's data.

As a result of his expertise, Peter learnt how to communicate his scientific theories with members of parliament and Western Australian Environment and Health ministers. He explained:

> I suppose I've had the time, and, I suppose, the fortune, to be able to sit down and really get my head around the technical stuff and that side of things [...] The hard part was learning how to deal with people I don't sort of know how to deal with, in so far as the bureaucrats in government and the ministers and those sorts of people which I, in my other life, would have rarely had any time for and any interest in speaking to.

The fact that Peter refers to the time prior to his activism as 'my other life' is testament to the extent of the transformation he experienced. The perceived injustice of corporate conspiracy and political negligence radicalized him, and produced a new kind of agent that was motivated to push for change.

In the context of the Kylanta chimneystack, the efficacy of official scientific processes to detect toxicity (for example through TLVs) was arguable and limited by current institutional knowledge. This form of science tended to disallow the possibility that undetectable emissions might have been hazardous to workers' and residents' health, which was discordant with the experience of illness felt and documented by community members. Peter and Jim consequently brought new forms of data into the dispute – which, akin to Brown's findings, might otherwise have remained latent – to demonstrate alternative explanations for toxic causality. This included an exacting analysis of the pitfalls of the current scientific paradigm.

Notably, however, Peter faced significant barriers. He represented the community in a group that was convened to address the issues surrounding the chimneystack, made up of workers, residents, OHS experts, government officials and Kylanta representatives. Kylanta's willingness to form the committee could be perceived as an act of openness and cooperation. However, Peter describes below the response he repeatedly received from his fellow committee members:

> Kylanta will agree [to providing information requested], and then say 'at a later date.' And so we'll mark that in our books and [put a] reminder next to it, and six months later, we'll ask the question, twelve months later we'll ask the question and on and on it goes until we get an answer: 'oh, sorry, we just don't have time to do that, so we'll have to remove that from this process and put it into another process.' And then you know that it's gonna go nowhere. (But I think you also know yourself then that you're onto something because they don't want to address it.)

Timing is crucial in environmental illness disputes due to the standards of proof in both the medico-scientific and legal fields. Medicine requires a *temporal* link between toxic exposure and symptoms, and legal decision-makers are searching for a causal association between negligence and damages, which again is a question of timing. Moreover, workers and community members whose health is allegedly affected by the plant's operations evidently perceive a great deal of urgency surrounding the issue – for their own physical, emotional and financial reasons as well as the health and safety of future employees. In controlling the timing in which emissions are measured and effects are monitored, defendant companies such as Kylanta can control the data that workers have access to for establishing a connection between their environment and ill-health. Since time is of the essence, the fact that – in Peter's words – 'it's all driven by [Kylanta's] timelines and nobody else's' represents an important power discrepancy that can limit the agency of actors such as Peter in the dispute over precaution. While popular epidemiology may yield important scientific data which otherwise may be lost, some of the crucial material to prove it can continue to be gate-kept by the companies implicated in the dispute.

Seeking political representation

Another strategy engaged by the community was to seek political reinforcement of their claims. A source of support came from a passionate local Greens politician, Hugh Porter. When the workers approached him and told him of their plight, Hugh explained to me:

> When these people came through the door, and I heard the labour party wasn't doing anything for them, the unions weren't doing anything for them, the State Department of Mines wasn't doing

anything, the Health Department wasn't doing anything, the Department of Environmental Protection wasn't doing anything, and then I started to hear all the dirty business that was going on in the background, and I thought…I'm that sort of person, I get very angry, and think, *I'll fix these bastards.* [He chuckles.] *At least, I'll give it a real go.* And so I did.

By helping to politicize the issue, he challenged Kylanta's dominance over the debate about emissions toxicity. He undertook detailed research, which involved, as he calls it, 'building up a good dossier' on the company. Hugh's investigations into Kylanta's history revealed some valuable pieces of information not only about the global company Kylanta International, but also about individual professionals employed or engaged by the local management. For example, one practitioner, who was flown from interstate to assess the workers' conditions, had determined that none of them were suffering from a chemically caused condition. Hugh's research uncovered that this specialist had in 1992 convened a group of scientists who concluded that 'the data in relation to "passive smok[ing]" and adverse health effects is weak and inconclusive'. Because the carcinogenic properties of passive smoking has since become normal science, the physician's prior record in denying toxicity somewhat weakened his credibility to neutrally assess the workers' conditions.

Hugh also harnessed the experiential data and expertise from members of the community and represented it in a public forum. In line with the Greens Party's philosophy of participatory democracy, Hugh explains his strategy: to gauge what was happening 'on the ground', collect the questions that the public want answered, 'print them out in parliamentary jargon', ask those questions in parliament, and give the answers 'back to the people'. Aside from empowering the public, this also meant Hugh went from having one person working in his office, to having 'hundreds of people flooding [him] with information' on different issues regarding the Kylanta dispute. Hugh's position as a member of parliament (though admittedly in the less powerful Greens party) facilitated the workers' access to the parliamentary process, and raised the political profile of their epistemological claims.

Popularizing the scientific debate

Another way in which the workers' bolstered their legitimacy was through the media. Media coverage can spread awareness and understanding about a contested illness (Aronowitz 1998: 29).The media played a particularly integral part in the Kylanta controversy, though they were initially delayed in taking an interest in the affair. When it became a hot topic, however, newspapers and current affair television programs supported the workers on a fairly consistent basis. A year after the chimneystack was installed, a local newspaper's front page headline was 'Kylanta in Health Risk Fear'. After that first article, over 400 articles appeared in local, national and international newspapers regarding the conflict. Many articles focused on the toxic health risks, including 'Chimneystack chemicals to blame: ill worker' (with a photo of Evan in a respiratory mask); 'Toxic fallout near Kylanta'; 'Experts stumped by cocktail of chemicals'; and 'Chimneystack ruined my life, claims worker.'

Often informed by Jim, press coverage frequently emphasized foul play from the company, with headlines shouting: '[Management] Memo told of Kylanta health risks,' 'Kylanta scare tactic works'; and 'Legal doubt on Kylanta breaches'. Some journalists sought to problematize the relationship between Kylanta management and the government departments who were supposed to be regulating them: 'Department of Environmental Protection reassures on plant emissions'; 'Ministers accused of ducking health talks: we want people with muscle, say Kylanta accusers'; and 'Govt. not serious about Kylanta health problems says [Greens MP, Hugh] Porter' Even though newspapers also printed company press releases that counteracted the negative press – for example, 'Kylanta denies emissions link to failing health'; 'Kylanta health cleared'; and 'Emissions at safe levels: Kylanta' – this reporting would always be juxtaposed with a discussion about residual community and professional fears regarding the emissions.

At the time of the Kylanta dispute, Clinton Bracks was a young and promising journalist at *The Perth Times*. As mentioned in the preface, Clinton heard about the Kylanta dispute by chance when he happened upon a letter in his chief of staff's office from a chemically sensitive elderly woman named Silvia living near the Kylanta operations. Clinton explains:

> I got in the car and just drove down to Forrestville and found the place, went to see her and just listened to the story. I took a photographer with me, made [the photographer] do a picture of [Silvia] with the smoke stacks in the background. Anyway, she's pulled out all this stuff, background information for me, you know, from the company and that. I thought, wow this is incredible, so drove back and I remember when I was driving home I needed to stop for a drink or something to eat, so I stopped in Milton, which is the other side of the [plant], and I got out of the car and I was like, hell, I can smell it from here you know? A heavy wet, chemical-type smell. I was like, shit, these people are living in these fumes. So I just drove back to the office and got a good story and rang Kylanta and got given a nonchalant, you know 'there's no problem, there's nothing happening, there's nothing to see here,' put that in the story and I remember, it ran as a picture story on the front page of the paper. So then I just...there was so much information that Silvia gave me that, you know, I just followed it up

and followed it up and followed it up and I spent two years working on the story. Did hundreds of stories about it.

In the ensuing conflict, Clinton actively engaged in the epistemological conflict between Kylanta and its workers and challenged the company's power to deflect responsibility for a growing health concern. When the dispute first began in the mid-1990s, he deliberately and systematically introduced the new concept of MCS and its link to chemicals to the Western Australian public:

> You can't just go splashing in with MCS does this and this, because they [the public] will just get overwhelmed and they'll go, 'oh it's too hard. I've read too many acronyms or too many long words'... and they give up. I was starting off from scratch, you know when no-one knew anything the hell about [MCS]... [*pretending to be a member of the public*] 'what? Kylanta, what? What do they do? Emissions, do they have emissions? Where's Forrestville? Who? Sick? What?' You know, I took it from zero to full information... I think by the end of it, just the average reader of *The Perth Times* would have read a few of my stories, they... they know... they now know Kylanta produces a [mineral, which] when it's produced, produces a lot of serious shit out of the smoke stacks that blows through those towns down there and makes people very sick [...] And it's happening and Kylanta hasn't done much about it. [The company]'s basically thrown a bit of money the way of some of the workers, you know, and have been absolute bastards about the whole thing.

Scholars writing on health social movements have emphasized how actors often utilize cultural ideologies 'to construct persuasive and culturally resonant frames' (Klawiter 2005; see also Epstein 1997). Clinton illustrated this point when he cynically 'made [the photographer] do a picture of Sylvia with the smoke stacks in the background.' A chimneystack is an easily recognized symbol of the risk society, and immediately conjures the link between industrial power and environmental risk. Visually juxtaposing this image with a sick, elderly woman completes a powerful metaphor of inequality.

Similarly drawing on culturally resonant themes, another journalist referred to Jim Herschovitz as 'Jim Brockovich' in order to compare him to Erin, the unlikely crusader for public health and victim of corporate conspiracy. Articles about a worker named David who was suing a different plant of Kylanta for chemical injuries referred to the company as a mining 'Goliath', capitalizing on the historically entrenched support for the underdog in the social imaginary. These are political tools that framed the workers' unorthodox scientific claims in a way that resonates in popular culture.

However, the simplified way in which tabloid newspapers represent health issues can be a double-edged sword for the categorization of new diseases. There exists a widespread belief amongst sceptics that the media fuels and facilitates hypochondria regarding controversial conditions, and, in relation to MCS, propagates unwarranted fears of toxicity (e.g. Showalter 1997). And this concern is not unfounded; Lofstedt and colleagues (2011) highlighted several instances in Europe in which the media amplified risks surrounding, for example, a cervical cancer vaccine, which gave rise to knee-jerk and unscientific policy reactions that made the public wary of products that were not only safe but also therapeutic.

Given this background, sympathetic coverage attracts attention to the condition that can evoke not only empathy but also disdain from the medical profession. For example, during the height of the Kylanta conflict, one of Western Australia's most prominent medical professors wrote a letter to the editor of *The Perth Times* entitled, 'Why do you scare the public?.' In this letter, he states:

> When medical claims are made about the negative impact of industry, it should be done at a responsible level which quotes documented research. Your so-called 'multiple chemical sensitivity' disorder is a disease which probably does not exist. If there really is a problem, please find some cases of people who really do have real diseases.

In turn media attention can negatively impact physician's attitudes towards the patients and ultimately adversely affect healthcare delivery (see Engel, Adkins and Cowan 2002). Yet suffice to say that journalists supported the workers' claims on a fairly consistent basis, which undeniably bolstered their legitimacy in the eyes of the public. Clinton was awarded one of the most prestigious journalistic awards in Australia for his investigative reporting on the Kylanta issue and later received a United Nations award for environmental journalism.

Government intervention and legal settlement

I have described above how the workers and the company jostled over the definition of toxic harm and the existence of disease. They both acted as 'risk entrepreneurs' (Lofsted *et al.* 2011), who capitalized on scientific uncertainty to frame risks in a way that suited their interests. However, I now turn to the state's involvement in the scientific controversy – through government regulation, parliamentary inquiries and the workers' compensation apparatus – to trace how the conflict eventually reached closure.

Several state departments in Western Australia were integral in the Kylanta affair. These included the Department of Health, the Department of Environmental Protection and the Department of Industry and Resources.

Since these factions are charged with regulating healthcare, environmental concerns and industrial production respectively, they were all approached by workers, community members and their supportive medical physicians to assess and regulate Kylanta's activities. However, for several years after the health complaints first occurred, there was very little communication between the departments and few changes to Kylanta's operations were enforced.

The inspection process undertaken at the Kylanta plant demonstrated elements of a 'medical-industrial complex', which is where doctors, industry consultants and government officials collude with one another. Such a complex has historically played a role in jeopardizing workplace safety, by suppressing information about industry risks and opposing legislative controls (Berman 1978; Brodeur 1974). In the Kylanta case, the Department of Industry and Resources is the division of government under which OHS issues at mine sites in Western Australia fall, as opposed to the Department of Health, which deals with safety in all other sectors of industry. The Department of Industry and Resources also deals with production (and therefore profits) from the mining industry. A number of players in the Kylanta dispute argued that this duality constitutes a conflict of interest, since safety precautions might be compromised in the interests of production. As one worker described the process of inspection, the workers' power to have their concerns heard over the interests of management was largely ineffectual:

> What we found was, [the government inspectors] would interview several workers and they would become very concerned. Then they'd go and have a meeting with the management of Kylanta and the management would just say, 'oh well, the very transient conditions that the workforce are experiencing, they just need to go to fresh air, there'd be no long-term health impacts from these emissions'. [Then] the mine's inspector would make some notes in a book at the site...and they never made very demanding requests of the company to improve the situation.

In this forum, corporate interests were listened to while those of the workers tended to be ignored, a claim that has been reinforced by earlier studies of workplace politics (Draper 1991; Pearce and Tombs 1998).

However, the combination of medical advocacy, community outrage and media publicity eventually led to a perceived social crisis. It was against this backdrop that Greens MP Hugh Porter succeeded in calling for the first parliamentary inquiry into Kylanta, which was led by the then Minister for Agriculture. The findings of this preliminary inquiry acknowledged that the Western Australian departments of Health, Environmental Protection, and Industry and Resources, needed to communicate more effectively to collectively address OHS risks, public health concerns and the regulation of industry in the future.

However, after this parliamentary inquiry, adverse health effects continued to be reported by workers and the community surrounding Kylanta's operations. Eventually, five years after the complaints had started – four years after the first media coverage of the affair – the Department of Health convened a discussion amongst medical and scientific experts on the Kylanta issue. The convention – called the Medical Practitioner's Forum – included 19 health and scientific professionals with an interest in the area, including doctors who had diagnosed workers and residents with chemical injuries, as well as doctors who worked for the Kylanta plant and who had previously rejected the harmfulness of the chemicals in question.

The forum was chaired by an expert in public health, Professor Willet James, because he was seen as an independent party who had no previous involvement in the contested area or stated position on the issues in question.[3] This group of experts conceded that there *was* a health problem that needed to be addressed, where previously it had been denied by those in authority. Although they concluded that there was not enough evidence to determine *which* chemical emitted by Kylanta's operations was causing the adverse health impacts, they unanimously agreed that:

> There appears to be an association between health problems and Kylanta's Plant. There were meteorological and temporal conditions that could connect the plant with health problems.

Professor James summarized the event to me as such:

> It was as if, finally, at last, they had been listened to by some group, you know? And I think it helped a little bit in starting some sort of healing process, or a more collaborative approach to the problem.

Simultaneous to the Medical Practitioner's Forum, Hugh was calling for a second parliamentary inquiry to be held, this time chaired by a fellow Greens member. This second inquiry was more extensive, taking submissions and questioning witnesses from the three relevant government departments as well as local residents, Kylanta workers, union delegates, and representatives from Kylanta's management and OHS departments. When the panel had completed a series of hearings at several locations between November 1999 and July 2000, the Standing Committee submitted a report of more than 400 pages. It made 29 recommendations regarding the structure of government regulation and the mining company's treatment of public health issues. Of most significance were the following two requirements:

The Government [should] review and report on the role of the Department of Industry and Resources as both regulator of mine safety and facilitator of mine developments with a view to determining whether such roles might be better addressed in separated agencies [...]

The Department of Health, as a matter of priority, [should] derive a hazard index for locations near to Forrestville in order to assess the health risks caused by the cumulative impact of the very high number of chemicals mixed together in the emissions from Kylanta's plant at Forrestville.

At the same time as the parliamentary inquiry, the first MCS compensation case against the company was about to reach trial, nearly five years after it had begun. It was in regards to the case of Evan, the worker whose life had 'changed forever' after the coughing fit in his workmate's car. Kylanta's legal team had submitted to the courts that they were intending to have Evan on the witness stand for 28 days. Evan's solicitor, Mark, who was acting pro bono for his client, was extremely anxious about continuing. The case was likely to cost more than a million dollars, as he needed to call witnesses from all over the world, but decided to 'call their bluff' and continue as if confident of a win.

Clinton and other journalists covered the conflict closely. One headline noted, 'Sick locals still waiting for compo [...] corporation digging its heels in to avoid pay-outs,' Another article asserted that:

> A Kylanta worker who is suing the company for making him sick says he was pressured to drop the case by a company executive just days before it was due in court.

The trial, however, never eventuated. Just before it was due to commence, Kylanta managers sought to settle not just Evan's but *all* of the sick workers' claims. To do so, they approached Jim in his quasi-consultant capacity, who described the interaction as follows:

> Basically Kylanta came to me one day and said, 'how do we resolve where we're at?' because a lot of bad publicity [was] being generated for them...they couldn't handle it anymore. And I asked for three things: a) that the sick workers get looked after financially, secondly, that the existing workers be protected from the emission and, thirdly, something be put in place for the community.

To facilitate the settlement, Kylanta called in their international medical director, Dr Matthew Stein, from the United States. Fortuitously for the workers, Dr Stein happened to be one of the world's leading experts in chemical sensitivities. Dr Stein interviewed all the sick workers, as well as the doctors who had treated them, and concluded that all of them were suffering from MCS. For one of the supportive specialists, who had received much scepticism from his profession and Kylanta management for so frequently diagnosing MCS, Dr Stein's visit reassured him that he was 'doing all the right things'.

Without definitively admitting Kylanta's liability for their illness, Dr Stein's finding was that the incidences of MCS had occurred 'at our plant, on our watch' (as quoted in *The Perth Times*). He concluded that, although it is impossible to isolate the cause of the condition, Kylanta had poorly treated a group of workers with chemical sensitivity for several years and he thus recommended that the best way for everyone to move ahead would be to find a financial compromise. Although this sounds like an admission of liability, there is a subtle difference. Dr Stein never identified a toxic cause nor directly blamed Kylanta for the incidences of chemical sensitivity. (A noteworthy aside is that Kylanta sponsors Dr Stein's research laboratory.)

Taking its medical director's advice, Kylanta management settled claims with all except one of the workers who had been diagnosed with MCS through the Workers Compensation Commission. They were each granted over $300,000 plus a total and permanent disability payout under their superannuation scheme, an unusually large amount according to workers' compensation standards.[4] The front page headline the next day was: 'KYLANTA IN $MILLION PAYOUT: Offer to sick workers.'

Financial recompense through the legal apparatus can be a powerful symbol of juridical recognition. As Das illustrates (2000: 284), the outcome of a medico-legal dispute – whether a payout is made, how much it is, and what this suggests about the negligence of the defendant company (and thus the validity and extent of the victim's suffering) – can significantly influence how litigants experience and cope with their illness thereafter.

The connection between legitimacy, compensation and healing is again illustrated in the Kylanta example. Where previously many of the workers had exhibited great anger and frustration, the perceived adequacy of the settlement dissipated these feelings for some of them. When I asked Jim if he felt the compensation was adequate, he said:

> I think for sick people there's no level of compensation – you can't put a dollar figure on health. On the other hand, I believe that the settlement that the workers came to with Kylanta allowed those people either to get on with their lives or stop being affected by the emissions and have a reasonable sort of money behind them to get on with life.

'Getting on with life' is part of the healing process, which often only begins when workers are given a sense of closure. In the previous chapter I used the word 'closure' as developed in science and technology studies, to refer to the point at which a controversy is rhetorically settled and closed off to further debate. Here, it has a similar meaning but it works on a more personal level: it is the point at which an individual psychologically places a conflict behind them. The workers illustrated that a sense of legal validation – a legitimate entry into the sick role and the social and moral value it confers – can assist in this process.

On the face of it, the course of events described above affirmed, to some extent, the workers' experiential knowledge about exposure to toxic emissions and its link to ill-health. And yet, from a more longitudinal perspective, it is clear that a more corporate version of science prevailed in the Kylanta controversy.

Closure: return to business as usual

Galanter (1994: 136) argues that when victims are compensated for workplace injury, the event can 'cumulate into a kind of knowledge that generates prevention'. In order to work as a prevention of future injury, information about the enforced compensation must be disseminated by court records, trade publications and the media. The information must be 'gathered into a kind of usable knowledge', such as in current legal publications, so that it enters the 'lore' of lawyers, insurers and risk managers. Other potential injurers (employers like Kylanta) must also pay attention to it and 'alter their behaviour in light of it'. Below I outline the social conditions that inhibited the dissemination of knowledge about compensation, potential risk and illness in the Kylanta case.

Despite the relatively large payout made to the Kylanta workers according to ordinary workers' compensation standards, the company continues to deny liability for their conditions, and the workers are now under a deed of confidentiality. This agreement restricts their ability to publicize their experiences to a large extent and the case is prevented from being used as a legal precedent.[5] As pointed out in the previous chapter, lawsuits can provide a form of civic education in which novel theories can be tested and scientific controversies can be resolved in the public eye (Jasanoff 1995; Lynch *et al.* 2010). However, an out-of-court settlement prevents the exposure of evidence that might favour a novel scientific explanation, and further undermines the potential for an emergent condition to be legitimized on the legal stage. Fully cognisant of this problem, a former pilot suing an airline for MCS argued that accepting an out-of-court settlement is equivalent to the defendant 'buying a win' and thus she rejected offers of settlement against the advice of her solicitor. Notably, however, chemically sensitive plaintiffs who can no longer work and who experience protracted and expensive legal proceedings often have dire need for immediate financial assistance, which can persuade them to accept the first offer of settlement irrespective of its adequacy. This trade-off between, on the one hand, immediate payment, and on the other, a longer arduous journey towards legal validation and a potentially bigger settlement, has also been observed in workers' negotiations regarding asbestos-related disease (Waldman 2011).

For Roger, who was the most disabled Kylanta worker with MCS and multiple sclerosis (which he believes is also work caused), the payout did little to assist him. His once two-income family has been reduced to relying on his wife's wage as a cleaner, which is minimal. Yet, the most hurtful outcome for Roger was the sense of betrayal at the way he was treated by his employer: 'They didn't believe [me] and they never once tried to help me, say, "well Rog, you got sick. You worked with us 22 years; we'll help you."' His wife explains that she has had to tell him to 'get over Kylanta' and has encouraged him to take up meditation. Roger nonetheless commented that he is 'not like Evan and Jim' because he is 'still angry'. The adequacy of financial redress is, therefore, subjective and dependent on one's circumstances. And for some, closure requires an apology, a symbolic recognition of their suffering by the injurer, and the role it played in causing it.

After their payout, the workers continued to be disbelieved and stigmatized by many sceptical experts, local residents, and Kylanta workers. The out-of-court settlement, and the lost opportunity for evidence of toxicity to be tabled, fuelled the perception that the workers were 'only in it for the money'. The sceptical infectious disease specialist said to me, 'these workers didn't get a whiff of chemicals, they got a whiff of compensation'. Far from settling the dispute over the condition, the agreement reached in the medico-legal dispute seemed to strengthen the already-existing rift between sceptics and sympathizers.

Furthermore, although the parliamentary committee brought to light some of the shortfalls of the government's and Kylanta's treatment of the health concerns, very few of the committees' recommendations were meaningfully implemented. To my knowledge, a hazard index has not been derived and the role of the Department of Industry and Resources remains unchanged.

Any perceived legitimacy for the workers arising out of the settlement was further depleted by the state approval of a $1.4 billion expansion of the Kylanta Forrestville plant. Although the plans were eventually placed in doubt after the global financial crisis, government officials and Kylanta management hailed the proposed expansion as an important source of new jobs and income for the local community and state. Unsurprisingly, the health impacts reportedly still arising from the emissions were not addressed in any of the company or government press releases or public notices surrounding the issue.

And finally, the media support for the Kylanta workers, which built momentum around the condition and its possible link to contaminants, has largely dissipated. Describing how this process unfolded, Clinton noted that his editor was concerned about the threats he received almost daily from Kylanta management regarding Clinton's coverage. Clinton was thus asked by his superiors to provide substantiating evidence for each of his claims. As he explained:

> When I wrote a story about Kylanta, [it was] not just, like, every line I'd have to justify, I used to have to justify every word. For example the word, 'toxic', right? I used to use the word toxic 'cause these things are toxic. And I'd be in there with my editors and they'd say, 'oh well the Kylanta people say that it's not toxic'...we'd get out definitions of toxic, you know, and I'd prove that it was toxic. Toxic things make you sick or it's harmful or if you have enough of it, it will kill you. We'd get it out, we'd go through it, we'd agonise and then my lawyers were trying to get me to take the word toxic out...

Clinton noted that the process became increasingly laborious:

> I'd be fighting to keep [the controversial details] in. 'Cause I'd be saying, look we can't sugar coat this, we...you know, that's what they want us to do, water the whole thing down so it's meaningless, right? And I said, that's not what this is about, I...I believe that they are harming people [...] and I'm out to prove it, alright, and so I'm not going to back off it, because I reckon I've got the evidence. And isn't it what newspaper is and what journalism should be all about?

Clinton remembers a Kylanta legal representative eventually travelled from the US to arrange a meeting with Clinton's superiors. After this point, Clinton's editor asked him to find another story to investigate and Clinton, in disgust, left the paper to join a family business. Thereafter, the media coverage about Kylanta and MCS all but dried up. Clinton's groundwork – wherein he had introduced MCS and its alleged link to chemicals until it was a relatively well-known concept – has in essence relapsed. Although residents such as Peter continue to inform the odd article about Kylanta, Peter expresses disappointment about what he sees as an overall failure of his committee to make any real difference to the impact of the mining plant on the community. One medical practitioner, who was optimistic for the recognition of MCS after the forum, was incensed about the approved expansion:

> I think it's outrageous. I think it's criminal. I think it's absolutely anti-social. I think it is exclusively financial for the benefit of the employer. I think it shows a weakness of our Government to stand up for the community who has voted it into power, because all they're doing is doing what the company says.

So the issue of MCS was for a short time politicized in Western Australia. However, the out-of-court settlement eventually negotiated by the company and the expansion approved by the government disqualified the Kylanta case from becoming a catalyst to meaningful change.

Conclusion

In order to raise the credibility of their experiential knowledge of disease, the Kylanta workers developed their own expertise in formulating and debating scientific theories. They forged alliances with sympathetic experts, politicians and the media to make their employer and regulatory authorities take their contamination claims seriously. Moreover, their stories highlight that these community alliances do have the space to contest and redefine risk, have been able to push for changes to mining operations to some extent, have solicited government intervention, and have sought redress for their emergent illness through the legal system. However, this glass-half-full perspective veils the ways in which inequality continues to exist in debates over toxicity.

Corporations accused of contamination can strategically shape the consensus about acceptable levels of risk by undermining the scientific credibility of workers' claims, magnifying uncertainties, selectively spotlighting parts of their operations that are environmental sustainable, and, ultimately, muddying agreement about toxicity.

As shown above, medico-scientific consensus was reached about the causal link between the Kylanta plant and community ill-health, and the controversy was legally settled. However, *closure* on the issue of Kylanta's toxicity (cleared as generally harmless) and the toxogenic explanations for MCS (deemed controversial at best) was *not* a result of scientific proof but, rather, a politico-economic arrangement in which Kylanta was permitted to return to business as usual. The case study emphasizes that because multinational corporations have increased leverage within the neoliberal status quo, they have a disproportionate influence in the social construction of medico-scientific knowledge.

Chapter 4

The medico-legal illness narratives

It's a huge impact on us to feel like we're fighting these kinds of things [the insurance company and the legal system] because, like David and Goliath, you feel like you're hitting your head against the wall all the time. [...] And in my thoughts, I was thinking, we're just putting ourselves through years of stress and heartache for something that we're not going to win. It's just going to drag out and drag out and cost more and more money along the way, and in the meantime, we lose our health and the time that we have together now [...]. And it's the person that's got the most money at the end of the day and the most clout that gets to make all the rules. And they've got more money and more clout than we have.

Jackie, wife of Ian Harvey, a plaintiff with chemical sensitivity

People with chronic conditions and their families often use narratives to articulate and give meaning to their experience. These 'before and after' stories demonstrate how people reconstruct their new selves after the disruptive event of sickness (Gibson 1997); interact with the broader medical structure (Klawiter 2005); and, in the case of chemical sensitivity, understand the new ways in which bodies react to the environment (Kroll-Smith and Floyd 1997). Stories told by MCS litigants have the unique narrative element of a workers' compensation battle, and thus provide an insight into how uncertainty is experienced and governed at the interface of medical science, law and the insurance sector. In this chapter I focus on the story of Ian Harvey. Drawing on illness narrative literature I firstly examine how Ian and other chemically sensitive participants experience the onset of MCS, engage help-seeking practices, re-evaluate their lives and deploy coping mechanisms. The chapter then introduces the workers' compensation system, and analyses how the chemically sensitive body is subjected to scrutiny in the medical clinic, the courtroom and by insurance inspectors in everyday life. It highlights the ways in which the workers' compensation apparatus is structured against recognition, financial assistance and healing for people with emergent conditions.

The onset of MCS

While I only knew Ian after he had been diagnosed with chemical brain damage, he was once known to his friends and family as a friendly, easy-going man who enjoyed partying. He always offered to help with his elderly neighbour's household chores, and, according to his sister, was 'just as a normal person is.' However, after working for several years as a trade assistant spray-painting for multinational company Vox Australia, Ian began to change when he was about 33 years old. He frequently became aggressive, constantly fell asleep at social events, looked pale and tired and, when helping his neighbour with the gardening, would often throw down his tools in anger. His sister recalls that he would get 'snappy' with her children and uncharacteristically refused to help with the care of his father, who had Alzheimer's disease.

Ian still finds it difficult to describe the nature of his condition and pinpoint its onset. He replicates a common element of illness narratives outlined by Arthur Frank (1995: 30) in recalling how his body began to act in unpredictable ways, rendering it contingent on forces beyond his control:

> It's like you're driving your car slightly beyond the range of your head-lights [*makes gesture of one hand moving just behind the other*]... And you hit a panic mode, or not a panic mode, you just hit a – your body's trying to go further than what your brain's allowing it to, and you tend to just snap... Just like a storm in a tea-cup and it's over. And once that situation's settled back down, to the distance that I can handle [*same gesture again*] I come back to here and everything seems okay.

The lack of control that Ian started experiencing led to anti-social behaviour, which in turn affected his relationships with those close to him. Chronic illness frequently forces sufferers and their families to rethink their relationships because it disrupts 'the normal rules of reciprocity and mutual support' (Bury 1991: 169). For Ian, the gradual and insidious onset of his condition meant that these social changes occurred *before* he understood what was happening to his body. His motivation was affected. This is emphasized in the following anecdotal excerpt, in which he had severely offended his girlfriend and she was about to walk out on him:

> I was just sorta [thinking], *Come on, get your act together boy, what's wrong with ya?* You know, *you love the woman, so get moving.* It was just like I was wading through sand. And she walked out the door of the bedroom [...]

Ian attributed the eventual break-up of this relationship to a combination of his constant tiredness, bouts of uncontrolled anger towards his girlfriend and her children, impaired libido and a lack of general motivation. Reflecting on it during one interview, he said, 'I was just a proper asshole when I was spray-painting.'

[At this juncture it is important to note some dissimilarity between Ian's case and the other stories I draw on. Ian was diagnosed with a toxic encephalopathy, or chemical brain damage, but was never diagnosed with MCS per se. He reacts to a few different chemicals, yet has not been labelled with multiple sensitivities. Ian's case also differs because he was exposed to lead-based spray-paint. Lead poisoning has been known to affect human health since the time of the ancient Greeks, although the way lead poisoning manifests continues to be a contested area of medical science, with many similarities to the MCS debate (see Widener 2000).]

Like Ian, all of the chemically sensitive people I spoke to only realised their health had changed retrospectively. Fiona, a former pilot, reflected on the onset of her condition, which she attributed to toxic cabin air:

> Because the symptoms would go away I didn't think too much of it [...] [Eventually] my voice got so bad I had to stop work because I couldn't do the passenger announcements...I would get like a tingling of the head, loss of concentration, short term – not good for a pilot [...] And I remember [when my condition got worse] I could hardly lift my nav bag across the car park to walk into work and then I [would] have to go out and fly. It was that bad and I didn't know that was chemical sensitivity [...] I had no understanding.

Seeking help

After two years of gradual deterioration, Ian says he realized something had to be done. 'I've gotta do something. Something's wrong, you know? This is not my normal...I'm doing things not in my nature. And I thought, God, I feel so goddamn tired all the time.' Seeking help is often a difficult and time-consuming process for people who suffer from conditions that have a contested causation. Their search to find a physician who understands their suffering in a way they agree with often entails a number of misdiagnoses, or labels that seem discordant with their experience (Dumit 2006; Reid, Ewan and Lowy 1991). One Kylanta worker, Evan, mentioned, 'I'd seen the local doctors and they just kept saying, "Oh look," you know, "it's probably allergies or this or that"'. In Ian's search for medical support, he thought he might have Ross River Virus,[1] so he consulted his general practitioner (GP), who assured him he did not. The doctor suspected he may be suffering from stress, and suggested Ian take a holiday. It was not until later that year that Ian discovered the filtered masks he was using for spray painting at his workplace were the wrong size and that they failed to protect him from the paint fumes. He remembered that he often finished work covered in lead-based yellow paint, and even coughed up yellow phlegm on several occasions.

Upon hearing his work history, Ian's GP suggested he see a specialist in occupational medicine with an interest in chemical injuries. The specialist listened to Ian's exposure history and the description of his symptoms and asserted that his condition was caused by exposure to lead paints and solvents in the workplace. This diagnosis was contested later in the legal dispute because the specialist had not found abnormal levels of lead in the blood tests. Sympathetic experts in Ian's case asserted that measurements of blood-lead levels do not necessarily correlate with the body's burden of lead; however, others engaged by the defence cite this reasoning as irrational and bad science.

Finding a supportive physician and being diagnosed are key events in a person's illness narrative, particularly for those with a contested condition previously shrouded in uncertainty (Reid, Ewan and Lowy 1991). For Ian and the other chemically sensitive participants I spoke to, the first confirmatory diagnosis validated their experiential knowledge to some extent, and encouraged them to seek compensation.

Re-evaluating lifestyle

Irrespective of a diagnostic label, when a person sustains a 'hidden' condition, they are often subjected to stigma and a lack of sympathy (Lipson 2004). This was the case for each of the MCS litigants I interviewed, including Evan, who experienced disbelief from some of his colleagues:

> Some of my workmates questioned me [...] I think they just couldn't understand why I was sick, you know, because I was fit, I was healthy, I was basically doing what I wanted to do. Like I was playing sport or I was into weights. I was a strong person – physically I looked okay – but I just wasn't. You know? [...] Unless you had a broken arm and a plaster, they can't put that relationship to your illness.

Another informant, Clyde, is a former engineer who contracted MCS when he entered his office having not been notified that it had recently been sprayed heavily with insecticide. Clyde says that after his MCS diagnosis, he distanced himself from his mother, who was sceptical of her son's condition because of his decision to take legal action:

> My mother saw it very much as me trying to make money by instigating some kind of compensation case, because I think that was her mindset. She had no real, no understanding or sympathy with these issues. And I think she was of the opinion that it was just a ramp to make money.

Another reason for incredulity from friends and family is their reluctance to accept that convenient, daily chemicals are harmful. Jim says, 'friends find it difficult to understand the impacts that it actually has on you. They can understand chemicals, but they can't understand, like, perfumes and that.' Clyde further estimates:

> Out of the public I'd say eight and a half out of every ten are total disbelievers. And of the remainder, perhaps three quarters of that remainder are people who are sympathetic but go ahead and use these chemicals anyway. They'll say, 'yes, yes, you know, it's very serious and these chemicals do cause bad infections' and so on and so forth and the next thing they're in the garden spraying organophosphates and organochlorins.

Clyde highlights that the chemically sensitive actually seek a redefinition of the sick role. They do not require temporary *exemption* from work but instead desire the workplace (and all public places) to be chemically free (Kroll-Smith and Floyd 1997).

After contracting a condition that is subject to stigma by many, people with a contested illness often necessarily establish a 'calculus' of friends and family (Clarke and James 2003: 1391). In other words, they lose touch with sceptical or apathetic acquaintances and develop closer relationships with loyal friends, or start to establish ties with new, understanding ones. This is further necessary when the friendship requires that those friends refrain from using daily chemicals in the presence of the chemically sensitive person. This aspect of the illness narrative is present in Ian's story too. In 2003, Ian re-encountered Jackie, an ex-girlfriend from many years ago, who had since married and had a son but was now divorced. Upon meeting her, Jackie immediately struck me as a caring, quiet and unassuming person who listened generously to Ian and accommodated his illness. Jackie and Ian re-established their relationship in 2004 and were engaged to be married in 2005 at a small wedding ceremony including close friends and family. Jackie thereafter largely supervised Ian's affairs and thus became a very central character in Ian's medico-legal encounter. Ian explained that Jackie helped him in the following way: 'by making allowances, and then, probably having that nature that's very giving. And kind enough to [be] patient. Because it does take patience.' He went on to say that she was the main source of support for him: 'if you don't have that, I don't think anyone would make it really.'

Aside from Jackie, another key person in Ian's illness narrative appeared at his new workplace. After terminating his employment at Vox, Ian started working as a trade assistant for a small, family-owned company. There, Ian was introduced to a fellow worker called Keith who became a lay advocate for Ian, since Keith's wife had similarly experienced litigation over MCS.

With chemical sensitivities as their common ground, the two became fast friends: Ian said they 'just clicked.' This feature was common to five of the chemically sensitive people I interviewed: they found support in conversations with fellow MCS litigants often encountered coincidentally. Akin to Dumit's (2006) findings, these acquaintances offered advice, assistance and empowering information to my informants, which assisted in their medical and legal interactions. Keith, for example, recommended Ian contact his wife's specialist in chemical injuries. This specialist thereafter became Ian's treating practitioner and a source of support for him. Keith also suggested Ian contact Jeff Carlson, the solicitor who eventually represented Ian's claim over the following seven years.

Thus far, the stories of the chemically sensitive align closely with the meta-narratives outlined in the medical social science literature on living with a chronic illness. However, their subsequent search for recognition from the workers' compensation scheme complicated their coping, and shrouded their experiential knowledge of illness in doubt.

The workers' compensation scheme

The system managed by WorkCover has undergone a number of reforms in recent years and markets itself as a workers' compensation and injury management scheme that is 'fair, accessible to injured workers and affordable to employers and the community' (see WorkCover 2014) The traditional adversarial trial system for resolving disputes was long criticized for its costliness and significant time delays (Grant *et al.* 2014; King *et al.* 2009). Moreover, it was recognized that an inherent power imbalance between disputing parties (for example, between the state prosecution and the accused, or between insurers and employees) could undermine a fair trial. In response to these critiques, all Australian states gradually introduced a number of non-adversarial justice measures to keep disputes out of the courts wherever possible (King *et al.* 2009). It is against this backdrop that WorkCover began to require disputed claims to undergo alternative dispute resolution processes such as mediation and arbitration before proceeding to trial. However, as illustrated below, the extent to which costs, time delays and power imbalances have actually diminished in the reformed workers' compensation system is questionable.

The scheme has also been strongly shaped by economic pressures on the insurance sector. As discussed in Chapter 2, in contrast to a welfarist approach to insurance – which conceptualizes insurance as a public good – when a neoliberal ethos pervades, insurance is understood as a product provided by corporate competitors in a (relatively) free market. Insurers thus seek to provide competitive premiums and therefore reduce claims wherever possible (Ericson and Doyle 2004: 108). Occupational medicine scholars have noted that the pressure to keep insurance premiums low has profoundly influenced the workers' compensation field, since there are increased forces against recognizing work-related injury generally (Osborne 2009). Researching disability insurance in Canada, Ericson and Doyle identified techniques that are mobilized by insurers to minimize payouts. Both injured workers and their treating practitioners are mistrusted by the insurance sector for either claiming for non-existent conditions, or over-claiming when the worker could have returned to work earlier. Consequently, compensation systems have become predicated on the value of 'work hardening', which is designed to return the claimant to work at the earliest possible opportunity (2004: 136). In fact, it is assumed that the worker is made a victim more by the iatrogenic compensation system than the accident itself and would be better off returning to work. This rhetoric and the economic imperative behind it has led to the emergence of a 'new cadre' of insurance inspectors who investigate 'every detail of the claimant's background, circumstances, and recovery' (2004: 136). Medical professionals are also co-opted into the policing of insurance claims and are required to undergo professional development courses that train them to detect fraud and malingering. This politico-economic context constitutes 'unique pressures' that can serve to transform the traditional role of healer into that of 'medical police' (Neimeyer 1991: 251). Additionally, since treating practitioners are seen as part of the 'social inflation' of disability claims, they too are placed under surveillance via the auditing of their diagnoses and billing practices. Ericson and Doyle (2004: 136) argue that the combination of efforts to police claimants *and* health providers 'heavily undercuts' the principles of welfare upon which the disability insurance system in Canada was founded. In the discussion below, I demonstrate similar neoliberal trends in the Australian workers' compensation system, how they have impacted health provision and courtroom encounters, and what they do to the epistemological debate over environmental illness.

The medical encounter

While the veracity of Ian's claim to a work-caused chemical injury was being assessed, Ian was subjected to confusing diagnoses, scrutiny in the clinic, and adversarial doctor–patient interactions. In turn, these influenced the way he understood and experienced his condition as well as the way it was diagnosed and treated by others.

Contrasting diagnoses

In all, Ian saw 12 different specialists before his case came to be heard by a review officer in 2005. This number is relatively small in comparison to the other informants; the others estimated that they consulted between 'two dozen' and 40 medical experts. Specialists provide medico-legal reports about the workers' condition and its relation to the workplace. However, there is a renowned divide between individual healthcare providers who tend to sympathize with workers' claims to injury, and experts who most frequently deny that workers' claims have any medical basis. Personal injury solicitors and insurance advocates usually have an established professional correspondence with those expert witnesses who are likely to provide an opinion favourable to their client's case; in other words they each seek 'injury brokers' (Grant and Studdert 2013). Moreover, solicitors tend to select health providers with a similar or greater level of expertise than their opponent's experts. For example, a GP generally has less standing in the medical field than a consultant psychiatrist, thus a solicitor will attempt to match a psychiatrist with a psychiatrist. This medical adversarialism is illustrated in the following account of Ian's medico-legal reports, which are supplemented by interviews with the practitioners.

Ian's solicitor Jeff first sought to understand his client's impairment by seeking advice from Ian's treating practitioner and an occupational therapist the lawyer had worked with previously. Because Ian was seeking access to compensation through common law processes (detailed in Chapter 5), Ian had to prove that he had suffered from a permanent disability affecting his functioning by at least 16 per cent to receive compensation. His treating practitioner reported that Ian had a 20 per cent disability, which included loss of mental function, an intermittent skin rash only occurring after his exposure to paint, and permanent disability from chronic fatigue, all resulting from chemical exposure in the workplace. Before Jackie re-entered Ian's life, the doctor reported that 'Mr Harvey currently barely manages to hold his life together' and that he needed an occupational therapist to help him weekly to look after his affairs. The occupational therapist, who spent several hours with Ian observing him in his home environment, noted that Ian's 'performance of managing home and personal life was poor' as a result of his chemical injury. She expanded that 'if deterioration occurs and is not identified and addressed in a timely manner, this man will become non-functional, and will eventually become a significant burden on society.'

Ian's solicitor then sought a specialist to comment on Ian's brain capacity: a psychologist who specialized in acquired brain disorders. After several tests, she made a finding that Ian's mental processing speed was in the borderline range and his reaction times were abnormally slow: 'a significant deficit for an individual with a high average general IQ.' The psychologist therefore believed that he 'has some cognitive defects which could well be explained by his exposure to a range of toxins.' She reported that Ian has a percentage functional disability of 15–19 per cent, and recommended a computer-based rehabilitation program, not as treatment (because his condition is apparently untreatable), but to help him manage his condition.

In response, the insurer's solicitor sought a report from a similarly experienced expert: a neuropsychologist. After this specialist scrutinized his colleague's report and conducted his own tests in consultation with Ian, he concluded that Ian's test results were 'excessively variable and [did] not in general make neuropsychological sense.' He went on to write that, 'If Mr Harvey has any cognitive deficits, [they] are related to non-organic factors such as depression, anxiety or stress,' and that it is 'not [his] opinion that Mr Harvey has or will be left with any permanent organically based neuropsychological impairment.' In terms of treatment, the neuropsychologist remarked that:

> It is not clear what [the supportive psychologist] would be attempting to rehabilitate and with this in mind it is possible that the undertaking of such a program could act to strengthen his belief system that he has serious cognitive impairment associated with his alleged exposure.

Ian also received contradictory diagnoses from expert occupational physicians, both of whom specialize in acquired brain injury in the workplace. The sympathetic physician, asked by Jeff Carlson to provide a report, claimed that Ian had a 'mild encephalopathy', or brain disease, which resulted from exposure to toxins at work and constituted an '18 per cent loss of effective use of his mental capacity'.

The sceptical specialist, on the other hand, who Ian was requested to consult by the defendant, disagreed. He wrote that there was a 'high chance of some of [Ian's] current symptomatology being due to somatization of unresolved stress and anger [towards the employer] into physical symptoms,' where somatization denotes the manifestation of physical symptoms due to a mental disorder. In other words, because Ian felt so angry towards Vox, he psychologically generated the symptoms. This sceptic 'did not find any evidence of disability sufficient to attract a [percentage] rating.' He went on to say that Ian should be assisted with 'stress and mood management, and try to shift some of his maladaptive patterns of thinking.'

Finally, consultant psychiatrists were also in disagreement over Ian's condition. One supportive expert, although acknowledging that he could not comment on whether or not Ian had a *toxic*-induced disorder because it was out of his expertise, reported that 'this man will have a permanent percentage psychiatric disability.' On the other hand, a sceptical psychiatrist claimed that Ian 'is almost certainly suffering from the equivalent of a depressive disorder with perhaps some degree of anxiety and prominent somatic symptoms and [a] little in the way of persistent sadness'.

This latter expert did not believe the condition was 'attributable to any physical or neuropsychiatric consequences of workplace exposure to chemicals.' He believed that Ian's depressive disorder was solely because of his break-up with his ex-girlfriend, which became a contentious issue later in the legal proceedings.

So Ian, along with the other workers I interviewed, was faced with polarized – but equally expert and specialized – 'evidence' on the condition from which he suffered. His rating in terms of percentage disability ranged from either nil by the defence experts, or between 15 and 20 per cent by the plaintiff's experts. The diagnoses did not merely differ; they fundamentally *clashed*, which exacerbated the epistemological uncertainty. And in half of these reports, what feels for Ian like a very real and disabling sickness caused by external things beyond his control, was reduced to a self-perpetuated affliction, or a non-existent one. MCS sufferer Hayley poignantly summed up the effect of this binary:

> you were in a position where you were being told that you were ill and [yet] you were constantly questioned and it was just...almost a schizophrenic position where you doubted, you know, you sometimes really doubted your own sanity.

Doctor–patient interactions in an adversarial system

Kroll-Smith and Floyd (1997: 32) discuss how 'the bioscience model of medicine has failed to provide the means for the patient [with chemical sensitivities] to act like a patient and the doctor to act like a doctor.' This is because 'the physician did not heal and the patient did not recover.' In the context of litigation, the consultations between Ian and physicians chosen by the defence were even more counterproductive: not only was the sceptical physician unlikely to heal and the patient to recover, but the two were more often than not in an adversarial relationship.

Ian, for example, spoke of the hurt and anger that he felt when one specialist, a dermatologist who he consulted about his skin rash, appeared to support his claims in the consultation and then produced a report asserting otherwise:

> [The specialist] said, 'yeah, I've experienced that. I know exactly what you're talking about.' And he said, 'as far as that itch goes, I've got a cream that can fix it.' I said, 'Really? It's been driving me nuts sometimes,' and he said, 'right,' he said, 'yep, it's a Cortisone and he wrote out a script and he handed it to me and said, 'get that.' And I said, 'if I wanted to start spray painting again – which I won't – if I rub this on my arm before I started, will that protect me?' He said, 'yes it will. It's good stuff...'. Funnily enough when [solicitor] Jeff Carlson rang me that night [the night of the consultation], he said, 'Oh how did it go with the specialist?' And I said, 'Oh, really great! You know, he's on the other side, but he knows exactly what he's talking about and he said he's prepared to help me and he's not worried about insurance companies.' So, yeah. But in his report, he'd done a complete back-flip and didn't

even mention any painting. He just said I get the itch when I get tired and upset. Or depressed. Or something...I forget how it went now. Something like that. And I looked and I went, 'what?!'...That's *crap.* Never said that at all. That was a downright lie, absolute lie.

Another example of dissatisfaction with medical encounters comes from Evan, who was also frustrated at the incongruity between the explanation he gave to defence doctors and the report they produced afterwards. Evan began to take his treating practitioner with him to any appointment with a sceptical practitioner nominated by the defence. Although Kylanta's legal department objected to this, Evan says he found a legal loophole which did not explicitly disallow the doctor to sit silently and take notes in the corner. This action, Evan believes, 'neutralized Kylanta,' in that 'they had to be careful what they wrote, then.'

Of course, Evan and Ian, like all of the litigants I interviewed, developed a rapport with doctors who were sympathetic to their cause, and experienced great comfort and relief from this support and reinforcement. However, I focus here on the defence practitioners because interactions with them had a lasting, negative psychological impact for the chemically sensitive. As a result of Ian's anger towards what he perceived as very unrewarding doctor–patient interactions with sceptical experts, he started to develop a strong dislike of the specialists he was expected to see by the defendant. Consider this excerpt from one of my interviews with Ian, which immediately followed him having told me that one of the experts he consulted with was 'a dickhead. An absolute sleazebag.'

TARRYN: What gave you that impression?
IAN: His whole manner and my instinct and what he was talking about. And when I confronted him with a question, and he couldn't answer it.
TARRYN: What question did you ask him?
IAN: My first question to him, when I was sent to him was, 'what's your score ratio [with chemical sensitivity patients]?'
  And he goes, 'Pardon?'
  I said, 'what's your score ratio?'
  'What do you mean?'
  And I said, 'well, how many patients do you let go through the system as are injured and how many do you knock back?'
  And he blinked and looked at me and couldn't answer and I helped him out. I said, 'Oh let's be fair, shall it be fifty per cent, you reckon?'
  And he said, 'Oh yes, yes, yes, it would be about that.'
  And I thought, *you're a liar, 'cause I know. I checked up on your records, it's practically nil.* And I thought, *alright, I've got you sized up, let's get down to this bullshit testing then.*

Like Ian, all of the MCS litigants questioned the motivations of doctors who reported that the workers were not chemically injured in the workplace. Interestingly, one defence specialist agreed that these sorts of doctor–patient interactions were unrewarding from the doctor's perspective. This specialist, who ascribed to the view that chemical sensitivity is iatrogenic, feels that interactions with patients like Ian are unsatisfying:

> The doctor and patient have to agree to part with different views about whether the patient is poisoned. And that's a very unhappy situation... it's not an easy process to go through from the patient's point of view and it's also a very unsatisfying process to go through from the doctor's point of view, because you can't satisfy the patient's expectations of you as a doctor. And at the end of it you're left in conflict with one more member of the human race. And there's enough conflict anyway.

This specialist, when engaged by the insurer, saw his role as one of 'giving [the patient] the reassurance that they're not poisoned.' When I asked whether he thought chemically sensitive patients might resent this 'reassurance' given their belief in the toxogenic nature of MCS, he said, 'The good news is usually very unwelcome.' He added that this is usually because they're 'locked in litigation', the outcome of which is contingent on them being confirmed chemically injured. On the flipside, Ian referred to this particular expert as '100 per cent [an] insurance man.' The workers' compensation system thus heightens the tension between doctor and patient, makes them question each other's motivations, and ultimately prevents productive therapeutic exchange.

Scrutiny in the medico-legal consultation

Although people with contested illnesses are often carefully scrutinized for malingering in their medical encounters (Kroll-Smith and Floyd 1997; Lipson 2004; Neimeyer 1991), a workers' compensation claim formalizes the scrutiny as an investigation into potential insurance fraud. The first way in which Ian was scrutinized by medical experts was with regard to his appearance upon entering the expert's clinic. If Ian did not embody the expected symptoms of a chemically poisoned person – as he claimed to be – he was perceived as exhibiting abnormal illness behaviour. Two of the reports that were written by defence experts described Ian as a 'well-looking' man, which immediately cast doubt on his claim to the sick-role. Dumit (2006) also found in his analysis of online chatroom conversations that people suffering from MCS and CFS were penalized in their medical interactions for trying to look their best despite how they were feeling. MCS litigant, Clyde, experienced a similar sort of stigma in his consultations:

I mean it usually starts with the raised eyebrow, you know, when they say, 'What can we do for you?' and you say, 'I'm suffering from the effects of toxic exposure of whatever magnitude.' The left eyebrow usually shoots up one and a half inches and you know immediately that there's going to be no rapport between that person and myself.

Another factor that worked against Ian's claim, identified by numerous insurance-engaged experts, was that he presented as 'an intelligent and articulate' person, which defied the expectations of a worker who alleged to suffer from a chemical brain disorder. Similarly, another litigant with MCS – Tony – was given an IQ test in a clinical encounter with a psychiatrist, and his high score was then used as evidence of his wellness. By contrast, sympathetic experts articulated that differing levels of intelligence in various parts of the brain is normal for people with chemical brain injuries because the toxins impact on some areas and not others.

Further, much of the MCS encounter relies on the doctor gaining an extensive medical and work history from the patient. These clinical guidelines are outlined in the work of Dr Mark Cullen (1987), the physician who initially identified the criteria for diagnosing the condition of MCS. Consequently, during their medical career, the chemically sensitive can become familiar with open-ended questions and tend to give more direct and well-practiced answers. Their rehearsed speech can pique the scepticism of doctors who might expect such a response from people who have an attachment to a particular diagnosis, and who have reconstructed their memory of events to allow for the onset of the condition. As a sceptical psychologist wrote of Ian:

This gentleman could access psychiatric or psychological care if he chose, however, that would require abandoning his disease conviction, which is likely to serve some significant positive psychological purpose in his, and his family's, life.

Experts were further reluctant to believe that Ian's condition was organically based when he referred too often and too emphatically to his employer's negligence as the cause of his condition. He thereby demonstrated anger towards the employer and a desire for redress, causing some specialists to regard these feelings as generative of his symptoms. By contrast, Ian's sympathetic experts tended not to focus on the anger Ian demonstrated except to imply that it was an understandable emotion in the circumstances, since they felt Ian's injuries *were* sustained because of Vox's negligence.

Notably, of the reports that suggested Ian's condition was psychosomatic, none of them explicitly suggested Ian was malingering. The term malingering is discouraged in a medical context since it is seen as a judgement and is 'extremely hard to prove' (Neimeyer 1991: 253). One defence specialist, after remarking that Ian's results did not make 'neuro-psychological sense' reported that 'this is not to be interpreted that I am suggesting Mr Harvey's performances to be invalid or not genuine.' Moreover, one expert remarked that the chemically sensitive 'are all genuine [in that] they all genuinely believe they are symptomatic' and further stated that a psychosomatic diagnosis does not reflect negatively on the patient's integrity. He chuckled at one point when saying that even though his 'bullshit-ometer is running off-scale here' there is nevertheless 'quite a lot of sensitivities involved in giving an opinion which you know is going to become public and [...] be transmitted to the patient.'

Yet, for Ian and other litigants, being told they 'genuinely believed' in a condition that only existed in their mind nevertheless countered their experiential knowledge, undermined their claim to financial compensation and cast moral judgement upon their trustworthiness. Despite the sensitivity that the above specialist attempted to apply in his reports, Ian still felt that he and the other defence experts were 'saying I was just a shifty bugger trying to milk the system.'

Ian's medico-legal experiences highlight how the workers' compensation system impacts health provision. Many of the clinical encounters were therapeutically counterproductive and actively worsened the illness experience for the chemically sensitive. Moreover, productive dialogue about the emergent condition, its cause and best treatment option was impeded by tension and scepticism between the provider and patient. For Ian and the other participants, the effect of the disability determination process was unsettling as their knowledge of their bodies, their legitimacy and deservedness were questioned, challenged and undermined.

The legal encounter

Ian started a legal action against his former employer, Vox, in the year 2000, with the help of a workers' union. Two years later, after feeling the union did little to advance his claim, Ian approached plaintiff solicitor Jeff Carlson to represent him. Renowned for dealing in chemical injury cases, Jeff felt that Ian's case was 'one of the strongest he'd ever seen' due to what he saw as a clear-cut case of negligence and resultant injury. After the case became complex and lengthy, Jeff (and the manager of his law firm – also his wife) agreed to work for Ian on a no-win, no-fee basis, although Ian continued to pay Jeff whatever and whenever he could afford. Jeff and Ian filed a claim for compensation under the common law, and Ian's case was heard in three courts over the next six years. First, in 2005, a review hearing was held to establish the extent of Ian's disability. The review officer found against Ian, determining that there was insufficient evidence to prove the relation of chemicals to his condition. Second, in his appeal to the

Magistrate's Court the following year, the judicial officer again found against Ian. Finally, the three judges who presided over the Supreme Court Appeal in 2007 similarly decided in favour of the defence (though not unanimously).

For the Supreme Court hearing, Jeff and Ian had hired a reputable QC to act as a barrister, paying him with some inheritance money Ian had acquired. After the decision against Ian, Jeff wrote to the barrister enclosing the judges' Reasons for Decision and noting that 'the principles of common law causation, which in my opinion should have got this man over the line, have been ignored.' Further, he ended with, 'there has been a disastrous miscarriage of justice.' At that point, because Jeff's small firm could no longer afford to continue acting for Ian without payment – the case had already cost the firm upwards of AU$200,000, which they would most likely never recoup – Jeff had to resign from representing Ian. Further, the writ against Vox had been discontinued because the defence threatened to make Ian pay their costs if he did not terminate his legal action. Although there were other clauses in the law which could allow Ian to pursue compensation via other routes, he lost his motivation for the fight, and Jeff was disappointed that 'yet another avenue [was] closing'.

Ian's case is an acute illustration of how workers' compensation proceedings are weighted against the recognition and compensation of occupational injury, especially one that is medically uncertain. Five sites of inequality are explored below: the burden of proof; economic disparity; surveillance; repressive governmentality; and emotional constraints.

Burden of proof

The burden of proof – the formal court rule that stipulates the party that is responsible for proving a claim – is one of the ways in which the law has been structured to manage uncertainty and mitigate risk. In criminal law, the burden of proof is traditionally upon the prosecution to prove the guilt of the offender. In personal injuries law, it is the worker's task to prove his or her illness and its relation to the employer's negligence.[2] The burden of proof essentially dictates 'wherever evidence cannot resolve a particular case [...] who is to be the winner' (Gaskins 1992: xv). In other words, if Ian could not prove his disability and its relation to his employment at Vox, then the default decision would be in favour of Vox. Moreover, plaintiffs must provide proof not only of general causation – that the chemicals in question have statistically been proven to cause ill-health, but also specific causation, that the chemicals in this case *did* cause *this* worker's ill-health, which is a much more specific, and complex, issue to prove (Jasanoff 1995: 122). This is also a problematic feature in cases of sexual or racial abuse, as Scheppele (1995: 996) points out:

> What [defence solicitors] now do instead of attacking people of color or women [as a whole] is to declare that they – public officials – would love to help women or people of color in general; it is just that […] nothing really happened in this *particular* instance. Or there is not enough evidence to decide one way or another. [*Emphasis in original*]

Having to prove specific causation is often a much more difficult task than disproving it, which places workers like Ian at a distinct disadvantage. This is never more evident than if the medical profession has not yet reached a consensus about the condition in question. Since the burden of proof fell to Ian, it was necessary that he pin-point the exact time of the onset of symptoms in order to demonstrate the chronological link between chemical exposure in the workplace and the resultant injury. However, by virtue of suffering from the insidious condition, chemical sensitivity, this point in time was difficult to isolate. Consequently, one of the arguments used against Ian by the defence was that if his symptoms did appear in 1997, when he and his family claim they started to emerge, why did he not see his doctor about it until 1999? Ian clarified that the process of realizing something was happening and seeking medical help took several years to occur. However, in cross-examination, the defence advocate unsympathetically summarized the situation for Ian: '[So you suffered from] really heavy fatigue that didn't concern you and you didn't go to the doctor's...?'

The claims put forward by the worker with contested illness and their medical and legal experts are usually unorthodox – a less valued, less recognized form of knowledge – which constitutes a further disadvantage in the litigants' quest to prove their condition (Gordon 1998). Ian's supportive psychologist argued that Ian had significant brain deficits in some areas but not others. For the defence neuropsychologist, this psychologist's assertions '[did] not make neuropsychological sense' and he put the condition down to depression. It is a significantly more difficult task for the worker's medical experts to prove that chemical exposure caused the chemical sensitivity, which in turn caused the depression, when the defence team uses the common and more easily understood argument that the depression came first.

This contrast is further highlighted in the disparity between the submissions put forward by the plaintiff and defence teams in Ian's case. As chemical injuries are shrouded in uncertainty, the worker's submissions are necessarily extensive and detailed. Ian's solicitor Jeff, for example, wanted the judicial officers in each hearing to be made aware of all relevant material: every fact arising from witness statements that emphasized Ian's condition; every aspect of case law that supported his argument; all of the relevant medical opinions that discussed the existence and nature of Ian's chemical injury; and the disparity in chemical injury expertise between his experts and those of the defence. Some of Jeff's submissions to the court were therefore extraordinarily lengthy and complex. On the other hand, since the defence are merely required to *deny* the allegations that implicate them, their submissions can be concise and need little in the way of detailed argument. In one hearing, Jeff's submissions filled 73 pages while Vox's submissions only totalled five. Gordon (1998: 75) concurs that, 'often, the debate by those denying chemical injury appears limited to, "We disagree with your conclusions."' Consider for example, the following excerpt from worker and defence submissions in Ian's case, which for ease of reading are abridged in Table 4.1.

As a consequence of this disparity in length and complexity, the judicial officer is faced with one argument that is complicated and time consuming, in contrast to another that is short, precise and follows an easy cultural logic. In my observations in the courtroom, three of the five judicial officers who presided over Ian's court hearings seemed visibly frustrated with the duration of Jeff's submissions.

In her Reasons for Decision, the review officer at Ian's first hearing demonstrated that she was aware that the medical complexity of the issue disadvantaged the worker: 'it may well be that as medical science increases its knowledge in relation to exposure to toxins, conditions relating to the effects of substances such as paint and solvents may be easier to diagnose'. While the review officer recognized the difficulty of proving an illness about

Table 4.1 Submissions from the worker and defence in *Ian Harvey v. Vox Australia*

Plaintiff's Submissions	Defendant's Response
Mr Harvey suffered at various times from: Mucous or nasal congestion; alcohol-like intoxication; a skin itch on his arm; restless legs; fatigue; irritability; mood disturbance; lowered sex drive/impotence; loss of motivation. He also suffered from decrements in intellectual functioning, such as speed of reaction time, memory, concentration, and learning. All of the above symptoms were suffered as a result of exposure to chemicals at work.	'The [defence] disputes Mr Harvey suffers from hazardous substance poisoning [and] the existence, nature and permanence of the alleged psychiatric and/or mental and/or behavioural disability; loss of mental function; toxic encephalopathy; "Fatigue;"Skin disorder' 'The [defence] denies the existence of a condition.'

which the medical profession is uncertain, she concluded that 'the worker carries the burden of proof in this regard and there is insufficient material' for her to infer that the worker 'was exposed to toxins at a high level' and therefore that he suffers from a chemical injury. She essentially agreed such a condition was *possible*, but was constrained from saying Ian suffered from it on the balance of *probabilities*. By default, she therefore found in favour of the defence's argument that Ian was suffering from depression.

Notably, the issue of expert evidence is an 'increasingly puzzling one, by virtue of the growing complexity of the evidence itself' (Kirby 2008: 7). Justice Kirby, (2008: 7) a High Court judge in Australia, emphasizes that judges are expected to understand the 'technicalities of the clash in scientific evidence' and then, in their Reasons for Decision, give 'convincing reasons for preferring one conclusion over another.' As I will further explain in Chapter 5, judicial officers are instructed to rely on theories that have a degree of consensus in the medico-scientific profession. Yet, one of the founders of legal realism, Jerome Frank (1974: 70), pointed out that people tend to protect judges' authority and wisdom by explaining that they are '*forced*' to make certain decisions (because of lack of evidence, burden of proof standards and so forth). In this case, the Review Officer herself implies that she was left with little alternative considering the 'insufficient material.' However, Frank (1974: 71) also emphasized the indeterminacy of law with the truism that 'the judge is a human being.' In other words, legal decisions vary and are not purely derived from statutes and legal principles, but can also be influenced by judges' social, political and moral prejudices and their own standards of proof, or evidence requirements. In Ian's case, only one of the five judicial officers who presided over his case were prepared to diverge from the mainstream position on MCS within the scientific field.

Economic inequality

Like all 'repeat players' in the legal system, insurance companies are often advantaged in disputes, due to their legal prowess and financial upper hand (Genn 1987; King *et al.* 2009). Moreover, the longer the legal process, the less likely it is for the worker to be able to afford to continue. In my research, all of the workers were represented by a relatively small plaintiff law firm – often working no-win no-fee, or sometimes pro bono, for their client – which had constraints to staff and resources. On the other hand, in each case, the employer was represented by the law firm of a large, financially backed insurer or, in the case of Kylanta, a multinational corporation, who were prepared to carry out long and expensive legal proceedings to avoid a reputation-damaging compensation claim against them.

In Ian's case a financial disparity manifested in several ways, the first during his initial legal proceedings. There is a regulation in the Western

Australian workers' compensation system that solicitors are not permitted to attend review hearings because the events are designed to reveal the factual evidence without being obfuscated by legal technicalities. Trained legal advocates, however, can appear on each party's behalf. While the defence employed a highly experienced legal advocate, Ian was unable to afford a professional to represent him in the review hearing. He asked his friend and fellow trade assistant, Keith, to represent him. (This concerned Jeff, but neither could his firm afford an advocate.) On several occasions Keith was reprimanded by the Review Officer for not following protocol, and I noted that – aside from the questions he was instructed by Jeff to ask of witnesses – his ad-libbed questions were often not helpful to Ian's case, where a trained advocate would have evinced more constructive responses and assisted Ian's case further.

Another example of financial disparity is that Ian and Jeff were unable to continue Ian's claim after the Supreme Court hearing due to lack of finances. As the burden of proof falls on the worker's team, it can be assumed that more staff hours and resources are needed to assimilate arguments that prove causality, hence a greater financial implication for the plaintiff than the defence. Such financial disparity in itself is not unique to people with contested conditions. The power differential between insurance companies and workers is well-known in compensation lawsuits. However, the financial implications for contested illness claimants are heightened when the medical contestation surrounding their condition makes proof more complex and time-consuming to obtain.

Surveillance

A further obstacle preventing workers from achieving medico-legal recognition is surveillance. Consistent with the neoliberal approach to insurance outlined above, insurers seek visual proof of malingering in order to minimize payouts. Surveillance can produce evidence of a worker's abilities (that is, lack of *dis*ability) in the tangible form of photographs, audio recordings and video footage. Most of my informants experienced some sort of surveillance attempt: one had their phone tapped; another's phone account was being monitored by the defence; two had an unmarked car regularly situated across the road; and several had footage obtained of them conducting everyday activities. Many of these surveillance strategies are, or are bordering on, illegal. In Australian courts, evidence gained through illegal surveillance methods is permissible if its 'desirability' outweighs the 'undesirability' of admitting improperly obtained evidence (see for example *New South Wales Evidence Act 1995*). Thus, while judicial officers have discretion to exclude such evidence, the definition of what is 'desirable' is ill-defined and open to subjective interpretation. No evidence obtained by insurers was excluded in my research.

In Ian's quest to prove his chemical injury, he felt he was exposed to four forms of surveillance, which took on great significance for him and his family throughout the nine-year dispute. The first indication for Ian was when he saw a silver car with tinted windows repeatedly situated across the road from his house, observed by both Ian and his neighbours. After noting the registration of the car and conducting some investigative work of his own, Ian traced the car to a private investigation company in Perth, which he suspected was hired by the defence.

The insurer also organized for a cameraman to be across the road and film Ian's and Jackie's wedding ceremony. They both felt this invasion ruined their special day. Ian said to me:

> We felt like, you know, viewing you while you're at work? Fair enough, you're fair game now. Or doing something out in the garden if you've got a crook back or whatever. [But] you *don't* go to a bloke's wedding. You know? I'd waited all me life for that. It's sort of like it's spoilt now, it's tainted. And things [were] hard enough as it was without them coming in and gate-crashing.

A third surveillance event, according to Ian, occurred when his car was broken into in the days preceding the first review hearing. Ian thought the 'attempted robbery' was suspicious, since the thief did not steal the coins visibly lying in the ash tray as one would expect, but merely rifled through the glove compartment. Ian feels this was a technique used by the defence to find incriminating evidence. The thief broke a pair of expensive binoculars that Ian kept in the car – but did not steal them – which Ian thinks was a token effort by the defence to make the event appear as petty thievery. Demonstrating the anger that this event caused, Ian said to me before the Supreme Court appeal: 'yeah, so, if we do get [the defence solicitor] at the bargaining table, I'm gonna wrap my hands about three times around that fucking tie of his and say, "you owe me a set of binoculars, mate"'.

A fourth suspicious incident of surveillance occurred for Ian after he had telephoned his friend, Ryan, in New Zealand, about a week before the review hearing commenced. Ryan was an ex-workmate of Ian's, and was thus to testify by telephone at the hearing the following week, since he had been subpoenaed by the defence. (United Insurers drew upon Ryan's comparatively healthy condition to argue that Ian's condition was individualized and psychological; a common technique by insurers – Draper 2000.) Jeff had advised Ian that since it was habitual for him to telephone his friend, it was permissible to continue to contact him, except immediately before and during the hearing since that might appear to be collusion. When cross-examining Ryan, the defence advocate's first question was, 'have you spoken to Ian recently?' This question was not asked of any other witnesses and it therefore seemed as though the defence were aware of the phone call. Ian and Jeff suspected that Ian's phone was tapped, which Jeff explained is, in his experience of chemical injury cases, a frequent (but rarely proven) technique of the defence. Ian and Jackie subsequently hired a detective of their own to 'debug' their house. Nothing was found, but the detective warned that tracking tends to be conducted digitally these days.

Throughout the legal proceedings, these surveillance efforts – whether genuine or perceived – have tangibly intruded into Ian and Jackie's lives in the form of adversaries across the road, uninvited observers at their wedding and, possibly, broken binoculars. Moreover, it has had a damaging psychological impact; they have been forced to live with a sense of being observed in their homelife, which, along with the rest of the medico-legal process, has caused significant emotional strain. Similarly, the Kylanta worker, Evan, received telephone calls nearly every evening during his legal battle that terminated immediately after he picked up the receiver. This sense of surveillance resulted in another litigant saying to me, 'nothing is safe for us here, nothing is as it seems'. Paranoia is a charge that is often levelled against the chemically sensitive. Sceptics suggest that paranoia about chemicals lies behind their psychosomatic reaction to toxins and argue that pre-existing mental instability often predates their condition. Yet in the context of private investigation efforts, in conjunction with the other forms of scrutiny they are exposed to in the medico-legal dispute, the workers' heightened fear of being observed seems somewhat inescapable.

Repressive governmentality

Aside from intimidation, there is another notable consequence of surveillance in the clinic, courtroom and by insurance inspectors. As observed in the case of RSI, sufferers of contested illness are forced to undertake a 'cultural performance' which 'forces them to be demonstrably and unremittingly ill' (Reid et al. 1991). This phenomenon harks back to the dilemma facing Indigenous land claimants discussed in Chapter 2, who needed to visibly adhere to traditional conceptions of Aboriginality to be deemed eligible for land rights (Strang 2004). For the chemically sensitive, in order for their illness to be recognized by medical expert witnesses and judicial decision-makers, injured workers are forced to represent themselves in a manner that meets medico-scientific and legal expectations of sick people. The need to exhibit signs of illness throughout the medico-legal process is not new: for over 200 years of compensation cases regarding post-traumatic stress disorder, 'the ability of the plaintiff to physically demonstrate his or her disabilities before the tribunal of fact [has been] of great importance to the outcome of the proceedings' (Mendelson 1998: 17–18).

The juridical definition of what illness *should* look like imposes a 'repressive authenticity' (Wolfe 1999) on claimants. The repressive effect is best demonstrated in an anecdote recounted by Evan. In spite of his condition, Evan continued to play football on occasion throughout his legal dispute with Kylanta. He explained to me that he was able to play only because he had a supportive coach and team who stopped using the chemical-based cream *Dencorub* and stopped smoking in the change rooms to prevent his exposure to toxins. Even though he experienced chronic fatigue – often for days – after each game, he continued playing in order to maintain some element of normalcy to a life that had otherwise undergone immense upheaval. Nonetheless, Kylanta notified Evan that they had obtained video footage of him conducting certain activities including playing football to undermine his claim to sickness. Evan explains how he felt:

> It was funny because, I mean, everybody [else] supported anything you could do that would bring your self-esteem up, or make you feel better. Whereas, Kylanta didn't […] they would use that against you. So it was like two different roads.

The metaphor of 'two different roads' that Evan speaks of here is a poignant illustration of the difficult choice experienced by workers under surveillance. He implies that he has the choice between building self-esteem – or 'making you feel better' – on the one hand, and proving permanent disability on the other.

In the lead up to his hearing, Tony mentioned a similar discordant feeling. He had found a treatment program that markedly improved his everyday symptoms, and thus became concerned about the implications this might have for his claim: 'It's like I'm warring within my mind, I feel like I'm denied the right to even get better'. Tony subsequently telephoned his solicitor and said, partly in jest, 'I think I'm getting better. Should I stay sick?' a question that supports Evan's experience of a crossroads. Tony's lawyer advised him to focus on his own health and continue with his life (also mentioning that an obvious and deliberate effort not to improve may be equally scrutinized and damaging to his claim). Despite this reassurance, Tony continued to express fear about the visible authenticity of his sickness.

Disability insurers justify their surveillance efforts because they are concerned about a nocebo effect, where perfectly healthy people generate illnesses, or people with mild injuries delay recovery time in order to receive workers compensation (Ericson and Doyle 2004). However, a different phenomenon was playing out with my participants. Those who sustain a chemical injury and the people around them develop coping strategies in order to manage day-to-day living with a disability (Lipson 2001). This might include getting married, socializing with friends and family, or playing football. Yet taking proactive measures to cope well or minimize observable symptoms can be captured on video footage, taken out of context and used to portray the worker as perfectly healthy. Their disability is not imagined or exaggerated, but rather their ability to cope *in spite of* injury is necessarily downplayed.

Therein lies an example of the stifling power of governmentality in medico-legal disputes, as workers practice self-surveillance to normalize their injury. These workers embody and reproduce medico-scientific and legal power when they adjust their experience of illness to conform to the institutional criteria for recognizable injury. By attempting to repress aspects of their experience that do not fit into legal categories, they reinforce (or at least do not challenge) the power of the law to define their illness and shape their recovery.

However, the case studies presented here also confirm the immense influence of the private insurance sector on this process. The insurer's investigation into each aspect of the worker's circumstances means that the scrutiny does not stop when they have left the medical clinic and the courtroom; the workers are subject to a panopticon as they know their telephone calls, home life and social events may be under observation at any given time. This underscores that insurance itself constitutes a form of governance that constrains the societal response to emergent disease, including the way sufferers themselves experience their illness.

There is, thus, another important source of inequality between the two parties in the workers' compensation process. Throughout the legal dispute, surveillance of the workers' conduct subjects them to close legal scrutiny to ensure they are good, morally upright, legal actors. On the other hand, the covert investigations practiced by insurance companies are relatively unregulated and beyond legal reproach, despite frequently being invasive and of dubious legality. The way in which legal force and, subsequently, governmentality, weigh unevenly upon the insurer and worker is another telling disparity between them in occupational disputes.

Emotional pressures

The final obstacle faced by litigants with a contested illness – a consequence of the first three – is the emotional pressures they face in the day-by-day unfolding of the adversarial medico-legal process. For Ian and Jackie – and to a lesser extent, Jeff – the case *mattered* emotionally, psychologically, professionally and, of course, economically. Jackie whispered to me during one hearing, 'the problem is that for the other side, it's just a game like tennis, and it's all about winning. They don't think about the actual lives involved'. Of course, in the event of a loss, the insurer may be liable to pay a sum of money and the employer may suffer a somewhat damaged reputation. However, in comparison to the worker, they have little to lose.

Ian initially articulated his impetus to fight for recognition and compensation as an altruistic choice on behalf of 'the next poor sucker that goes up against [the legal system]'. He was prepared to provide private and embarrassing details about his condition in the court hearings (for example, in relation to his sex-life) because 'I felt it was important that that sort of stuff should come out, because this stuff, even in worse injuries than mine, it's so often shoved under the carpet because of the embarrassment'. Other chemically sensitive litigants expressed a similar notion of acting on behalf of a broader cause for MCS sufferers everywhere.

And yet, there are emotional consequences for taking this avenue, for rallying against the mainstream paradigm. Ian's wife, Jackie, expresses these sentiments in the following quote, which was uttered in a conversation before the Supreme Court hearing:

> Ian feels like he has this moral obligation to do the right thing, to be the forerunner. Not to be a martyr, but to set a precedent for other people, to sort of break the ground. I think he's probably feeling if there's anyone in a position to at the moment, it's him. [Other people], they give up. But Ian won't give up. And that's a good thing, I suppose. But it's really detrimental to us. And I just feel like, look, let somebody else be the hero. Don't...you know, let us have our life. [*Jackie looks ashamed*] Which is not, really the right thing to do [...] Well you're caught, you know? You wanna support them, and I do, a lot. But you have times when you think, *this is too hard. This is just too hard.*

The toll of 'setting a precedent' was eventually felt by Ian, too. Several months after the Supreme Court decision had been handed down against him, Ian explained that the pressures had worn him down. When I asked him whether the lawsuit had impacted his marriage, he said:

> Strained it. [In] every way. Every way that you could think of. You're just always unhappy. You're always under pressure, most of the time [...] it's bloody hard work. And you know you get those little...just like another bag of sand chucked on you and you just sink a bit further and you just push up, and eventually both of you just fall in a hole and you throw it off and you stand up again...

He went on to express disillusionment with his struggle for compensation:

> If anything, you know, I'm shagged out, I don't want [my solicitor, Jeff] to be pressured anymore and I don't want my marriage to be pressured. And the instinct...the common sense thing is for me to, you know, just walk away from it. Let it go.

So irrespective of any initial desire to fight for the common goal of chemical sensitivity recognition, emotional pressures can eventually impede a
worker's desire to continue in their battle. Evan explained that one of the
only reasons he was able to endure the medico-legal process was saying,
'there's gonna be an end to this':

> I used to wake up and the only thing that kept me going some days
> was that, I know that everything comes to an end. Good things or bad
> things, so I know this will end one day. I just didn't know when [...]
> 'cause you never see the light at the end of the tunnel when you're in
> the middle of that.

As demonstrated in the Kylanta case, legal settlement can and has brought
a sense of closure for some of the Kylanta workers, which has aided their
healing process. However, for Ian who never received resolution, for Roger
who did not agree with his settlement, and for others who are still fighting,
emotional strain endures.

Conclusion

Ian's story vividly emphasizes that the worker's compensation process can
be therapeutically counter-productive for litigants. The psycho-social
process of understanding and coping with chemical sensitivity is rendered
particularly complex in the context of an occupational dispute. The quest
for medical diagnosis and treatment becomes more problematic when the
insurer denies the existence of a condition and seeks medical evidence to
counter it. In turn, due to the uncertain and contested nature of medical
diagnosis surrounding the illness, the legal process is lengthened and
complicated.

Furthermore, the stories above demonstrate that the medico-legal
process is heavily weighted against the recognition of new environmental
illnesses. Despite attempts that have been made to implement non-adversarial reforms in the compensation courts, these measures do not
necessarily prevent an acrimonious battle (whether it proceeds to trial or
not), and power imbalances still permeate through to more informal
processes. Insurers have a privileged position within the workers' compensation apparatus, which gives them significant leverage in fighting against
the physiological categorization of disabilities, particularly those that defy
medical consensus. Whereas, workers seeking recognition for MCS are
disadvantaged with respect to the nominal status of their epistemological
claims and the economic capital available to them. Moreover, constraints at
the medico-legal interface – the burden of proof, the cost and delays of
legal proceedings, the repressive effects of surveillance, and emotional
constraints – reproduce this inequality, and make it more likely that MCS

litigants will lose their claim, or abandon the case before it reaches completion. The combination of these many factors makes the path towards recognition – if it is to occur – a long one.

Chapter 5

Medical, legal and insurance reasoning in the governance of uncertainty

Medical science is predicated on a positivist worldview, which places trust in the scientific process and requires a logical, mathematical standard of proof. It values proven scientific 'facts' over theories that are merely speculative, or have not yet been tested or observed. There is a long tradition in the social sciences of critiquing medico-scientific positivism, and the ways in which this mode of reasoning disqualifies the recognition of subjugated knowledges about illness (Foucault 1973; 1976; Lupton 1994; Pols 2013; Romanucci-Ross and Tancredi 2007). Subjugated knowledges are those that are unqualified – or have been actively disqualified:

> naïve knowledges, located low down on the hierarchy, beneath the required level of cognition or scientificity [...] such as that of the psychiatric patient, of the ill person, of the nurse, of the doctor, parallel and marginal as they are to the knowledge of medicine – that of the delinquent etc.
>
> (Foucault 1976: 83)

Criticisms of positivism are useful to highlight, as I do below, the historical development of a narrow paradigm for understanding disease causality, which presents an extremely powerful barrier to the legitimization of emergent conditions, or their potential to reach the required level of 'scientificity'. However, in this chapter, I analyse how medico-scientific understandings of the body intersect with – and are reformulated by – insurance and legal frameworks. First, I demonstrate how medical assumptions about disease become reified as 'fact' by the neoliberal insurance apparatus and closed off to further debate, which restricts the way emergent complaints are understood thereafter. I then analyse what happens when judicial decision-makers arbitrate over medico-scientific controversies. Legal modes of reasoning can counter dominant medico-scientific assumptions, bypass rigid insurance categories, and recognize unorthodox epistemologies as probable. However, the MCS case study illustrates that a dynamic of medico-scientific positivism, insurance schemes, and legal conservatism tend to restrict decision-makers from entertaining new epistemological possibilities.

Medical reasoning and uncertainty

The mainstream medical dismissal of MCS in Australia is informed by a historically entrenched set of assumptions about disease and its cause, visibility and measurement. Although there are competing paradigms and alternative voices in the medico-scientific field, there is nonetheless a dominant body of knowledge and mode of reasoning that defines medical practice, which we can generalize about (Brown 1992: 272). This mode of reasoning, traced historically below, goes some way to explaining why chemical explanations for MCS, and lay experiences of environmental risk, are incommensurable, or do not make sense, within the current medico-scientific paradigm.

Positivism and disease: valuing the visible

Christian beliefs about purity and sin once dominated Western medical understandings of health and illness. Yet during the enlightenment period that took hold in eighteenth-century Europe, a cultural shift towards an ideal of *reason* began to take root. People began to seek rational solutions to social problems, including the provision of healthcare. An emerging category of medical 'expert' and the development of a medical 'profession' led to the formation of the clinic and hospital. In his seminal work on the development of the clinic in France, Foucault (1973) highlights two aspects of contemporary Western medical practice that can be traced back to this period. First, biomedicine localized disease to particular organs of the body, where previously it was popularly accepted that diseases attacked the entire being (188). Second, disease became perceived as a material and visible entity, in contrast to a more spiritual or unseen affliction, as it had thus far been understood. With this new knowledge, combined with the advent of medical technology such as microscopes, stethoscopes and the post mortem, doctors could see the pathological entity itself, and the specific local impact it had on the body (Lupton 1994). Disease thus became *measurable*. This conceptual shift towards measurability was linked to the highly influential philosophy of René Descartes (1596–1650), who encouraged a stark distinction between the body (which is natural, observable, and can be measured) and the mind (which is considered intangible and can foster a distorted version of reality – Gordon 1988). Medical science therefore became, specifically, the study of the body and the measurable, which to a large extent still characterizes its practice today.

Critics of positivism also highlight that, in medicine 'that which cannot be measured is deemed, more or less, not to exist; at best it is ignored in any notions of causality' (Romanucci-Ross and Moerman 1991: 368). Medical science thus demarcates a narrow set of requirements about what can be recognized as a causal mechanism of illness:

> Contemporary ideology in biomedicine includes the following values: first, causation is temporal, reductionist and essentially metonymic, that is, the part represents the whole and/or cause is taken for effect and effect is taken for cause. The metonymic style looms in importance as it forms the primary structure for treatment. One 'treats' the 'cause' of illness, not the 'symptoms' of illness.
> (Romanucci-Ross and Tancredi 2007: 28)

These historically entrenched beliefs about localization, measurement and the primacy of cause partly explain the reluctance of most of the medical profession to grant MCS legitimacy without further proof. The cluster of medically unexplained physical symptoms (MUPS) claimed by people with MCS – headaches, nausea and chronic fatigue, for example – cannot be isolated to a particular organ and are not objectively measurable in the clinic, nor in the laboratory. It is, thus, the persistently intangible nature of MCS that makes it so indefinable. This is not unique to controversial chemical injuries, either: the same problematic is found in the treatment of chronic back pain patients. Like those with MCS, those with back pain can be disbelieved by health providers when they articulate suffering that is inconsistent with the lack of measurable pathology in their bodies (Niemeyer 1991). With regard to MCS, for epidemiologists (and most health providers), 'problems of measurement are secondary to the more fundamental problem of knowing what to measure' (Wing 2000: 32). It is for this reason that Kroll-Smith and Floyd (1997: 33) refer to MCS as 'subclinical' to denote 'the absence of a diagnostic technology capable of identifying the quantity of chemicals that probably change the bodies of the chemically reactive'. So the causal relationship between low-level toxic substances and ill-health is currently invisible, or beneath cognition, and is thus non-existent from a positivist scientific lens.

However, there is a more multifaceted explanation for why a chemical aetiology to MCS is rejected by the mainstream scientific community. It must be remembered that there is a growing minority of scientific experts, also trained as positivist scientists, who entertain the possibility that MCS *is* toxogenic. The scientific community is not unanimous on this issue, and there is a movement of experts attempting to improve knowledge about, and technological detection of low-level toxins in the body. This iterates an important point made by scholars of scientific controversies, which is that the scientific community has never been as inflexible, as narrow-minded, and as blind to the social construction of scientific 'facts', as social commentators have sometimes accused them of. Overly reductionist critiques of positivism also overlook the fact that 'good positivistic contributions' have been responsible for debunking old scientific myths and leading to paradigm shift (Barnes 2009). Barnes (2009: 55) further notes that most formal scientific awards and honours are awarded for theoretical innovation.

Thus, while conventional reasoning certainly contributes to the mainstream medical dismissal of MCS validity, politico-economic factors external to the scientific community also constrain ongoing scientific debate. Part of the reason for this is that scientists (and, indeed, experts from most fields including insurance, cost–benefit analysis, and the social sciences) have to justify the worth of their expertise to the outside world by proving its objectivity and trustworthiness. Pressured to prove the truth of their theories, they usually *quantify* their evidence, responding to (and reinforcing) a culturally embedded trust in the logic of numbers (Porter 1995). Numerical evidence is also politically convenient: as Foucault emphasized (1973), governments tend to favour measuring tools that allow them to quantify – and therefore more effectively know and control – social activities. For social theorists of DNA profiling, the numerical probability of DNA matches has not only been persuasive because of its quantitative strength, but also because it is a politically useful form of measurement: it ostensibly proves and thus justifies the need to monitor and contain those members of the community who were, already, politically troublesome (Cole 2002; Lynch *et al.* 2010). Lynch and colleagues explain the extent to which scientific tools of measurement and identification have been coopted in this way:

> measurement regimes are key elements of social reform movements and government schemes [...] The numbers become reified, and are used as proxies for what they purport to measure. Economies form around them, and political reforms are leveraged by means of them.
>
> (2010: 157)

Similar politico-economic reforms using codes of measurement are noticeable in the health arena. Below, I demonstrate how such schemes have forced changes to medico-scientific practice and inquiry, which has made its assessment of illness more standardized, rigid and inflexible.

Actuarial changes to diagnosis: codes, categories and evidence-based medicine

As the institution that is responsible for the provision and rationing of healthcare, there is a political expectation that the medical community will uphold a rigorous standard of proof before approving medical benefits for a new class of injury. There has also been an increasing acknowledgement of, and discontent with, the margin for error and inconsistency in clinical diagnosis, both internally from members of the medical community as well as those scrutinizing it from the outside (including insurers, legal decision-makers, political actors and patients). As a consequence of such dissatisfaction, there have been some notable efforts to remove some of the ambiguity in medical care and to regulate more closely the way in which diagnoses are made. These processes, outlined below, have been adopted by the global medical field – and its local Western Australian branch – in the interests of providing more cost-efficient and effective healthcare on a large scale. In doing so, the positivist notion that illness must be objectively evidenced and measurable in order to be legitimate has been further reinforced in the medico-legal field.

One recent attempt to standardize diagnosis is the global trend towards 'evidence-based medicine.' In the second half of the twentieth century, the search for the best available evidence in the medical field has led to the advent of randomized control trials, or RCTs (Ecks 2008; Williams and Garner 2002). These trials produce statistical information based on research conducted on large samples, where the results are compared to placebo control groups and the findings are considered a benchmark for 'best evidence' (Ecks 2008; Timmermans and Berg 2003). Over the latter half of the century, databases that summarize the results of these trials – many thousands of RCTs are conducted every year – have been made increasingly accessible to medical clinicians. Subsequently, there has emerged a trend towards evidence-based medicine, which has also taken hold in mainstream Australian medical practice (Willis and White 2004).

This trend is an effort to make available consolidated research findings for busy health providers. Ecks (2008: S80) notes that 'doctors are [now] trained to believe more in statistical evidence than what they observe in clinical practice' (S80). The ideology of evidence-based medicine is to move away from the individual doctor-based diagnosis that the old model of medicine promoted. As Gandjour and Lauterbach (2003: 161) conclude, 'the goal is to substitute reasoning that relies on intuition and personal experience by reasoning based on solid foundation on the results of clinical research'.

Australian physicians are also regulated by clinical practice guidelines, which ideally standardise the treatment of emergent conditions. Within the Australian medical context, practitioners are directed in their diagnosis by clinical practice guidelines. The guidelines are consensus documents that are developed after complex negotiations have taken place between healthcare providers, patients and consumer representatives, and they are subsequently presented to practitioners as best practice standards (Ankeny 2003). This process occurs in areas with emerging or changing diagnostic and treatment principles, such as in the case of CFS. These documents serve as guides, which, like evidence-based medicine, are similarly designed to take away the idiosyncratic nature of clinical diagnosis.

However, in the case of a controversial illness such as MCS, clinical practice standards tend not to be released, since there remains too little consensus in both the medical community and the broader social body. Physicians are thus not given guidelines for determining causation and providing treatment. Moreover, the existing scientific 'evidence' from RCTs supports both sides of the toxogenic/psychogenic debate. Returning to a previous example, studies focusing on the olfactory system (sense of smell) as a mechanism for MCS are divided. One strand concludes that if the chemically sensitive person smells chemicals before experiencing symptoms, then the condition must be psychosomatic (e.g. Van Diest *et al.* 2006; Winters *et al.* 2003). The other school of thought supports the contention that the symptoms are caused by an organic reaction between the olfactory system and the brain (e.g. Ashford and Miller 1998; Bell *et al.* 1993; Pall 2007). This differential interpretation of the same evidence emphasizes the interpretive nature of evidence-based medicine, despite its aura of objectivity and consistency.

A further danger of evidence-based medicine is that it has an inherent conservative element where it privileges established concepts over newer ones, since less research has been conducted on emergent phenomena (Ecks 2008: S81). If, for example, more research has been carried out by experts who interpret their data to support a condition's psychosomatic causation, then the summarized findings on the evidence database will favour that conclusion. By virtue of being unexplained, contested and in its infancy, the lack of available (numerical) evidence on MCS continually disallows MCS credibility within this system.

Standardization of diagnosis also occurs at the legislative level as governments regulate and reform the insurance apparatus for assessing occupational injury. According to the Western Australian Workers' Compensation and Rehabilitation Act, people who allege to have a chemical injury must provide sufficient proof that they are legitimately ill. The first action that workers must take after sustaining an injury at work is to inform their employer of the event and then consult and nominate a doctor. This doctor is then required to fill in the 'first medical certificate' (see Figure 5.1), which asks the expert to circle the worker's 'affected area' on a picture of a person of ambiguous sex.

With this certificate, doctors are expected to localize the diseased area. This excludes the illustration of conditions that might be perceived as affecting the whole person, such as aggression or a lack of motivation, which are symptoms suffered by many chemically sensitive people. The compensation scheme further reifies injury into that which is measurable and visible, and works to automatically disadvantage those who suffer from a condition that cannot be mapped on, in Foucault's (1973) terms, medicine's 'anatomical atlas'. A further example of this codification of disease can be found in the schedule of disability (see Table 5.1).[1] This table

WorkCoverWA

Workers' Compensation and
Injury Management Act 1981
(Sections 57A(1)(a), 57B(1)(b) & 61(1) and 73(1)(b))

Workers' Compensation *First* Medical Certificate

1. Worker's details
First name(s):   Surname:
Address:
Telephone: 08   Date of birth: Occupation:
☐ I have provided a WorkCover WA Injury Management brochure to the worker.

2. Employer details
Name & address of worker's employer:

3. Consent authority *(to be signed at the option of the worker)*
I authorise any doctor who treats me (whether named in this certificate or not) to discuss my medical condition, in relation to my claim for workers' compensation and return to work options, with my employer and with their insurer.

Worker's signature: ....   Date: ....

Affected Area

IMPORTANT: FAILURE TO PROVIDE YOUR SIGNATURE ON THE AUTHORITY ABOVE MAY DELAY A DECISION BY YOUR EMPLOYER ON YOUR CLAIM.

4. Details from worker
Date of injury:
Workplace location where incident occurred:
Worker's description of the injury:

Worker's description of how the injury occurred:

5. Medical assessment
Clinical findings / diagnosis *(include possible complications, effect of prior injury or medical condition)*:

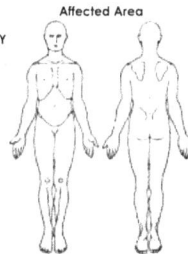

In my opinion the above diagnosis ☐ **does / does not** ☐ correlate with the injury described to me by the worker.

Injury management

6. Fitness for work It is my opinion that as from the date of this certificate the worker is:
Fit
☐ Fit to return to pre-injury duties, no further treatment required.
☐ Fit to return to pre-injury duties, **but** requires further treatment.
☐ Fit for restricted return to work **from:**   **to**
     ☐ restricted hours *(please specify)*:
     ☐ restricted days *(please specify)*:
     ☐ restricted duties.
☐ Work restrictions:
     ☐ No lifting anything heavier than   kg.   Other restrictions:
     ☐ Avoid repetitive bending / lifting.   ☐ Avoid repetitive use of affected body part.
     ☐ Avoid prolonged standing / walking / sitting.   ☐ Keep injured area clean & dry.
☐ **Unfit** Totally unfit for work for   days from   to   *(inclusive)*.

*(2. First and final certificate.
See reg 7 and s. 61(1) of the Act)*

7. Medical management
☐ Medication
☐ Approved allied health treatments *(specify type and include number of sessions recommended)*:   ☐ Imaging:
☐ Referred to hospital/specialist *(name)*:

Other treatment:
Next appointment *(Unless "First & Final Certificate")* Date   Time

If the worker is reviewed within 14 days, the worker cannot be required – under section 64 or 65 of the Act – to submit to a medical examination by a medical practitioner provided by the employer, on a day chosen by the employer that is within one month of the date of this certificate.

8. Medical practitioner / employer contact
☐ I have made contact with the employer and discussed alternative work options.
☐ The worker will be off work for more than **3 working days and/or is unable to return to normal duties.**
     Employer please fax your contact details as I will contact you to discuss return to work options.
☐ The worker is able to return to normal duties. Contact with employer not necessary at this stage.

9. Medical practitioner's details
Name: Registration no.
Address:
Telephone: Fax:
Time & date of examination: Signature: ....

**For workers' compensation and injury management information or assistance contact
WorkCover WA's Advisory Services: 1300 794 744**

Figure 5.1 WorkCover 'First Medical Certificate' (available from WorkCover 2014)

Table 5.1 Maximum percentages prescribed under the *Workers' Compensation and Rehabilitation Act 1981* (adapted from WorkCover 2008: 87)

Item	Nature of Injury or Impairment	Maximum % of PA	Conversion Factor
	FEET		
69.	Impairment of both feet	100	100 x WPI/44
70.	Impairment of foot	65	100 x WPI/25
71.	Impairment of great toe	20	100 x Lower extremity/2
72.	Impairment of any other toe	8	100 x Lower extremity/2
73.	Impairment of 2 phalanges of any other toe	5	100 x Lower extremity/5
74.	Impairment of phalanx of great toe	8	100 x Lower extremity/2
75.	Impairment of phalanx of any other toe	4	
	BACK, NECK AND PELVIS		
76.	Impairment of the back (thoracic spine or lumbar spine or both)	75	100 x WPI/60
77.	Impairment of the neck (including cervical spine)	55	100 x WPI/40
78.	Impairment of the pelvis	30	100 x WPI/15
	MISCELLANEOUS		
79.	Impairment of genitals	50	100 x WPI/20
80.	Impairment from facial scarring or disfigurement	80	100 x WPI/50
81.	Impairment from bodily, other than facial, scarring or disfigurement	50	100 x WPI/95
82.	AIDS	100	N/A

defines the maximum percentage of compensation to be received by injured Western Australian workers suffering various forms of impairment, and is further intended to simplify diagnosis in actuarial terms for doctors engaged in the compensation scheme.

Here, if a worker suffers impairment of one foot due to a work accident, the maximum compensation he or she can receive under the scheme, is 50 per cent of the capped amount of compensation for that year, which in 2009 sat at AU$168,499.00. Percentage disability – or 'whole person impairment (WPI) rating' – encompasses not only the direct physical injury sustained by an accident, but also the flow-on effects such as damages that are psychological, sexual or the result of scarring of the skin. Despite these clauses, this system nonetheless privileges the measurable injury – one that can be easily quantified and converted. Notably, many physicians were confused by this conversion system when it was first established, and judicial officers in my research expressed frustration with the inconsistent ways in which experts were using the formulae.

Yet the workers I interviewed feel they suffer from an illness that affects multiple organ systems and causes largely immeasurable complaints – such as anxiety, anger, fatigue, limited fitness and a loss of libido – none of which are neatly described in the impairment guide or included in the above tables. If an expert feels that Gerard, for example, is genuinely injured by toxins, she can interpret this table by noting that if he has lost his libido, Gerard has lost 50 per cent of the use of his genitals. In accordance with the table, this would entitle him to receive 25 per cent of the maximum amount. If, however, the doctor reads the table more rigidly – if in her opinion Gerard's symptoms are unable to be described under this table – Gerard will not be able to prove his eligibility for compensation.

As mentioned, workers also have the right to sue their employer under the common law if the workers' compensation scheme is inappropriate for their claim. Yet in 1999, the Western Australian State Liberal Government incorporated restrictions to common law access such that claimants would have to prove that they had suffered a permanent disability above a prescribed percentage. Like Ian in the previous chapter, workers now had to prove that they had lost 16 per cent of the use of their body; if they could not, they would not be eligible for common law access. Once this 'whole person' disability is proven to be within this category, then the claim goes to the District Court to determine whether the employer is negligent. If negligence is found on the balance of probabilities, compensation is awarded by the judicial officer in accordance with his or her evaluation of the case, and the amount of compensation that can be awarded – depending on the judicial officer's discretion using common law principles and precedent – is unlimited by statute.

For this task, the Western Australian branch of the Australian Medical Association (AMA) developed a guide, in conjunction with WorkCover, to help practitioners determine a worker's percentage disability (see Guides for the Evaluation of Permanent Impairment 2008). Tellingly, this comprehensive guide to occupational disability provides little assistance with regards to toxic exposure. It gives one case history of a fictitious patient who is exposed to spray paints in his workplace, yet the man only suffers from a small amount of temporary dermatitis on his arm and practitioners are therefore instructed to label him with 0 per cent permanent impairment.

In 2004, with financial pressures and lobbying from insurers, the Western Australian parliament decided that the current system was not working. A large number of workers were successfully gaining access to lengthy and expensive common law processes (see Report on Common Law Proceedings 2007). The parliament again changed the requirements for workers seeking access to common law with some noteworthy reforms. Under the previous system, medical experts invariably disagreed about the percentage disability of each worker, so the 2004 system was modified in an attempt to make the determination of impairment more rigid. Medical specialists who certify workers for compensation now have to be trained and approved by WorkCover, and the new impairment guide for determining percentage has substantially narrowed the scope for medical discretion. Although the categories for common law access have been reduced from 16 per cent and 30 per cent to 15 per cent and 25 per cent, it is more difficult now for workers to prove 25 per cent than it was for them to prove 30 per cent under the old system. Consider the graph at Figure 5.2, which is adapted from information in the 2007 Common Law Proceedings Report.

From 1999–2005, legislative changes reduced the amount of workers annually meeting the threshold to access common law proceedings from an average of 864 to only 56 workers. Assuming there has not been a radical improvement in workplace safety over this period, for all injured workers the changes in legislation have most certainly made their quest for common law access and, ultimately, for substantial compensation, even harder. For those with a controversial condition, about which the medical community is uncertain, the situation is likely to be more challenging again. The legislative changes have, however, been a radical improvement for insurers and has improved the cost-efficiency of the worker's compensation system (WorkCover 2007).

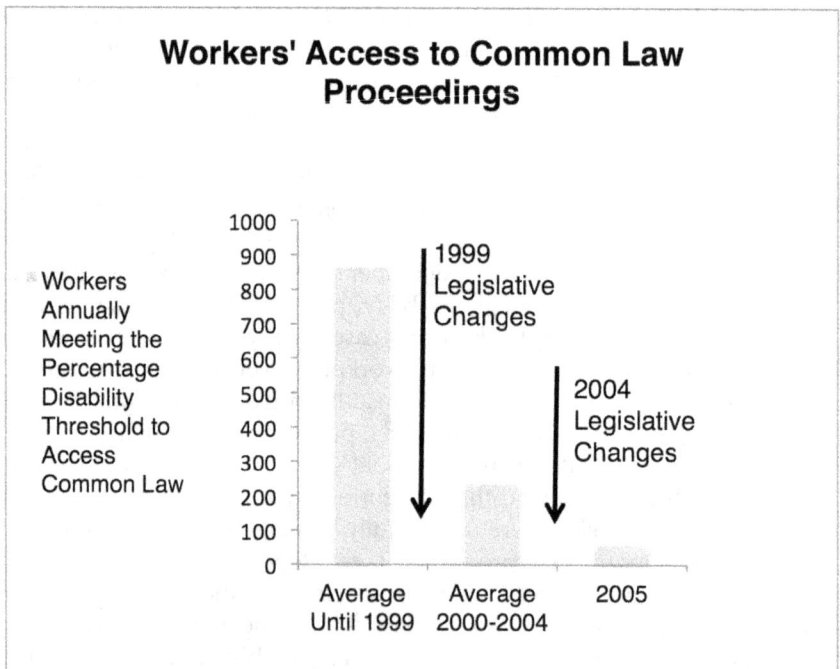

Figure 5.2 Effect of legislative changes on workers' access to common law proceedings in Western Australia (adapted from WorkCover 2007)

At this juncture it is important to consider the treatment of other immeasurable conditions in the Western Australian medico-legal system. Take, for example, stress resulting from employment. Although the process through which stress has received increasing biomedical attention and legitimacy is an intriguing study in itself (see for example Horwitz and Wakefield 2007), it is now considered a compensable condition in Australia, which is referred to and validated in the above tables and diagrams. Anecdotal evidence suggests that stress is generally considered a *less* valid illness than a physical injury and it is consequently more difficult to justify exemption from work and compensation on the basis of stress. Yet, unlike MCS, stress has been accepted at the legislative level and many workplaces now allow their employees to take 'stress leave', which entails (usually paid) exemption from work. However, people who suffer from stress rarely request exemption for longer than six months, and often only for a few weeks. On the other hand, the chemically sensitive in my research tended to be applying for total and permanent disability payouts, since they could no longer maintain employment. Unlike MCS, stress is widely researched, has a definable category and case definition, fits into the workers' compensation scheme, and is included in workplace agreements (see for example WorkCover WA 2001). The chemically sensitive who seek compensation are thus making much bigger demands than those requesting stress leave: they not only require sufficient financial capital to allow them permanent exemption from work, but also require the historically established categories of illness to be expanded and redefined in order to encompass the disability they claim to suffer from.

The evidence-based databases, clinical practice guidelines and worker's compensation forms and tables described above – intended to standardize medical diagnosis – are reifying categories of illness, which then become 'proxies for that which they purport to measure' (Lynch *et al.* 2010: 157). In other words, it is not the individual or their experience of illness that is treated, addressed and compensated by the insurance apparatus, but rather the code they are ascribed. This recalls the notion of black-boxes from science and technology studies: a 'black-box' is a term used to describe concepts that are presumed to be true and bracketed off. The uncertainties, or socio-political disagreement that once surrounded them, either get suppressed or collectively forgotten and the concepts become taken for granted (Latour and Woolgar 1979; Lynch *et al.* 2010: 15). Unlike what was witnessed in the laboratory by Latour and Woolgar (1979), it is not an isolated scientific laboratory that is responsible for glossing over ongoing disagreement and stabilizing facts about the body and how it interacts with the environment. Insurance technologies and political pressures are further drawing 'black-boxes' around medico-scientific knowledge about occupational risk. In turn, this overrides ongoing contestation, and inhibits epistemological flexibility amongst practitioners, further narrowing the potential for the recognition of contested emergent illness in the medical arena.

Legal reasoning and uncertainty

What role, then, does legal reasoning play in the struggle over emergent scientific knowledges? The Anglo-American legal system is, like bio-medicine, very much entrenched in the rationalist tradition. Contemporary Western law was also developed during the intellectual crisis in Europe, where people started to aspire to rationality. After trials by ordeal were deemed barbaric and irrational, the set of laws that gradually replaced them required that, for a claim to be proven, it must be deemed probable (Shapiro 1991: 7). Probability remains the standard of proof today: in criminal courts, a claim must be proven 'beyond reasonable doubt' whereas under civil jurisdiction – in which personal injuries law falls – evidence is required to prove a conclusion on the balance of probabilities.

Legal reasoning historically diverges from medico-scientific standards of proof in several crucial ways. In the first instance, causation in the common law has historically been approached differently than it has in biomedicine. The difference lies in liability, which is described by Mendelson (1998: 234–5):

> The law looks at causation from the stand-point of determining legal liability in negligence [...] the plaintiff has to establish not merely a scientific, philosophical or medical cause of the harm, but a *legal connection* between the particular breach of duty by the defendant and the actual injury of which he or she is complaining. [...] Therefore, although scientific and medical explanations of the causes are important, the attribution of liability is ultimately a matter of legal judgement.

Furthermore, Cartesian philosophy, which 'devalued the disciplines dependent on experiment or testimony' and was fundamental to the medical tradition, was not so influential to the legal system (Shapiro 1991: 7). Although the law does not allow hearsay, the law does rely to some extent on lay personal accounts to determine whether something did or did not happen. It also allows evidence dependent on testimony when it is based on specialist training or expertise. However, the veracity of a lay or expert's 'knowledge' of what happened in any given case is not proven until it has been subjected to rigorous examination and cross-examination in the adversarial courtroom (Henry 2013). This legal test is perceived as an 'extremely powerful machinery for discovering the truth' (Lynch *et al.* 2010).

Legal decision-makers consequently have tremendous authority in determining whether a person's experiential knowledge is valid, which is an important consideration in cases of workplace negligence and occupational injury. Social critics have long problematized the ways in which courts have historically reproduced the narrative of the dominant majority or the elite, and dismissed (or accorded less weight to) the counter-narratives of subordinated groups (see, for example, Henry 2013; Scheppele 1995). In determining whose explanations, or 'manners of imagining the real' (Scheppele 1995) are factual – (in this case, the workers' account of toxicity and injury, versus the employers' account of safety and harmlessness) – courts pronounce judgments on events that construct a powerful (if contested) narrative about what did or did not occur (Henry 2013).

Moreover, as the DNA story so neatly illustrates, legal decision-makers play an important role in arbitrating over conflict between expert knowledges, and can shape the direction and timeline of scientific controversies. Courts are thus an important site from which to examine the potency of legal authority to shape what we know about the natural world. And yet when a new illness is on trial in an adversarial system, judges (and sometimes juries) are expected to weigh-up contradictory medico-scientific evidence to determine which conclusion is most probable in a process of adjudicative fact-finding. In the context of MCS lawsuits, judges are faced with testimonies from equally qualified experts giving opposite 'evidence' regarding the onset, severity and causation of a plaintiff's medical condition. OHS professionals are also called to provide expertise regarding negligence and foreseeable harm of the toxic exposure in question. The ensuing conflict, as we will see below, presents myriad of problems for judicial officers determining the 'truth' about disease, particularly in a field of science that is complex, in its infancy, and an area in which the judicial officer is not trained (Kirby 2008; see also Chapter 4).

Importantly, several politico-legal attempts have been made to ensure judicial reasoning is not arbitrary or wayward in response to scientific uncertainty. In the US, the Supreme Court ruling in *Daubert vs. Merrell Dow Pharmaceuticals, Inc.* imposed requirements on judges to examine the scientific method underlying the expert evidence submitted 'and to admit [only] that which is both scientifically reliable and relevant to the issue at hand' (Melnick 2005: S30). This case involved a trial in which the parents of two children born with birth defects, allegedly as a result of the drug Bendectin, took legal action against the pharmaceutical company that produced it. The plaintiff team submitted evidence to support that the drug was harmful and the defence team highlighted that there was no scientific study alerting to any ill-health effects from Bendectin specifically. The court found in favour of the defendant company on the basis that the plaintiff's claims were not yet accepted by the scientific community, a decision which is increasingly common in areas of scientific uncertainty (Edmond and Mercer 2004; Shearer 2011).

Although there are obvious advantages to the Daubert standard because it prevents unfounded theories informing erroneous decisions, such a ruling disadvantages illnesses about which the science is 'incomplete' (Melnick 2005: S30). Evidence arising out of unorthodox theories that cannot be backed up by quantitative proof is likely to be excluded, and thus made invisible. Although the Daubert motion has not been so influential in Australian law, the widespread dismissal of novel allegations of chemical injuries in Western Australia demonstrates that judicial officers still tend to privilege established science in their judgements. There have, however, been a number of cases interstate and internationally where legal reasoning has led to the recognition of MCS and similar conditions. In contrasting the decision-making in these exceptional cases with that of the norm, I explore below: first, the legal concepts that facilitate the recognition of emergent knowledges and, second, why these decisions are not made more often.

As mentioned in Chapter 1, some chemically sensitive people are achieving recognition from the law in the US via the *Americans with Disabilities Act* (Kroll-Smith and Floyd 1997). Because disability relates to function and not cause, the chemically sensitive need only document their impairments to prove they are disabled, rather than providing evidence of pathological causal mechanisms as they are required in the narrow medico-scientific model. In this context, once disability is documented, 'the search for cause in the legal arena is far more flexible than a similar search in the medical arena' (1997: 165). Consequently, Kroll-Smith and Floyd are optimistic, since there is 'sufficient evidence that the existence of a new body is recognized with some regularity in decisions and deliberations of the courts' (169).

Moreover, in some outlying common law cases, controversial chemical injuries have been successfully proven in the courts despite ongoing medico-scientific contestation over their cause. In 1997, three shearers came before the Supreme Court of New South Wales in a combined negligence case against their employer, Allambie Pastoral Company, who they were suing for over-exposing them to 'sheep dip', which is a substance used to control disease on fly-blown sheep [*McKenzie, Johnson and Tiedemann v Harper and Ors T/as Allambie Pastoral Company* 1997]. Contained in this product is Diazinon, which is an organophosphate similar to those that are used in the nerve gas that is employed for chemical warfare. The latter substance lies at the heart of the controversy over Gulf War syndrome from which many veterans from Desert Shield and Desert Storm engagements allege to suffer, a condition that is similar in many ways to MCS (Donnay 1998). During the trial, the symptoms of the three shearers reportedly matched those of returned soldiers, including burning throats, headaches and memory loss. After a long and involved medico-legal battle, in which the defence mainly relied on evidence to suggest the plaintiffs' symptoms were from alcohol abuse, Justice Grove nevertheless found in the shearers' favour. In his Reasons for Decision, the judge explained that in order to form his opinion, he had to disregard the debate unfolding between plaintiff and defence experts over the controversial condition to some extent:

> Claims and counter claims made by 'experts' will inhibit any rapidity in reaching an accepted analysis of the situation [...] I refer to these matters of debate because a considerable proportion of the hearing was devoted to the expression of and cross-examination upon contradictory views about the possible after effects of organophosphate exposure. I emphasize that it is neither my task, nor within my abilities, authoritatively to resolve an issue upon which learned medical practitioners, scientists and chemists are in disagreement.
>
> (1997: 13)

Furthermore, on the issue of causation he noted that:

> As the hearing progressed and large volumes of scientific evidence were being adduced I formed an impression that breakdown product [from Diazinon] was a likely culprit in this instance but in the nature of things that cannot now be scientifically demonstrated nor do I need to make such a finding before the plaintiffs are successful in their case.
>
> (16)

Justice Grove went on to report that the lay evidence – the experiential knowledge – was particularly persuasive:

> I would not have expected the plaintiffs to be as pernickety about recounting detail as scientists (or lawyers) but their actions impressed me as that of honest working men initially mystified by what had befallen them.
>
> (15–16)

So despite the lack of consensus amongst the scientific community regarding the workers' conditions, he felt the 'evidence [was] well nigh overwhelming' (15) that organophosphate poisoning had occurred and was a causative factor to the workers' conditions. He thus awarded them full compensation for damages. The plaintiffs were awarded up to AU$277,000 according to the extent of their disabilities and other factors that contributed to the amount of pecuniary damages, or future loss, they would sustain. Interestingly, in this case the illness narrative was regarded as stronger evidence than that put forward by the experts. This is an interesting example of how an imbalance of social, cultural and economic power – which, as the previous chapter illustrated, places workers with a contested illness at an extreme disadvantage – can be overturned to some extent by legal decision-making.

Another example of a successful chemical injury lawsuit, also in New South Wales, is a Compensation Court case [*Wignall v. State of New South Wales Department of Education,* 1995] in which a high-school science teacher alleged to have contracted MCS from being exposed over several years to chemical emissions. The emissions emanated from the classroom and the adjoining preparatory laboratory, which was at times used as a staff room for him and his colleagues. In this case, again, there was vehement medical debate over the possibility of chronic symptoms developed from long-term, low-level exposure. (Although, as with all the cases I studied, the extent of the exposure was under debate: the defence relied on it being 'low-level', whereas the plaintiff's team argued that it was in fact a more substantial dose over time.) The judge in this case, Hon. Justice Campbell, also found in the teacher's favour: He wrote in his Reasons for Decision:

> [The defence barrister] did argue that the evidence did not establish that the initial causation was exposure at the school, however, I think the evidence establishes that to be a probability. It is true that [the plaintiff barrister] did not lead much evidence on that particular point, however there is sufficient such evidence, particularly in the light of the histories taken by the doctors [and] the reasonable inferences which may be drawn as to the nature of the atmosphere in the preparation room.
>
> (18)

So we start to see a difference emerging between what constitutes evidence in positivistic medical science on the one hand, and legal definitions of probability, or 'reasonable inferences' on the other. Similar reasoning regarding chemical injury litigation was engaged in the Irish Supreme Court in 1988. In this case an Irish farming family – the Hanrahans – sued the local plant of an American-based pharmaceutical company, Merck, Sharp and Dohme, for damages to their health, livestock and property stemming from the emissions from the factory [*Hanrahan v. Merck, Sharp And Dohme,* 1988]. The arguments of the defence were strikingly similar to those against the workers' claims in the Kylanta case. The family lost their case in the high court and then appealed to the Supreme Court of Ireland. After considering the evidence they were faced with, the three Supreme Court judges held that:

> A consideration of the scientific evidence as a whole given on behalf of the defendants leads me to the conclusion that, even if accepted in full, it only shows what *could* or *should* have happened in the way of damage by toxic emissions. In the light of what *did* happen in the way of toxic damage, I consider that the defendants' evidence could not be

held to rebut the plaintiff's case. Theoretical or inductive evidence cannot be allowed to displace proven facts. It was proven as a matter of probability that John Hanrahan suffered ill-health as a result of toxic emissions from the factory (1988: 645).

All of the judicial officers cited above are making a distinction between the evidence upon which medical science relies, and facts that are proven to be *legally* probable. As I describe later, medical inductive reasoning is itself probabilistic (see also Fox 2000). However, the data traditionally needed to prove something in medicine must be measurable according to scientific standards, which is not necessarily the case in the law. The case against chemical disorders, which emphasizes a lack of evidence for the condition within the traditional medical framework, can be discounted by legal decision-makers in favour of testimonial evidence (from injured workers and supportive specialists) which, to them, proves the workers are *probably* suffering a chronic illness from chemical exposure. This finding is consistent with Jasanoff's (1995: 125) outline of toxic torts, in which she notes that:

> The courts seemed inclined in each case to favour a holistic (or medical) to a reductionist, toxicological model of illness. The holistic view focuses on the suffering individual and asks whether, given the totality of circumstances, this person could have been affected in the stated way by the stated exposure.

In Jasanoff's work, many legal decisions in favour of the plaintiffs in toxic torts can be due to the fact that court processes privilege the testimonies of treating medical practitioners (who are often sympathetic) over that of defence physicians who have not examined the patient (1995: 123–125). This trend was not evident in the cases I studied: for example, the limited time that sceptical medical practitioners had spent with Ian (some not consulting with him at all) was not considered when judicial officers sided with them in dismissing his condition (see Chapter 4). Moreover, the cases cited above reveal that sympathetic judges are to some extent opting out of the medico-scientific debate altogether. They are basing their decision on *lay* accounts of illness and exposure to form their perspective on the specific causation and 'totality of circumstances.' They did not require the worker to align with scientific norms to the extent of the medical paradigm described above, but rather sought to make 'reasonable inferences' of their own regarding the extent of the exposure and 'what *did* happen in the way of toxic damage'. So, medico-scientific requirements for proof of pathology, and inflexible insurance categories, have to some extent been bypassed, and this has been facilitated through the law's potential to engage with a more flexible category of legal probability.

Thus, in the context of chemical sensitivity, the law has shown its ability to deem lay experiential knowledge as factual and legitimate where medical science has largely been unable. There are, understandably, some actors that bemoan non-scientific legal reasoning in lawsuits regarding toxicology. As Jasanoff (1995: 136) notes:

> Proponents of greater professionalism in toxic tort process [that is, 'primarily scientists, industry representatives, and some academics'] emphasize what they view as unscientific features of judicial thinking, such as excessive reliance on treating physicians, undue scepticism toward statistical evidence, and disregard of issues relevant to general causation.

The medical and legal positivists who 'accord more weight to what is statistically probable' (Jasanoff 1995: 126) believe that the legal system should undergo reform similar to the Daubert standard such that legal probability *cannot* bypass medical uncertainty. However, for litigants with emergent illnesses who are made invisible by medico-scientific positivism and insurance codes, legal flexibility provides a rare avenue for recognition.

If recognition of emergent, uncertain conditions is legally possible and there is precedent of sympathetic outcomes, what is preventing judicial officers from engaging this reasoning more often in MCS cases, particularly in Western Australia? For example, of the five judicial officers presiding at various times over Ian's case, four of them were unable to find in favour of the chemically injured worker on account of medical uncertainty and 'insufficient evidence'. While I highlight how a broader neoliberal pattern constrains the legal response to emergent concerns in Chapter 8, it is necessary here to discuss several aspects within the legal system that discourage judicial flexibility in this context. First, even though the above legal cases illustrate a different ideological understanding of what *can* constitute legal proof of causation, most judges pragmatically rely on – or are pressured not to steer away from – mainstream consensus about illness, and are not prepared to make inferences that bypass medical scepticism. As one plaintiff solicitor theorized, 'the law is well equipped to deal with it, but the experts aren't.'

Second, as illustrated in Chapter 3, confidentiality agreements and a lack of admission of liability prevent out-of-court settlements from becoming precedent. It could be argued that it is these cases where the evidence is most persuasive that MCS can be work-caused – even the liable employers thought so and thus settled before reaching trial. (Notably, though, corporate representatives claim that they are often forced into settling with 'possibly undeserving claimants' because 'legal inconsistency and haphazard standards of proof contribute to a climate of uncertainty' – Jasanoff 1995: 14). Nonetheless, a settlement cannot greatly publicize the legitimacy of a toxogenic explanation, and it does little to create and sustain momentum around sympathetic legal reasoning with regard to emergent knowledge.

Third, the rigid way in which injury and disease must be codified and understood as percentage impairment in the insurance apparatus means that medical uncertainty cannot be sidestepped by judges in favour of legal probability. Many workers with MCS are unable to access common law avenues and therefore are denied the potential for recognition that is enabled under the more flexible common law precedent.

Finally, as legal anthropologists make clear, in focusing on disputes, we must not forget those who are unable to bring attention to their complaints (e.g. Krygier 1980). In my research network it was evident that a large proportion of MCS cases in Australia and those of similar chemical disorders do not reach trial due to a range of reasons: a lack of medical support; a lapse in the time limit under the statute of limitations due to the period of latency of the illness; or cases where the plaintiffs give up their battle to prevent further financial and emotional strain. These people have attempted and failed to have their claims tested on the legal stage. Such omissions are also relevant when considering why there is continually 'insufficient evidence' for the courts to elevate chemical sensitivities from possible to probable.

Conclusion

Medical positivism determines that a theory will not be recognized until it has exceeded the threshold of scientific certainty. This requirement delays the medico-scientific orthodoxy from agreeing that an emergent environmental risk – and an associated illness – might be valid. Yet, as the following chapters illustrate, medico-scientific experts of both supportive and sceptical persuasion admit that medical science is by no means complete in its understanding of environmental impacts on the body. However, politico-economic pressures and legislative changes to the insurance apparatus take current medico-scientific reasoning, quantify it and fix it into categories, which rhetorically glosses over residual uncertainties and discourages ongoing questioning.

In the courts, the category of 'legal probability' does allow space for the recognition of lay experience of illness when medico-scientific experts reject the possibility or disagree amongst each other. However, decision-makers tend to privilege tried and tested medical theories when faced with scientific uncertainty. In essence, there is a dynamic interaction between medical, legal and insurance ways of assessing truth-claims that makes each field conservative in their evaluation of new epistemologies. This, in turn, confines medico-legal outcomes to a narrow set of possibilities.

Chapter 6

The deviance of sympathetic experts

I'm a crusader for truth. And if I believe something and I can look for evidence to prove it, you know, I'll go with it. That's just the way I am [...] It doesn't always win you friends, you know.

(Sympathetic genetics expert)

Sympathetic medical and legal practitioners who side with lay plaintiffs and advocate for reform in the understanding of emergent conditions present a challenge to mainstream science. In the first half of this chapter, drawing on interview data, I illustrate how sympathetic practitioners were first introduced to MCS, and analyse how they deviate from the dominant medico-scientific perspective. They are, I suggest, driven by both an epistemological stance about the inadequacy of the current scientific paradigm, and a different moral conviction about their responsibility as health providers. The second part of the chapter examines the sanctions these experts face for their oppositional stance. As theorists in science and technology studies have highlighted, those who are on the losing side of a scientific controversy often endure economic and professional consequences (Collins 1975; 2004; Latour and Woolgar 1979; Lynch *et al.* 2010). The stories below mirror this trend, since sympathetic experts of MCS have, to some extent, been 'bankrupted' by their professional communities for their deviance. However, the present controversy emphasizes that, along with reductions in money and professional credibility, there are also powerful psychosocial barriers that coerce medico-scientific practitioners into abandoning unorthodox lines of scientific inquiry. These disincentives can pose an insidious form of governmentality, in which practitioners can self-moderate, deradicalize their intellectual resistance, and retract their level of support for sufferers with uncertain conditions. The social dynamics of professional communities therefore can pose a significant constraint to the recognition of emergent knowledges.

Here it is important to qualify why I include such a range of disciplines in this discussion. As mentioned earlier, the health providers I interviewed were from diverse sub-fields, including general practice, toxicology,

psychology and occupational therapy. Yet for supporting a chemical explanation for MCS, the six sympathetic experts felt not only ostracized by the
wider medical profession but also marginalized by their immediate disciplinary peers. Moreover, although the two plaintiff lawyers I interviewed
came from a non-scientific background and a different professional
community, there are some intriguing similarities in their reasons for taking
a stand on the MCS issue, as well as parallel patterns in their career paths
thereafter. This is a reminder of the extent to which medico-scientific orthodoxy has authority in many realms of social life, even though the
sovereignty of this knowledge is ever-changing and oft-contested. It also
highlights the diversity of actors that play a part in the unfolding of scientific controversies.

Accidental mavericks: specialising in contested science

For sceptical commentators and those who assess insurance claims, the
motivations of plaintiff experts in contested illness lawsuits are questionable, and can even be fraudulent (Huber 1991; see also Ericson and Doyle
2004). Peter Huber, who coined the term 'junk science', refers to clinical
ecologists as 'cranks' and 'mavericks,' and qualifies that:

> Not every investigator who has fallen hard for pathological science is
> weak-minded, sloppy, or inclined to fraud. Some are seduced simply
> because they are irrepressible rebels, compulsively driven to dispute
> orthodox views, whatever they may be.
>
> (1991: 31)

However, the sympathetic experts in this research demonstrated a very
different set of motivations than fraud or irrepressible rebellion. In the first
instance, all of them developed an interest and reputation in MCS after they
had been approached by several people with a history of chemical exposure. One doctor, for example, was erroneously placed on a list of
sympathetic doctors disseminated amongst people with chronic fatigue
syndrome and chemical sensitivity. Despite her initial lack of experience in
the area, the doctor explains, 'the jungle drums beat, and someone else
comes, and someone else comes, and before you know it, it kind of
snowballs.'

Another medical expert, a geneticist, followed a similarly unplanned
career path. After conducting an epidemiological study on an unrelated
project, her team stumbled upon an unforeseen connection between chemical exposure and male fertility. The study received unprecedented media
attention, and, as a consequence, she explains, 'being involved in toxicity,
I sort of found myself being referred a lot of people who were ill from
chemicals.'

Plaintiff solicitor Jeff also happened upon his career in chemical injuries after negotiating compensation for a woman whose husband had died from workplace chemical exposure. He estimates that between 50 and 100 chemically sensitive people consulted him in the following years.

Despite the fact that their reputation in MCS was initially unintended, all of the supportive experts then made a conscious decision to be vocal in their advocacy for the chemically sensitive. Aside from the lawyers' obvious role as advocate, some medical practitioners received media attention for opposing mining operations where MCS allegations arose, most have published research surrounding the condition, and all of them continued to provide medico-legal reports for people with MCS who were embroiled in litigation.

To some extent, the sympathetic practitioners I interviewed *were* radicals, in the sense that they resisted the long-established orthodoxy of the medical profession. Yet Huber implies deliberate, pro-active, self-assured dissent. As I describe below, those I spoke to did not seek to rebel but rather found themselves specializing in a controversial condition and (often somewhat reluctantly) arriving at alternative conclusions. What, then, motivates sympathetic experts to disagree with their sceptical colleagues about MCS when faced with the same evidence?

[Importantly, sympathy and scepticism lie upon a spectrum. They are complex and can co-exist. As I will illustrate in the next chapter, experts can be sympathetic towards the physiological basis of one contested disease while being sceptical about another and change their views over time. For now, however, I seek to analyse what distinguishes the reasoning of those who identify as steadfastly sceptical or sympathetic in relation to MCS].

Epistemological rationale

Uncertainty poses a problem for a scientific paradigm. Since there is a lack of consensus and unorganized array of theories in the current medico-scientific debate over MCS, it could be deemed a period of *crisis science*, which harks back to the Kuhnian model of science. Kuhn (1962) emphasized that, when a field of scientific investigation is emerging and uncertain, the various works being conducted into the field are often chaotic and disorganized. At some point, a remarkable piece of work appears which, in turn, provides a model for further investigation, and thus a new paradigm begins to be established around this work. When an anomaly emerges, however, and the current paradigm offers no plausible explanation, this period is called crisis science, wherein the scientific community is in a state of insecurity. Some medical scientists working on MCS and similar conditions have explicitly argued that a paradigm shift is needed, or is underway, in the scientific understanding and clinical treatment of unexplained 'somatic' symptoms and 'functional syndromes' such as CFS, and MCS (Pall 2007; Sharpe and Carson 2001). However, the conflict between sympathetic and sceptical experts in my research extends to (and partly arises out of) contention around this very point. As I will illustrate below, the sympathizers believed that MCS posed a predicament to current scientific fundamentals, where sceptical experts believed that no crisis was present and the condition could be explained by current knowledge.

Learning to deal with uncertainty is an inherent part of the way medical students are 'intellectualized' (Fox 1959; 2000). Medical students are taught inductive reasoning, which is a form of problem-solving that requires a practitioner to make inferences from the evidence at hand, which, combined with medical knowledge and previous experience, leads him or her to make a rational diagnosis (Gandjour and Lauterbach 2003). This is mainly carried out through 'differential diagnosis,' whereby the physician examines the raw material, the signs and symptoms of the patient, uses his or her education and clinical experience to work out all that could *possibly* be affecting the patient, and then isolate what is *probably* causing the illness (Beck *et al.* 2003). Medical students develop collective defence mechanisms to suppress the possible perils of the uncertainties they deal with. Practitioners sometimes avoid uncertainty, since the medical profession 'foster's belief in the superior effectiveness' of the treatments developed in their field (Fox 2000; Katz 1984). This means practitioners are able to work within the confines of their professional paradigm, have faith in its efficiency and thus evade the notion of uncertainty altogether. For example, a sceptical toxicologist exhibits this confidence, and lack of uncertainty, in the excerpt below:

> MCS is a condition that presents itself solely with symptoms . . . there is never anything wrong that you can measure. So you can never find anything wrong on physical examination, you can never find anything wrong on laboratory examination, and even methodologies of neural imaging which are so sensitive that they can see you think *still* don't see anything going wrong . . . In some circumstances it's justifiable to measure specific toxins [. . .] But only where there has been a half-way plausible exposure history. If [not] then those tests are never abnormal, so they're not pursued. At the end of that kind of assessment – which is a pretty laborious process – most cases which present with MCS you can give them the reassurance that they're not poisoned – they've got MCS, but it's not to do with any poisoning syndrome.

This toxicologist has a strong belief that the current measures of toxicity used in his field, such as neural imaging, are effective. Similarly, a consultant occupational physician, in his testimony to the Kylanta parliamentary inquiry regarding MCS asserted:

> I was left with no choice but to conclude that, with the measured quantities [of emissions from the chimneystack] in both workplace and the environment, there was no potential for long-term health effects... The scientific data left me with no alternative but to come to the conclusion that there was no evidence for an association [between ill-health and Kylanta emissions].

This expert adheres to and trusts the mode of reasoning and technologies of measurement permitted within the risk assessment paradigm, which in turn leaves him with only one correct and 'rational' decision regarding the chimneystack: that it does not cause ill-health. All the sceptical experts I spoke to, or analysed reports from, came to the conclusion that MCS cannot be physiological because their scientific measures provided no evidence to suggest that this was the case. Consequently, they offered alternative causative mechanisms for the condition. As mentioned, many subscribed to the theory that MCS was a belief system – 'similar to a cult' in the words of one expert – which is perpetuated by supportive doctors, the media, and popular culture. Another expert suggested that for evolutionary reasons the human population has developed a bodily response to bad odours and that chemically sensitive people have an extraordinarily intense reaction. By fitting the anomaly of MCS into existing frameworks or theories that they do subscribe to – such as the idea that it is a socially communicated condition – sceptical experts are rejecting uncertainty. Rather than approaching the condition as a 'problem' for which biomedical science may not yet have the solution, they are instead approaching it as a 'puzzle' to which they only need to apply their existing paradigmatic knowledge.[1] From their perspective there is no Kuhnian crisis; no need to question the fundamentals of their medical knowledge or training.

By contrast, the supportive experts demonstrated less faith in current paradigmatic assumptions about disease and toxicity. A supportive occupational physician, for example, asserted:

> MCS is different [...] there is needed a change in the way we think about diagnosis and pathology [...] It is demanding of medicine that the doctors are prepared to think perhaps our pure pathological approach to illness doesn't apply. Given that MCS lacks the nice heart-attack-heart-in-a-bottle-that-you-can-see, given that it lacks overt physical findings such as a tumour on the chest or a paralyzed limb, given that it lacks test tube laboratory tests such as full-blood counts being down, or serum sodium being up, we are left with a diagnosis which is based on the history, which is, 'how were you before all of this happened? When did you get sick? What was the event? When did the symptoms start?

Sympathetic experts, like this man, thus illustrated a very different reaction to uncertainty. A clinical neuro-psychologist – who has specialized in chemical brain injuries for over a decade, treated hundreds of chemically injured patients around the nation, and regularly acts as an expert in MCS litigations – had the following response when I asked how MCS worked:

> Oh, how does it work? [*Laughs*] Well, I suppose I'm not exactly an expert on it. But it seems that the person who suffers from MCS generally has an exposure to one chemical [...] and then after some time, their system tends to break down, because they were overloaded with chemicals [...]

Another practitioner answered emphatically in response to what causes MCS that 'medicine doesn't know'. These experts believe that MCS *is* an anomaly, and medical science is uncertain about toxicity, yet they are reluctant to attempt an explanation. They do not defend their profession's efficacy in detecting poisoning, unlike the sceptical toxicologist who commented on the wonders of neural imaging. They do not attempt to explain the condition with existing theories, such as those regarding psychosomatic conditions or odour aversion. They imbue less value in current scientific consensus. Instead they say 'medicine doesn't know', and in doing so, exhibit a lack of confidence in the existing paradigm that medicine has for understanding the effect of chemical exposures on health.

Part of the reason for this disparity between sympathisers and sceptics was the extent to which they adhere to a positivist mode of reasoning when determining the legitimacy of an emergent condition. A sceptical infectious disease specialist noted that, when he first heard of MCS due to the publicity surrounding the Kylanta case:

> I researched multiple chemical sensitivity and I went to a lecture by the expert from America [*Professor Mark Cullen*] [...] And I thought that his lecture was very nice, however, it had no data in it as far as I could tell. He didn't convince me, he didn't actually have any evidence that it existed. Now the thing about chemical sensitivity is that there's not a scientific basis for it.

By requiring data and a 'scientific basis,' this specialist emphasizes his positivist requirements for believing in the organic nature of an emergent environmental condition. Objective, credible evidence of pathology must be provided for the condition to adhere to the mainstream canon of scientific knowledge, and to exceed his own standard of proof. (It is common in scientific controversies for experts to claim their perspective is more scientific than the other side – more logical, objective and closer to 'pure description' – because it 'affords an impregnable position from which to snipe at the enemy' – Barnes 2009: 166).

Sympathetic specialists, on the other hand, accorded more weight to experiential knowledge; both in terms of their own perceptions in the clinic and the narrative of their patients or clients. A clinical psychologist said, for example:

> I've interviewed many, many people and I've seen how adversely chemicals [...] have affected a person's overall functioning. Not only neuro-psychologically, but emotionally, physically, and in a number of ways. [...] I've seen them first-hand, and know how much they suffer.

An occupational therapist further iterated the importance she places in her own empirical observations:

> What I tend to do is when I'm looking, I go to [the MCS patient's] home and I look at what's happening in their home and I just start putting two and two together and I try and analyse what's actually going on. Yeah, I can't believe people would purposefully make their lives so miserable. I just...these people are struggling. These people aren't happy.

An occupational physician emphasized the significance of the patient's story. For him, those with MCS:

> ...usually [have] normal health to begin with, then the occurrence of illness developed in association with some recognizable chemical exposure, and for which there is a reasonable, temporal, time-related, relationship. So, exposure, followed by symptoms. The evidence that is of the most importance in thinking about the patient with MCS, is the patient themselves. It is the symptoms they've got. It is their story. It is their history. It is what they tell you of their experience. It's the experiential data that is absolutely crucial.

Interestingly, these experts are engaging the legal understanding of causality outlined in Chapter 5 – in which something can be deemed probable if cause and effect can be reasonably inferred – in contrast to scientific standards of proof, whereby something must be measurable, or statistically relevant to exist.

Moreover, the two solicitors I interviewed, who believed MCS is organic, did so for similar reasons. Both lawyers developed their opinion based on the perceived genuineness of their clients' narratives. Mark said of one of the Kylanta workers he represented:

I believed he was a very credible person and I didn't believe that he was making anything up at all, and that he genuinely suffered from the complaints he said he had. People don't generally...there's certainly no suggestion that [this worker] or the other [MCS] clients I've dealt with, had any mental or other sort of difficulties which would make them...lead them to fabricate something like this. It's just too far-fetched.

Despite an absence of objectively measurable evidence for the patients' condition, if the supportive experts believed the patient to be genuine – that there was a temporal link between chemicals and ill-health – then they would conclude that what needs to be placed in doubt is the medical profession's understanding of toxicity and standards of proof, rather than the patient or client's claims.

Importantly, although I suggest supportive experts acknowledge uncertainty more readily, they are not so flexible in their professional beliefs as to immediately change them upon being confronted with an anomaly for the first time. The supportive physicians I talked to took a long time to accept the physiological causation of MCS. All of them remarked that when they were first introduced to patients with the condition, it took a number of consultations before they began to truly develop their own understanding of what was happening. One expert mentioned that with each patient presenting with symptoms consistent with chemical sensitivity, he would go through all other possible explanations before considering the possibility of an MCS diagnosis. Another expert explained that if someone presents with a conviction that they have MCS, she will first rule out alternative medical explanations. She has, for example, diagnosed people who thought they were chemically sensitive with depression, anxiety, and pregnancy. So for these experts, straying from the paradigm in which they were trained – which has intellectualized them to have confidence in the efficacy of current medical knowledge and to circumvent uncertainty – is not a frequent, nor light-hearted, decision.

Essentially, supportive and sceptical experts are problem-solving in a similar and equally inductive way – they are both using evidence-based logic, taking data from their surroundings and then abstracting conclusions from them. However, the sceptics privilege those forms of evidence that are more credible according to current consensus, while sympathetic experts turn to the patient's experience as valid data if the condition seems, to them, to present an anomaly to the current paradigm. Each therefore has a different (rational) outcome to their scientific reasoning, and both believe the other is being irrational. Sceptics consequently have their certainty unshaken, while sympathizers are left feeling dissatisfied with their profession's knowledge-base.

Moral rationale

And yet, like any scientific controversy, the debate over MCS is not just an epistemological conflict – a simple disagreement over facts – although it is usually expressed by experts in that way. There is a moral conviction that underlies sceptics' reasons for believing the condition is psychosomatic, and the sympathizers' rationale for supporting a chemical explanation. In the expert disagreement over RSI, Reid and Reynolds (1990) argued that the medical science engaged by experts to explain their viewpoints constituted 'desocialized facts'. Supportive experts applied 'objective' scientific discourse essentially as a disguise for their compassion for people with RSI. Equally, sceptical experts used the language of hard science to simply veil their moral outrage at, in their view, non-deserving people receiving compensation. Akin to their findings, compassion and outrage were also expressed by sympathetic and sceptical experts regarding MCS. Consider, for example, the following interview excerpts:

SCEPTICAL INFECTIOUS DISEASE SPECIALIST: I think these [workers] get a whiff of compensation rather than a whiff of chemicals. So they have . . . the situation is they have an illness of some sort which cannot be diagnosed. They look around, they say, "What is the cause of this? My God, what's that smell? That must be the cause." And this is the process that people go on with. And then they switch on Foxtel, what do you know? *Erin Brockovich* is on TV.

SYMPATHETIC CLINICAL PSYCHOLOGIST: [Sufferers] withdraw themselves from society really. And I've seen them first-hand. I've visited them in their homes, and know how much they suffer. So that's why I'm prepared to take a stand.

In conjunction with compassion and outrage, these medical practitioners are each expressing an affinity to a different facet of the medical practitioner's role. On the one hand, the sceptics are, in the case of MCS, according more weight to their role as invigilator of fraud and gatekeeper to funds, which, as illustrated in Chapter 4, is an obligation that is heightened and enforced in neoliberal insurance apparatuses. By contrast, sympathizers are engaging a more traditional rhetoric of altruism; that of patient advocacy above all else (Pearson 2000). The occupational physician, for example, said:

[When] I speak to an individual and I feel that I'm talking to a genuine human being who has got a real problem and who is worthy of medical help, that's where the support is. And it comes from the . . . it's like distilled whisky. It's pure. You see the patient who is not phony, who is not trying to manipulate the system, who is not dishonest, who has got an absolutely genuine problem, who has got something which is not their fault, and who is receiving all sorts of opposition to getting what any normal person under calm circumstances would feel is the logical, right thing to do; namely, help someone who is sick.

Another expert, a toxicologist, alluded to altruism when stating that his decision to be an advocate for the chemically sensitive was not likely to lead to scientific innovation or career success:

> I do it to help people. I actually would like to think there is something sort of special we can find and then look forward to a cure [but] I actually don't think there is. I think if there was we would have found it by now.

Just as there are the dual roles of advocate and gatekeeper in the doctor's toolkit, so too are there different ethical approaches to lawyering. Where some lawyers might interpret the law in a positivist, black-letter manner, others may be more focused on the spirit of the law – what it ought to be achieving, in their view – or on the law as a tool for social justice (see Parker 2004). The solicitors in this research demonstrated an affinity to an explicitly moralistic style of lawyering which, they felt, differed from their colleagues who worked for insurance companies. Jeff, for example, said chemically injured people deserved help because they were:

> ...up against large corporations and insurers behind them [...] and they [the insurers' legal team] tended to fight, not necessarily for the truth, but fight every single technical point and attempt to burn off each individual accident victim, and I was incensed about that and I had a passion for justice and I enjoyed fighting on behalf of genuinely injured people.

Moreover, sympathetic experts explicitly mentioned the lack of significance they attach to financial reward. A sceptic from the UK once iterated to me that he believed MCS specialists tended to have very lucrative practices on Harley Street specializing in treating wealthy patients with MCS. However, in my study, for specializing in representing litigants of a controversial illness (most of whom could not afford high medical or legal fees) sympathetic experts often lowered their fees or did not charge for services. In Ian's case, for example, the total cost for him to consult all of his supportive medical specialists, of which there were six, was approximately AU$1500. The cost of the defence specialists' fees in Ian's case – of which there were also six of similar qualifications – was approximately AU$15,000. (Importantly, I saw no evidence that sceptics' decisions were in any way driven by financial reward, although it is unassailable that the financial mark-up for providing a sceptical opinion for the insurer is a bonus of their position.)

Lawyers who represent MCS clients similarly do so at a financial risk, since they often act on a no-win-no-fee basis. Jeff explained that one of the impacts of his decision to represent people with chemical injuries is that:

> ...on a mundane level, to some extent it's kept me poor. The difficulties in succeeding in chemical injury cases are so mammoth that your remuneration is sometimes nil...there've been several cases where we've been paid poorly, if at all, for the work that we've done in chemical injury. So to that extent, there's been some impact on my lifestyle. But I'm not the slightest bit troubled about that because money doesn't bring happiness.

So the supportive experts emphasize that financial gain is insignificant. Jeff in particular has opted out of financial security in order to seek 'happiness', which he intimated is obtained from the internal satisfaction of following one's internal moral code. (Evidently, the extent to which professionals are content with compromising financial gain for the benefit of the MCS cause can vary. One solicitor who acted on behalf of a chemically sensitive informant, Fiona, tearfully tried to convince her client to accept a settlement rather than continue to trial because, 'we won't get paid.') Nonetheless, unlike the accusation of entrepreneurialism often directed at them, I witnessed only financial *dis*incentives for acting as a sympathetic expert.

Sympathetic experts thus disagree with the mainstream position on the issue of MCS on both an epistemological and moral basis. Although they are faced with the same evidence as their colleagues, they have a different reaction to the uncertainty presented by the chemically sensitive, and less faith in the current explanatory models for disease causation and toxicity. They also have a moral conviction that for them justifies and reinforces the 'rightness' of their unorthodox stance.

Sanctions for deviance

When people breach their professional community's standards they are often punished for it. Like any social group, a professional community creates a sense of 'affinity and belonging' in its members, who on the whole have mutual interests and therefore, relatively shared values and norms (Freidson 1970; 1986; Daniel 1998). Yet, there are also surveillance and sanctions imposed in the professional communities to ensure doctors and lawyers conform to medical and legal codes of conduct. According to Daniel (1998), the professional community is usually a tight-knit, autonomous group that largely shelters its members from outside scrutiny, but only until a member transgresses professional standards in a way that threatens the profession's public image. When a colleague is caught deviating – overcharging clients, for example – professional representative bodies then ceremoniously demonstrate to the public that they will deal with the renegade(s) in an appropriately harsh manner so that the public will once again feel justified in trusting the profession to regulate itself according to the public's best interests. Daniel's (1998: 3) concern, however, is that sometimes, 'one person [gets] chosen for exemplary punishment to carry away the guilt of many and deter others from wrong-doing.' The manner in which these situations are handled and the offenders punished by the profession can denote a kind of scapegoating, such that their collective reputation is upheld and other members are deterred from disobeying the code of conduct in the future.

The treatment of clinical ecologists might also be seen as a case of scapegoating of professional deviance, but the transgression is epistemological rather than an instance of behavioural misconduct. The public's trust in the scientific process of accruing knowledge, and devising medical treatment (a faith which, admittedly, has changed – Hess 2005; Willis and Coulter 2004) is in part strengthened by its rigorous peer-review system and evidence base. This system of review, which, at least in rhetoric, is to ensure the credibility and trustworthiness of scientific research, has an inherently conservative element: reviewers tend to be reluctant to support unorthodox and high-risk research, which in turn encourages scientists to be 'mainstream' and risk-averse in their projects (Laudel 2006). Moreover, the medico-scientific community, who, for the most part, have established their careers on the basis of a particular set of fundamental assumptions, have a strong personal and collective interest in protecting the status of their paradigm. Indeed, anthropologists Romanucci-Ross and Moerman (1991) refer to medicine as a 'closed system of knowledge' and further iterate that:

> It has many vested interests in remaining that way. Physicians who stray too far from the properly defined and encoded clinical perspective, or from what is generally deemed to constitute proper basic research, are likely to be shunned, or at least ignored, by peers and superiors.
>
> (1991: 368)

As the following cases will illustrate, the sympathetic experts in my case studies clearly breach their profession's system of knowledge by questioning what constitutes proper basic research – by challenging the importance of traditional ideas of 'measurability' and numerical 'proof' – debates which have long ago been largely agreed to and closed off.

We cannot be overly reductionistic about the closed nature of medico-scientific knowledge; as mentioned, certain innovations and even paradigm shifts have been enabled and eventually rewarded in medical science.

When a proposal for a paradigm shift is successfully tested, legitimized and becomes a mainstay of 'normal science', its proponents are often rewarded by career success and formal accolades, as their professional fame begets funding and personal wealth, and vice versa (Latour and Woolgar 1979; Lynch *et al.* 2010). But, when a theory is disqualified or subjugated to the status of 'unscientific', its proponents can suffer damaged reputations, which correlate to a lack of capital to support their careers (Collins 2004).

Sympathetic experts in environmental health controversies have often experienced such disenfranchisement. In the disease outbreaks of Love Canal and Woburn, Massachusetts, scientists who 'aligned themselves with citizen alliances' and acted as whistleblowers against the mainstream scientific and political perspective were initially punished for it, both financially and in terms of professional credibility (by having, for example, grant applications continually rejected – Brown and Mikkelson 1997). Below, I highlight how these same sanctions were imposed on sympathetic experts of MCS, which distinctly impacted their ability to follow unorthodox lines of inquiry.

One expert in genetic science developed a controversial technique for detecting toxins in the chemically sensitive body. For her, it was a definitive moment; 'proof' of the physiological basis of MCS. Yet, soon afterwards, her laboratory stopped receiving funding. She argues the evidence she produced was too contentious and, in her words, 'upset some very powerful people'.

> Basically they sent me out of business. I have got beaten down because I lost all my money [...] I haven't been able to do the things I used to do so I've dropped right back.

Although she omitted details because she was 'too frightened of being sued for defamation', her experience emphasizes the infrastructure that is needed by researchers – particularly in a field of science that is in its infancy – which includes financial and institutional support. If and when that assistance is not forthcoming or is terminated, the practical implications are that one may be forced to 'drop right back' in attempting to act on behalf of MCS litigants. This is irrespective of whether one feels a drive to be altruistic and rejects the importance of money on principle.

There are, moreover, social consequences for supporting an unconventional scientific claim. All of the medical practitioners felt very alone on the issue of MCS amongst their professional colleagues. The sympathetic toxicologist decried the 'monolithic refusal' of certain sections of the medical industry to agree that there is in fact a condition'. Another expert, an occupational physician, explained his marginal position:

TARRYN: Do you have many colleagues who share [your] belief about the condition?

PROFESSOR: [*Smiling*] No.

TARRYN: Any?

PROFESSOR: Some, to varying degrees. I've got one who I think agrees with me. I've got one or two others who I think are sympathetic, but who I think would hold strongly to the view that I'm wrong [...] and ah, will make a bit of a joke of it really. But in essence, I am in a minority.

Similarly, plaintiff solicitor Mark recalled his experience with the medical majority from his legal vantage point:

The most profound feature of [the Kylanta case] was the reluctance of medical authorities to see that this condition existed [...] I remember it being difficult to find experts that would comment on MCS [...] it wasn't easy to find people that would talk about that.

For unconventionally privileging experiential knowledge over proven scientific facts, these medico-scientific and legal experts were often mocked by their contemporaries. Mark said, for example, 'amongst my other legal colleagues, there was sort of a little bit of a laugh as to whether something like this really existed.'

A sense of humour is a self-preservation mechanism adopted by practitioners, as well as a central part of the cohesion of a professional community (cf. Fox 2000), and thus being laughed at in a joking manner can be harmless. However, for some, friendly mockery became more severe isolation for choosing an unconventional area of specialty. As an occupational physician noted poignantly, 'this area is very difficult and lonely.' She articulated the stigma she experienced from her colleagues after developing a reputation in the MCS area. The psychologist remarked:

I find that I've been almost blacklisted as a person who's sympathetic to the cause. [...] You find that if you're sympathetic to the worker that is affected by chemicals [...] you're almost like a leper in the community because you take the stance that you do.

Related to this, most sympathetic experts suffered not only a lack of social support from their colleagues but also institutionalized questioning of their credibility. The following anecdote narrated by one expert illustrates this clearly. Each year, it is compulsory for members of professional communities to ensure they sustain currency in professional development, through conferences and workshops. For attending these, they receive credit in the form of points for 'professional attainment'. Some of the supportive specialists I spoke to have attended a number of conferences of the Australian Chemical Trauma Alliance (ACTA). These are meetings of a not for profit organization where chemically injured people convene with advocates and experts, including environmental, occupational and toxicological scientists, to discuss recent findings about chemical injuries. The expert in question said ACTA conferences are among the best and most informative conferences to which he has ever been. By contrast, he explains that he has never learnt 'one single thing useful about chemical injury' from the various conferences that he has attended within his own discipline. Yet when he applied to his representative college of medicine to receive professional attainment points for attending the ACTA conferences, he was promptly notified by letter that such meetings would not accrue points because they did not further his medical knowledge. This case study typifies the forms of surveillance that exist in the medical profession to ensure doctors do not deviate from the standard medical knowledge framework. This expert expressed his belief that people should be encouraged to 'step outside' of what they know, because otherwise it is 'just the same people recycling the same old stuff within the family'.

Aside from loneliness and institutionalised sanctions, several practitioners felt they had been labelled 'quacks' amongst their colleagues for diagnosing numerous people with MCS. This loss in credibility can have ramifications for the perceived credibility of their expertise in a legal setting. Jasanoff (1995: 132–134) highlights how judges have discarded evidence from clinical ecologists because 'the leading professional societies in the specialty of allergy and immunology...have rejected clinical ecology as an unproven methodology lacking any scientific base in either fact or theory.' Dissident medical experts who are treated as 'quacks' and 'lepers' by the scientific orthodoxy have reduced authority as credible witnesses, which then inhibits their ability to meaningfully assist the legitimization of emergent conditions.

Damaged credibility was also experienced by plaintiff solicitor Jeff for his passionate advocacy for chemically sensitive clients. When I first became involved in Ian's legal conflict, Jeff was fairly confident of a win. However, Jeff was confronted with defeat after defeat during the process of seeking compensation for Ian. Although Jeff had experienced extreme disappointment and frustration with the unfavourable findings of the Review Officer in 2005 and Compensation Magistrate a year later, he remained optimistic before the Supreme Court hearing in 2007. Ian's case was to be represented by one of the most senior QCs in Perth, a well-respected barrister within the Perth legal community. Jeff explained to me that if the judges were to listen to and understand *all* of the facts, then they could do nothing else but find in Ian's favour. I attended the Supreme Court on that day, during which Jeff whispered to me minutes before the event that he and the barrister had a difference of opinion as to how to approach the case. The barrister felt that the way to win this appeal was to argue that the Review Officer who had previously decided against them had made an error on a legal technicality.[2] Jeff, on the other hand, felt that since this was their last chance, it was dangerous to rely solely on a minor legal detail. He wanted to emphasize what he felt were the substantive issues: that the science in the area of chemical sensitivity is still uncertain; to reiterate evidence that he felt proved that his client was legitimately sick; and to highlight the fact that the defendant's experts had less experience in identifying chemical brain damage than the plaintiff's experts did.

Below is an excerpt of my field notes written immediately after the Supreme Court hearing:

> As the barrister was winding up his final submissions to the bench, after which the hearing would be over, I saw Jeff [who was sitting next to the barrister and advising him on certain matters] tug at the barrister's robe and whisper something to him urgently. The barrister seemed to wave Jeff's point away as unimportant or inappropriate, and completed his submissions. As the judge sitting in the middle, the chairperson, was about to say the hearing is over, Jeff got up suddenly, impulsively, and said, 'Your Honours, can I raise some final matters?' Everyone, including Jeff's barrister, the three judges and the defence looked very surprised at his action. The judges looked at each other and tentatively allowed him to speak, a little bemused at his request. Jeff said he had three final points to make: he talked of the toxicity of the chemicals that the employer had failed to monitor, and went over the discrepancy between the expertise of the plaintiff and defence expert witnesses as well as the difficulty of scientific uncertainty.
>
> In the middle of Jeff's plea, the chairperson said to Jeff that it would be unfair for Jeff to be able to submit further arguments if the defendant was unable to respond to them. Jeff said then, a little urgently, that it would be good if the defendant could be given the opportunity to respond to this because it was 'a matter of critical justice for his client' and he continued... After he had finished talking, the (disgruntled) judges talked amongst themselves and eventually agreed that they could not allow these new points to be accepted. The chairperson said they would reserve their decision. We all bowed as they filed out of the courtroom and the hearing was finished.

While I was speaking with Jeff, Ian and his wife Jackie outside the Supreme Court immediately after the hearing, Jeff explained why he had stood and made what he referred to as a 'passionate plea'. He said:

> I thought, 'blow it'. I got egg on my face. The judges were singularly unimpressed. It's not the done thing. But it was my last chance. I'm very glad I did or I would never have forgiven myself.

In the appeal court, Jeff is expected to fulfil a 'junior barrister's' role. Jeff had disregarded the code of conduct that is expected of him as a solicitor in the Supreme Court – particularly the convention for when and how to present arguments – and his actions therefore displeased his superiors. The judges disallowed his submissions and months later, two out of three found against Ian. The case was, essentially, over. The 'egg on Jeff's face' seems symbolic of the way in which lawyers who take a strong stance can be faced with professional sanctions, not only for straying from behavioural norms for solicitors, but also for deviating from the mainstream medico-scientific knowledge framework.

Although supportive practitioners feel professionally isolated within their local discipline groups and in their daily professional lives, it is notable that they are respected at international toxic injury conferences, as well as in email contact with the chemically sensitive and other dissident supportive professionals for challenging the status quo and acting on behalf of 'genuinely injured people'. For example, although Jeff received disdainful looks from the panel of Supreme Court judges for his unconventional plea, his client, Ian, revered Jeff. He and his wife Jackie emotively expressed thanks for Jeff's show of commitment to Ian's cause. Ian said that Jeff was 'one of the best blokes he knew' and that he had 'looked everywhere to find a lawyer who would do the kind of thing Jeff did.' Thus, even though supportive professionals forego some forms of capital, such as their reputation within the broader professional community and certain financial benefits, their decision to advocate for the underdog acquires them a different form of kudos, a bolstered legitimacy in alternative arenas.

Ultimately, though, as in scientific controversies over gravity wave science and leukaemia clusters, sympathetic researchers of emergent and uncertain conditions also face social isolation, reduced professional credibility and financial consequences. Furthermore, an intriguing discovery in my research was that in the face of these pressures, the experts consequently adjusted the nature of their support for the chemically sensitive. As described below, some became emotionally burnt-out after years of facing these pressures and abandoned their line of work, others reduced their emotional attachment to the outcome of the quest for MCS legitimacy, and still others continued to practice but de-radicalized their once passionate resistance.

In conversations with the supportive MCS experts, there was a palpable sadness that arose when they discussed their experiences with the chemically sensitive. Despite their initial motivations, they seemed jaded with the cause, and unconvinced of its potential. A prominent example of dissatisfaction is again illustrated by solicitor Jeff. When I first formally interviewed him in 2006, Jeff clearly felt inspired by his work. He had decided to specialize in personal injury law because, 'I had a passion for justice and I enjoyed fighting on behalf of genuinely injured people.' Yet two years after this interview and with his law business now closed, I noticed a significant change in Jeff. His wife and the manager of his office, Margaret, says of their experience in chemical injury cases:

[We received] no satisfaction at all. [It's] very soul destroying in that way. And gradually I think it wore me away. You know, I've been quite angry about it in later years, just because it's very hard to keep going at something where there is no reward.

A lack of professional satisfaction for Margaret and Jeff, coupled with financial constraints – they lost approximately AU$250,000 in working no-win, no-fee for Ian – played a large role in the Carlsons' decision to give up their practice. At the time of writing, Jeff was still working in personal injury law but worked for another firm in another city. I watched Jeff's romanticism about justice in his profession diminish after Ian's case, about which he said, 'it's hard to imagine a more gross case of injustice'. He went on to say that he is 'losing confidence that the law, as it is currently structured, can handle the complexity of [Ian's case]'. In our most recent interview, I asked what he would advise me to do if I were to suffer from a chemical injury. He explained:

In the past, I would have recommended that you consult those people who are most skilled in Western Australia in that area [of] the medical profession to see whether they consider you have an injury, and the extent of the injury and whether it is caused by toxins at work. [Then] I would look at whether or not you had a common law action in terms of being able to prove negligence or breach of statutory duty [...] But, my recent experience has been so grim of the law and the way it worked [...] So now I'd have to reconsider advising anybody to do anything but ignore the law altogether and try to get as much quality of life as they can through medical treatment.

Just as this solicitor has begun to feel disillusioned with his profession's capacity to deliver justice, so too are the medical specialists questioning medicine's ability to recognize, heal, and discover treatment for toxic injuries. One specialist, for example, mentioned that engaging with the quest for MCS legitimacy denied him emotional 'nourishment':

One area of support does not come from getting success in these cases – success in winning the case – because mostly you *don't* win the case. Most of the people I see with MCS and with other conditions, there is in some concrete way a loss that they sustain, and therefore I can't get any nourishment as a doctor from waiting or seeing their recovery and their success in all of this. So one thing I do not do is have any attachment to a successful outcome. I have commitment to trying to help them. And doing what I can and knowing that I've done what I can, and then I try and let it go. Because if I don't, I'll sink, because I see one person, two people, three people, twenty people etc. And they all have difficulties.

A typical response to this exhaustion is for experts to emotionally distance themselves such that they are desensitized towards the outcome of their advocacy. Just as the occupational physician tries to 'let it go [or] I'll sink,' the toxicologist remarks:

> In my early days it was gruelling, because I found I was trying to help the plaintiff. I was involved in a class action…and the lawyer there said, look, you're not here to help the clients, you're here to help the court. So now I just go in and just say what I think. And I was in court last week…and the [plaintiff lawyer] didn't ask the right questions so I couldn't help her. And I wanted to say, 'no, don't ask that, ask this!' But it's not my problem. Yes it was my problem because I wanted to help her […] but I don't worry about it anymore. I used to in the past, but I don't anymore.

In essence, these stories show the capillary power of governmentality at work. Professionals who challenge the mainstream scientific paradigm, like all of their colleagues, are under the gaze of their professional community. None of these sympathetic experts have lost their licenses to practice or been denied membership to professional societies. The sanctions imposed on them are more subtle, but nonetheless disempowering. Decisions handed down by professional accrediting associations, social gatherings between colleagues, and courtroom dramas are all sites where institutional norms are challenged and debated, policed and reinforced. Through these modes of surveillance, those members who deviate in a way that challenges the current paradigm, and are deemed to threaten the credibility of the collective, are punished for their transgressions and deterred from future nonconformity. It is thus not just the risk of financial and reputational loss that discourages intellectual risk-taking, but also a desire to conform – or, rather, an awareness of the sanctions for resisting the norm – that provide powerful disincentives against experts supporting unorthodox theories. One practitioner showed the discomfort she was made to feel by saying, defensively, 'I never wanted to be a quack! I want to do just good medicine. Mainstream, good medicine.' As one of the sympathetic experts has closed down his law business, another has 'dropped right back', and others have chosen 'not to worry about it anymore', these normalizing deterrents weaken the involvement of supportive specialists, such that their challenge to scientific knowledge and practice is deradicalised.

Conclusion

Medical and legal professional communities play an important role in governing emergent forms of knowledge within their ranks and can disqualify unorthodox theories from gaining recognition. In the case of

MCS, sympathetic specialists tend to accord more weight to the experiential knowledge of the patient than their sceptical colleagues, and emphasize their responsibility to advocate for the patient's interests. Yet such experts can be deterred from continuing to research or represent sufferers of emergent conditions, not necessarily because an environmental cause has been disproven once and for all, but rather because of the social, economic and psycho-emotional risks they face for deviating.

Sympathetic experts – although they specialized in MCS accidentally, initially – are listening regularly to the narratives of the chemically sensitive and therefore begin their interest in the condition as motivated players in the quest for understanding it. By disenfranchising these experts, the medico-legal field can inhibit productive debate and advancements in understanding about contested illnesses. This emphasizes another powerful constraint to the recognition of emergent forms of knowledge about disease.

Chapter 7

Non-legal governance and epistemological possibilities

When a disease comes to the fore of political debate, this can provide a forum for alternative knowledges to mobilize and achieve recognition, where standard medical and legal understandings of risk and disease may subjugate or disqualify them (Waldman 2011). For example, when asbestos-related diseases became implicated with race politics in South Africa, Waldman argues this paved the way for more public participation in the discussion over asbestos and its governance, which arguably led to more just compensation measures and better regulation than in other contexts such as the UK and India. In this chapter, I compare the governance of the scientific debate over MCS in the medico-legal field with its treatment in other sites. On the one hand, the adversarial legal system prevents dialogue and the sharing of data between medical scientists, germinates suspicion between them, polarizes their opinions further, heightens uncertainty and further delegitimizes new forms of knowledge. On the other hand, partial scientific consensus about and recognition of MCS has been reached in alternative sites in Australia and internationally, such as in medical panels, disease classification bodies and health centres. However, I illustrate below how these avenues can have less weight than a landmark legal decision, and can depoliticize the disease, in turn deflecting attention away from crucial questions about toxicity and contamination.

Medico-legal polarity

As illustrated in the previous chapter, the process through which the scientific community internally agrees upon or rejects new theories is not just about observation, discovery and refutation. Rather, knowledge is also given value and disqualified through conflict over professional credibility, moral convictions, and money. Litigation, in turn, refracts and exacerbates controversies between scientific experts. There were, for example, some surprising nodes of agreement that existed between sceptical and sympathetic specialists on the MCS issue, but these were obscured and forgotten when they became involved in the medico-legal process.

The medico-scientific practitioners I spoke to perceived each other as at opposite poles of a spectrum, between sympathy and scepticism and between diagnoses of deserving and unwarranted. Yet both groups simultaneously expressed discomfort with representing the science over MCS in a simplified binary. For example, despite some of his acerbic comments regarding the 'unreason running through MCS' and his 'bullshit-o-metre running off scale' the sceptical toxicologist does not believe in a solely psychological causation of the condition. Rather, he qualifies that:

> The purely physical/mental divide doesn't really exist in medicine anymore, and explanations for any illness like MCS [that] would say that it is purely psychological and purely under the control of the patient wouldn't be accepted as consistent with the general foundations of modern medicine and psychiatry.

The professor made it clear that he subscribes to a *predominantly* psychological causation, however his beliefs about physiological and psychological elements of MCS are more finely grained. Sympathetic professionals also acknowledged that there is a psychological element to the condition (even though they think this too may be caused by toxins). The geneticist who often works on MCS cases as an expert for the plaintiff, admitted that she sees a convergence between the different elements of the condition:

> [When the condition is characterized by] a psycho-emotional sort of reaction where the person is *feeling* sick, you know, it might be hard to convince people that it's real [...] We don't really know how it works. And since people involved, you know, are often suffering some, let's say, brain dysfunction by this stage [when they are seeking medical support], they may appear to be unstable and so therefore a sort of psycho-emotional explanation is appealing.

Most of the chemically sensitive I spoke to also accepted the existence of a psycho-emotional element to their condition. Michael, who was awarded compensation by Kylanta after being diagnosed with MCS, said, 'there [is] a small percentage of the whole equation of MCS that is a mental part of it. And anyone who says there isn't is not being honest with you.' He went on to acknowledge that 'that's why some doctors think it's psychological.'

Moreover, one sympathetic expert recounted an anecdote in which he coincidentally met a renowned sceptic at a medical event, who had in the past been a vocal opponent of his in MCS lawsuits. He said he had imagined this man to be irrational and mean but in person found him to be reasonable and open-minded, and that there was surprising common ground between them.

There is, thus, some consensus about the multi-factorial nature of MCS; that MCS affects the body through an interaction between emotional, psychological and physiological responses to chemicals. This resonates with a theme emerging from the literature on chronic fatigue. Researchers from both the medical and social science fields have sought to understand the continual 'battlefield' that is the CFS provider-patient encounter (e.g. Banks and Prior 2001; Huibers and Wessley 2006). The research approach and conclusions differ in the range of studies conducted about CFS (e.g. compare Bradley, Ford and Bansal 2013; Snell *et al.* 2013). However, all of the authors agree on several fundamental points. First, they agree that CFS and other similarly contested conditions are a combination of factors (Afari and Buchwald 2003). Increasingly it is recognized that the condition is a physiological one with psychological elements, rather than the reverse; and, moreover, that if psychological illnesses are present as a cause, consequence, or comorbidity, they are still nonetheless part of a complex biological interaction (Wessely, Hotopf and Sharpe 1998). Second, they agree that the current clinical approach for treating unexplained somatic conditions continues to be therapeutically inadequate on the whole. Finally, and most importantly, experts are not comfortable with the contestation surrounding these conditions (Engel, Adkins and Cowan 2002). Ultimately, all researchers into CFS wish to reconcile objective evidence of pathology with the patient's experience of disease and arrive at a therapeutic outcome.

The same areas of agreement exist amongst sympathetic and sceptical experts involved with MCS litigation in Perth. However, when health practitioners form a tentative belief about it being *predominantly* psycho-generated or toxogenic, this places them (sometimes reluctantly) in a position to support either the plaintiff or the defendant in a worker's compensation dispute. Once embroiled in the legal apparatus, the division between sceptical and supportive experts on the MCS issue is reified, through several mechanisms, which are explored below.

First, although workers are not required to prove the negligence of their employer under the statutory workers compensation scheme, they must nonetheless establish that the injury was work-caused, or at least that the workplace contributed to its onset to a recognizable degree. Medico-scientific experts are thus engaged by legal teams to opine on whether the condition is genuine and work-related. So, when providing expert opinions, practitioners necessarily commit to positive or negative answers on these issues. They are consequently automatically positioned to one side or the other, and the scientific debate over the condition's cause is forced into a binary.

Second, the correspondence between medical experts for the plaintiff and defence in a legal context is combative and polemical. As highlighted in Chapter 4, when plaintiff lawyers request a medico-legal report from a qualified practitioner to establish the toxogenic nature of the worker's condition, the defence's legal team usually engages a similarly qualified expert who can a) attest to the condition being psychosomatic or non-existent; and b) discredit their sympathetic colleague's argument and expertise. Plaintiff lawyers, of course, do the same thing in reverse. Then follows more correspondence amongst the experts and the solicitors, in which the medical practitioners seek to falsify each other's contentions. Consider the following excerpts taken from four different reports that were written by plaintiff and defence experts on the subject of Ian's condition:

> Ms [*Sympathetic Psychologist*]'s reliance upon a now aged, qualitative and quite impressionistic interpretation...would appear to be poor scientific practice...Her quotation from Tulsky is erroneous. Whilst it is probably a typographical error...these errors suggest [she has] had little if any experience with the [psychological test she used].
>
> I will respond to only some of the comments made by Mr [*Defence Psychologist*] regarding my assessments and reports, as I feel that other comments made by [him] do not really warrant my attention.
>
> Dr [*Sympathetic GP*] claims to have read widely on the subject and attended national conferences (but she does not say which) and to have communicated with national and international experts in the area (but once again does not indicate who and for what issues).
>
> The reasoning of Dr [*Sympathetic Physician*] seems to go from consistency to conclusion without much in the way of evidence or experienced rational analysis in between.

These experts are, as encouraged, attacking each other's expertise and the methods through which it has been obtained. While these reports to some extent mirror the differences in opinion that already exist within the medical expert community, the lawsuit restricts scientific debate to polemical correspondence, which increases the antagonism between the two sides. The similarities between their equally scientific and inductive approach are thus obscured.

Third, the experts' bills are paid by the side that has engaged them in the workers' compensation system.[1] This monetary exchange contributes to the perception amongst both lay and expert participants that expert witnesses for the opponent are acting under financial incentive, and diagnosing accordingly. For example, a supportive physician commented that:

> There are doctors out there who work for employers and the insurance industry and they've got their affiliations [...] They get paid by these companies, and when you look at the dynamics of medical opinion regarding MCS, you pretty well only get people who are unaffiliated and are independent to say there's a [health] problem. And you nearly

universally get the people who are working for the employer saying, 'no, there's no problem.'

And then, the sceptical toxicologist mentioned:

[MCS patients] do seem to have seen a certain number of people and they do seem to have ended up with the same label regardless of what the real diagnosis is. So [...] there is this certain big concern about the litigation process, in that it forces people to suppress the real diagnosis, in favour of the one that is going to hopefully pay off in the end.

The litigation context leads experts to believe that there are entrepreneurial reasons for the other side's diagnosis. Put simply, lawsuits strengthen each expert's view that their colleague is practicing bad science for unethical reasons.

Finally, adversarial proceedings foster simplified ideas about scientific objectivity. The way in which scientific uncertainty and the potential for human error can be pushed aside in the courtroom was emphasized by Lynch and others (2010) in their analysis of how DNA criminal profiling evidence is presented. As discussed in Chapter 2, expert proponents of the DNA technique are encouraged to present incriminating evidence in terms of how *im*probable it is that anyone other than the accused would match the crime stain, rather than a discussion about the possibility for error (Lynch *et al.* 2010: 178, 250). Yet the incumbent degree of uncertainty is glossed over, which in part has contributed to the increasingly unquestioned admission of DNA evidence around the globe.

This removal of uncertainty and aura of objectivity in the presentation of evidence also shapes and constrains the MCS controversy, but in a different way. The agonistic nature of cross-examination pressures experts into 'professing greater certainty than they really feel' (Good 2008: S48). The experts above who acknowledged the complexity of the psychosomatic/physiological spectrum are unlikely to emphasize this ambiguity when being cross-examined about individual cases, since it would make their perceived ability to make an authoritative assessment vulnerable to attack. Legal proceedings veil the unknowns that plague medical knowledge about the condition, which makes the contrast between the two epistemes seem starker.

Given these restrictions on scientific debate at the medico-legal interface, is there greater potential for productive dialogue about controversial new diseases outside of the legal arena? Below, I highlight some of the epistemological possibilities – as well as the pitfalls and pretences – in other modes of conflict resolution and recognition that appeared in my research.

Deliberative interactions

Deliberative interactions are one way of acknowledging and, to some extent, reducing, exaggerated medico-scientific polarity. This kind of event is best illustrated by the Medical Practitioner's Forum, which was set up by the Health Department of Western Australia when the Kylanta controversy over MCS became a political hot topic. The potential opened up by deliberation can be illustrated in the story of Willet James below, the professor who was chosen to chair the panel.

Professor James used to be sceptical of a physiological explanation for MCS. He initially developed his view of the condition through experience with chronic fatigue, which he refers to as myalgic encephalomyelitis (ME). Professor James said:

> The thing that really struck me about [ME] was that there was a particular doctor who really believed in that particular condition, and who developed really quite a lucrative private practice around it...[*He laughs*] And I suppose the cynic in me tended to, you know, it raised questions in my mind as to whether this was a physician-induced illness. So I suppose my early exposure to the concept of MCS syndrome was probably coloured a bit. Especially when it also seemed to have its champions: particular members of the medical profession who saw lots of patients with this [...]

Illnesses that emerge at a similar time often become interdependent in the socio-medical mindset and get conflated with each other in the clinic and elsewhere (Aronowitz 1998). Clearly, scepticism about MCS arises not only because it defies medical standards of proof, but also due to individual practitioners' experiences with associated conditions, and preconceptions about entrepreneurs. Yet Professor James was then asked to chair the medical panel into MCS, which was an innovation of the Western Australian Department of Health. The process was similar to a technique lauded amongst political scientists, called 'deliberative democracy' which seeks to achieve consensus amongst disparate groups through adequate discussion and debate (e.g. Walmsley 2009).[2]

The forum included nineteen health and scientific professionals with an interest in the area, including experts who had diagnosed Kylanta-related chemical injuries, as well as doctors who worked for the Kylanta plant and had rejected the harmfulness of the chemicals in question. In his capacity, the professor facilitated a discussion amongst sympathetic and sceptical health providers and assessed a number of Kylanta workers and community members who had allegedly contracted chemical injuries. At the first of two meetings in late 2001, the group gathered to determine first whether they were dealing with a significant public health problem and second, whether the problem related to Kylanta. Professor James explains that the experts sat around a table – for eight hours – and each was given a chance to say everything they thought was relevant until no-one had anything else to contribute.

The first surprising outcome of this meeting – in distinct contrast to the controversy that had thus far played out on the legal stage – was that, in Professor James' words, there was 'quite a degree of consensus' amongst practitioners. The forum, moreover, concluded that there was a public health problem and that it was related to Kylanta's operations. There was, eventually, a unanimous decision that the health concerns were real and that they needed addressing.

The second unusual result of the forum was that it changed the professor's own opinion about the aetiology of MCS. He explains:

> I try to be very much aware of my own potentials for bias, as well as the potential for biases in other people. I'm that sort of scientist. So, naturally, I brought that ethic to the process, and then it was just a matter of, kinda, 'well [...] let's go through and make an assessment of what we have here.' And I was particularly swayed by the consistency of the stories, the number of people involved, the wide variety of doctors – not just the ones who, you know, seemed to be making a bit of a practice out of it, [but] other people who might see an occasional patient or whatever – the extent to which *they* were impressed by some of these patients, these people suffering. So... yeah, I was just impressed by the amount and consistency of the material.

Although the volume of material was persuasive for the professor, it is notable that it was largely the experiential data – the stories of the chemically sensitive – that 'swayed' him to rethink his prior beliefs and to consider MCS as a predominantly organic condition. The illness eventually met his standard of proof for a legitimate, physiological disease (though, notably, on the issue of CFS, he remains sceptical).

Gathering experts in a non-adversarial setting is a possible way of facilitating more medico-scientific consensus about the cause of MCS. One can only imagine what would have – or would not have – been achieved if Professor James had instead asked all of the experts to express their opinions in medico-legal reports. Arguably, the forum was made possible because it was such a politicized case at the time, which led to Government sponsorship. Such facilitation would probably not occur when individual workers have relatively small claims like Ian's. Yet the advantages of this exceptional event between experts highlights the inefficiency of the usual adversarial legal proceedings for surpassing debate.

There have, moreover, been some reforms in Victoria, Australia, which have acknowledged and responded to the problems of polarization amongst expert opinions in accident claims, and sought to improve deliberation in this regard. In personal injury and work accident litigation, medical panels have been established, which contain independent experts who assess a claimants' impairment in the case of uncertainty or disagreement between the parties over the alleged condition. This sort of initiative is an apparently positive reform, since it is an attempt to increase face-to-face deliberation and reduce combative, lengthy and costly medico-legal correspondence. Yet, as we saw in Ian's case, informal, non-adversarial meetings do not necessarily overcome structural inequalities between insurer and worker, or between experts with unorthodox environmental concerns versus mainstream scientific scepticism. Moreover, how medical panellists are selected for the panels is not transparent. A balance of representation is an important consideration, given some experts consistently support the insurer, while others almost always sympathize with the worker (Grant and Studdert 2013). And, since insurers and neoliberal governments favour policies that limit workers' access to legal avenues for compensation, the extent to which these panels are truly independent, and a fair avenue for claimants, will need to be continually evaluated.

MCS policy in Australian hospitals

Although MCS has not achieved medico-scientific, legal or sustained political recognition in Australia, there have been some alternative sites in which the suffering of the chemically sensitive has been recognized. Hospital guidelines for managing inpatients with MCS have been developed by the Royal Brisbane Hospital in Queensland and have subsequently been endorsed by the Western Australian and South Australian Departments of Health. These documents deliberately do not engage with the epistemological debate surrounding the condition's cause. Indeed, they specifically mention: 'These MCS hospital guidelines are not provided as a definitive MCS text or to argue the aetiology of the condition' (SA Health 2010). However, they do acknowledge the potentially debilitating physical *manifestation* of the condition and highlight to hospital staff that careful adherence to the needs of the chemically sensitive – to be free from toxins at any level – will improve individual health outcomes and reduce the length of their stay in hospital.

Anecdotally, the extent to which these guidelines are followed vary amongst health providers. Some chemically sensitive people I have spoken to have been impressed with the compassionate and therapeutic way in which they have been treated in the hospital after these guidelines were introduced. Others, however, have experienced disregard for their expressed needs by nursing staff, despite the policy's existence.

The introduction of hospital guidelines constitute a *partial* recognition of an emergent condition like MCS. De Graff and Bröer (2012) have emphasized that policies which focus on care rather than cause in the context of contested illness, while they may be perceived as humane, may also be attempts to depoliticize the issue. By accepting that the chemically sensitive do suffer, and that the suffering may be triggered by the environment, policy-makers may be attempting to improve cooperation in the clinic and establish smoother health provision in this context, without having to concede anything regarding cause or liability. Pamela Gibson (2010) emphasizes the problems associated with individualizing the struggle over MCS. A narrow focus on care could take attention away from the bigger, 'upstream' problems regarding toxic production and the contamination of public space, work-places and homes (cf. Nadeau and Lippel 2014). The dilemma, then, for emergent illness activists becomes a question of whether to subscribe to an initiative that does not fully recognize their claims to an environmental cause, may ignore the crux of the problem, and veil any need for measures to prevent them further. Furthermore, these initiatives can ignite the anger of those who perceive the condition as illegitimate, its sufferers as non-deserved, and dedicated services as a waste of finite state resources and, consequently, lead to a backlash (De Graff and Bröer 2012). Notwithstanding this complexity, it is notable that many chemically sensitive people, and the local MCS society, talk about the existence of these guidelines as marking a turning point in which their symptoms and what triggers them, at least, have been publicly acknowledged to some extent.

Dedicated environmental health centres

In some parts of the world, medical treatment programs and research centres devoted to environmental illnesses have been established. Specialized clinics dedicated to environmental illnesses have been set up in Japan (Hojo *et al.* 2003) and the Netherlands (Amsterdam Kliniek 1997). In Nova Scotia, Canada, a government-funded environmental health centre can be accessed by patients with chronic MCS, CFS and fibromyalgia, among other conditions 'triggered' by the environment (Joffres *et al.* 2001). One of the centre's objectives is to advise policy-makers in recognizing, preventing and treating environmental sensitivities. The centre has a 'no scent policy' making it a friendly environment for sensitive patients, and it takes a patient-centred, evidence-based and holistic approach to treatment. Treatment programs focus on both psychological improvement (such as mind-body awareness programs, and counselling), as well as toxicological mechanisms (such as pharmaceutical prescriptions and evaluations of toxins in the home and workplace). Researchers affiliated with the centre have argued that, irrespective of the aetiology of MCS, successful treatment relies on a recognition that the condition is multi-factorial: in other words, 'psychological and physical aspects are part of the problem and the solu-tion' (Joffres *et al.* 2001: 165).

However, the Environmental Health Centre was not established without negative media attention (Joffres *et al.* 2001). The centre is devoted to a set of illnesses that have limited legitimacy in the orthodox medical community in Canada, similar to Australia. Further, its establishment did little to alleviate the stigma directed at the chemically sensitive population in broader Canadian society, as demonstrated by the ethnographic work of Lipson (2001; 2004).

Disease classification

There have been a number of instances where authorities internationally have officially recognized MCS as either multi-factorial or specifically physiological. In 2005, the Danish Environmental Protection Agency reported that sufficient evidence existed to suggest that MCS resulted from environmental contaminants, and the agency subsequently sought to establish measures that would prevent further sensitivities (Danish EPA 2005).

Further, in a letter to the Chemical Sensitivity Network in Germany in 2008, the German Institute for Medical Documentation and Information reported that the category 'Multiple Chemical Sensitivity: Allergy, not otherwise specified' had been classified under code T78.4 in the German version of the WHO register of diseases, the ICD-10 (DIMDI 2008). Including the condition as an allergy is controversial, since there is much debate even amongst sufferers and sympathetic experts as to whether 'allergy' accurately describes the mechanisms of MCS in their view (Kroll-Smith and Floyd 1997: 128). However, by including MCS in the chapter on 'Injury, poisoning and certain other consequences of external causes', the German classification authority implied their belief that the condition has physiological causal components and is not purely psychogenic.

However, the classification authority of Germany and the Danish EPA were not necessarily acting in concert with mainstream medical thought, nor did they widely publicize their actions. It is mainly through chatrooms, email lists, support groups and sympathetic websites that these documents have been shared and discussed by the chemically sensitive themselves. No experts mentioned them in my research, and they were not discussed in legal correspondence. Consequently, quasi-acceptance at this official level in Germany and Denmark has not manifested in greater on-the-ground support for sufferers of MCS in those locations. An activist who founded and writes for the Chemical Sensitivity Network (2010), wrote about the ongoing, alienating experience of MCS:

> For other countries, it often looks like chemically sensitive patients in Germany get more medical help than anywhere else since MCS is recognized as a physical disease in our country [...] But the reality for people with Chemical Sensitivity is hard and bitter. Many are fighting

at court to get their disability recognized, but even when having numerous medical reports confirming their condition, they usually loose [sic]. Because, like in other countries, sickness from chemicals and modern living is not truly recognized but rather swept under the carpet even though we exist and suffer every day [...] Further, in Germany, people with MCS are neglected by society. There are people who are homeless because of MCS. Many have lost their jobs and houses. [...] Further still, the chemically sensitive people here in Germany are systematically declared mentally ill or having only psychosomatic symptoms.

A post from a Danish subscriber at the bottom of the piece replies 'I truly recognize the story from my own "MCS-situation" in Denmark' (Chemical Sensitivity Network 2010).

The reports or classifications from DIMDI and the Danish EPA have not reflected or substantively affected significant change in medical, legal or community thinking with regards to MCS in those countries. Possibly, these events will accumulate into a groundswell of support for a chemical explanation for MCS. However, for the moment, they have not led to any substantial improvement for the chemically sensitive population in terms of an increase in scientific credibility, social support or financial assistance.

Conclusion

The unresolved epistemological battle over MCS in Australian courts can be usefully contrasted against other contexts in which the debate over the condition has been governed differently. As we have seen, the legal process refracts medico-scientific debate by reinforcing bitter divisions between experts. In turn, the internal politics of the scientific community gets re-expressed and re-understood in epistemological terms: proof, evidence, expertise, irrationality, (and, more informally, 'bullshit'). The polemical language used in the legal context reifies their polarized opinions, further exacerbates the perceived incommensurability of their theories and obscures points of consensus. The legal process is thus alienating from each other the two groups of experts who have a principal interest in understanding MCS. As shown in Chapter 3, experts involved in these cases go on to act as consultants for the plaintiff or defendant in future lawsuits, inform media representation of the condition and advise Government departments about industries in which the condition occurs. These specialists are, consequently, 'brokers of information' (McCormick 2009); they are not only key players in the local construction of MCS but also contributors to the global medico-scientific debate. Adversarialism in the courtroom thus contributes to scientific uncertainty and contestation in the broader community. And, since a degree of consensus is required before emergent knowledges will be considered recognizable, uncertainty increases the likelihood that legal decision-makers will fall back on default, mainstream science, which currently delegitimizes them. The polarizing effects of litigation therefore disadvantage proponents of new and unorthodox theories seeking recognition.

Other modes of governing scientific disagreement did open up different epistemological possibilities, and alternative forms of recognition. Hospital policy and dedicated health centres re-framed the issue of MCS as one of care, which meant that the scientific controversy over its cause could be bypassed and the suffering of the chemically sensitive addressed nonetheless. However, when MCS is reframed and governed in this way, the political debate over the continued existence of toxic risk and the problem of corporate negligence can be downplayed or overlooked.

Deliberative interactions between sympathizers and sceptics, such as in medical panels, seem to encourage experts to share and analyse data in a less polemical manner and open a forum where the experiential knowledge of the sufferer is given more equal weighting to scientific research. This opportunity, in turn, can lead all parties to better understand each other's viewpoint, and lead them to recognize the disease as more nuanced and multi-factorial than the legal process permits. It would appear, then, that consensus meetings should be encouraged in the face of emergent uncertain illnesses, ideally before lengthy occupational disputes over these conditions are played out on the medico-legal stage. And yet, as the Kylanta case warns, the extent to which these modes of governance and moments of consensus lead to meaningful, *sustained* recognition, the curtailing of industrial toxins, and the prevention of future suffering, must be continually interrogated.

Chapter 8

Neoliberalism, scepticism and toxic knowledge

In the previous chapters, I have outlined the structural elements *within* the medical and legal fields that present barriers to the recognition of new knowledge. However, in this chapter, I show how the medico-legal response to knowledge about emergent disease can be implicated in a broader risk-management pattern in this society. In the first section, I illustrate how the unfolding story of MCS and the history of asbestos-related disease are reminiscent of a global trend, whereby claims of toxic crime or negligence are often dismissed as 'unproven' until there is a visible crisis. In the second section, I contrast this to recent sweeping reforms in criminal law, where controversial 'proof' about risky individuals is used to justify a swift and pre-emptive response. I show how the difference in the visibility, recognition and perceived urgency of these problems is justified not because one is riskier than the other, necessarily, but by a neoliberal logic that constructs them in this way. Thus, in the final section, I illustrate how the dismissal of emergent diseases by medico-scientific decision-makers on the basis of 'insufficient proof' must be understood within the context of a broader neoliberal approach to uncertainty and precaution.

A sketch of what I mean by 'neoliberal logic' is required here. As discussed in Chapter 2, neoliberalism is a politico-economic ethos which values capitalism, individual 'responsibility', free trade, and a withdrawal of state intervention from affairs in the private sector (Wacquant 2009). While it is contested by critical scholars and decried by social movements, the current neoliberal focus on the economy in the Anglo-American world is in many ways historically embedded as common sense; the most natural order of things. It informs policy decisions about, for example, the regulation of markets, the privatization of public services, work-for-welfare schemes, and the jurisdiction of the workers' compensation apparatus. But neoliberalism also manifests as a form of governmentality, a persuasive logic that can to some extent mould people's subjectivity and inform their decision-making (Larner 2000). Some theorists see the positive potential in how neoliberalism shapes subjectivity. For example, being perceived as more responsible for one's healthcare may lead a patient to be empowered and encourage him or her to critically engage with medico-scientific knowledge and risk (Pols 2013). Others, however, are more pessimistic about the creep of neoliberal logic and its insidious effects. Pearce and Tombs (1998), for example, are concerned that 'the ideas associated with globalization become predominant to the extent that they seep into popular consciousness, ruling out alternatives' (1998: 52). Moreover, Rose (1996b; 2007) has pointed out how neoliberal ideas of responsibility and consumerism shape decision-making *as though* they are choices, which cunningly veils the way in which decisions may be delimited. Like these theorists, I am interested in how neoliberal ideas 'prove' some forms of knowledge about risk and prevent alternative knowledges from reaching the threshold of visibility – thus the exploration in this chapter. First though, it is necessary to outline how a neoliberal value system can be seen in society's macro response to different types of risk.

Risk-management and toxic knowledge

In Australia, at least, the risks associated with toxicity in food, home objects, water and soil is a frequent theme of the media, local pamphlets in letter boxes, and dinner party conversations. In their early work on the 'risk society', Beck (1992) and Giddens (1990) argued that the processes of modernization had exposed large numbers of people to previously unknown levels of risk, particularly hazardous side effects from man-made disasters. Although Beck conceded that risks were 'not a modern invention' (1992: 21), and Giddens (1990: 123–4) believed that day-to-day life was not inherently riskier than before, they suggested that modern society was distinctive for its awareness of – or 'methodical skepticism' about – widespread industrial risks. Indeed, they implied that the modernizing process had exposed *everyone* to latent and ubiquitous risks. Since hazards were inescapable and could not be 'distributed away' (i.e. by the privileged) this meant the risk society to some extent transcended traditional social divisions (see Beck 1992: 99).

But later scholars disagreed, emphasizing that the political economy very much shapes how risks are distributed in the first place. Indeed, the way risks unevenly burden certain communities tends to *reproduce* traditional cleavages of inequality, such as socio-economic status (Pearce and Tombs 2000; Smallman 2000), gender (Draper 1991; Nadeau and Lippel 2014) and race (Evans and Kantrowitz 2002; Waldman 2011). Evans and Kantrowitz (2002), for example, document how disadvantaged communities often bear the brunt of man-made risks. They catalogue an inverse relationship between, on the one hand, socio-economic status, and, on the other, exposure to environmental harms such as pollutants, low water quality and poor work environments. Poorer environmental quality strongly contributes to lower physical and psychological health outcomes among economically disadvantaged groups (Evans and Kantrowitz 2002). Moreover, class is inextricably linked to other axes of inequality: in the American context, non-white individuals are more likely to live in neighbourhoods with higher levels of pollutants and toxic waste from industry. Zoning decision-makers can be discriminatory when they approve sites for potential polluters, and corporations can prefer neighbourhoods where they are unlikely to be faced with (costly) collective action against their expansion (Hamilton 1995). In Australia, for example, there is a long history of disregarding Aboriginal inhabitants when making policy decisions about the potential locations of toxic mining operations (Short 2008). The alarming correlation between this and health outcomes lead Evans and Kantrowitz to argue that income and environmental exposure 'cannot be disentangled from racism' (2002: 304).

Additionally, the disproportionate burden of risk in poorer neighbourhoods of wealthy countries is consistent with a global problematic, in which those living in the industrializing world are more likely to be exposed to pollutants and waste than their counterparts in the developed world. When dangerous chemicals or toxic industrial processes are banned in wealthier countries, corporations can relocate their operations to lower income countries where there is often more relaxed environmental regulation, weaker restrictions surrounding occupational safety and less collective action around workers' rights (Grossman 2006; Waldman 2011). Many suggest that corporate exploitation of pre-existing socio-economic disparities by both industry and neoliberal governments constitute a form of environmental racism, which only reinforces global inequality further (cf. Westra and Lawson 2001). Put crudely, the political economy exposes certain groups to more risks than others, both locally and globally.

And neoliberal values go on to shape when and how knowledge about those toxic risks is heard, heeded and responded to. To examine this further, it is useful to outline the 'risk-management' process more broadly and the extent to which it has changed over time. Nearly two decades ago, Hood (1996: 212–3) argued that the hegemonic framework for risk-management – in both businesses and in communities – could be termed 'social pre-commitment to rational acceptability thresholds'. In this model, 'consensus' is reached about a level of acceptable risk, and a commitment is made that this threshold will not be exceeded. The company, or the community, will ideally activate or enforce systemic changes when that agreed-upon threshold of danger is reached.

Yet there are significant pitfalls to this system of agreeing upon risks and responding to them (Hood 1996; cf. Smallman 2000: 58). In the first instance, it does not account for the variable ways in which a community or a company might reach consensus about what is risky, and what is an acceptable threshold of danger. Further, as illustrated in the discussion of 'threshold limit values' in Chapter 3, the idea of a 'threshold' quantifies danger and makes it seem more certain, which ostensibly removes uncertainty and veils the fact that the figure arrived at is a subjective social construction. It also overlooks the possibility that groups (such as industry and government officials) may strategically set *convenient* thresholds in the interests of cost efficiency and economic growth. There is, furthermore, an important disparity between what those 'in control' – corporate managers, town planners, legal decision-makers – deem to be acceptable levels of risk, versus what those at the receiving end of the risks are prepared to endure. So, this 'consensual' approach to risk management tends to be elitist, and based on a style of regulation 'in which policy-makers and industry [meet] behind closed doors and [make] regulatory decisions' (Lofstedt *et al.* 2011). Finally, this process for managing risks tends to be slow, unwieldy, and cumbersome to change. Indeed, it often only responds to crisis (Hood 1996).

Pearce and Tombs (1998) illustrated this elitist management of risk in their sweeping study of the chemical industry, in which they specifically examine the social conditions that led to Bhopal, among other crises. They argue that accidents caused by the chemical industry should be understood as 'safety crimes', which, for them, is a subset of corporate, white-collar, crime. (Corporate crime refers to injuries and deaths caused by businesses to workers or consumers through criminal breaches of safety legislation, where risks were known and ignored. It includes workplace accidents, exposure to illegal pollution, and poisoning due to the sale of unsafe food, beauty products or pharmaceuticals. Scholars have documented how corporate crime causes many times more instances of severe harm or deaths than interpersonal violence – (Slapper and Tombs 1999; Whyte 2012)). More than just 'accidents', Pearce and Tombs believe safety crimes like Bhopal are enabled because of the value placed on economic efficiency and growth in the capitalist economy. In turn, this prioritization shapes what kind of knowledge about chemical safety and risk is allowed to come to light: managers communicate certain aspects of knowledge, where the workers' experiential knowledge of risk is silenced or overlooked. This disparity, they argue, leads to an overly complex technological setup and a calculation of, and 'consensus' about, risk that is amoral. Although crises are preventable, under these conditions they are somewhat inevitable.

Yet, given the very visceral horror of the Bhopal disaster and later safety scandals, the lay public have arguably become more distrustful and interrogative of the way experts manage public risks. The crisis of Bovine Spongiform Encephalopathy (BSE, or 'mad cow disease') in the UK, for example, was widely perceived as a knowledge that was mishandled by government and health officials.[1] Partly due to mad cow disease and other food safety scandals, disenchantment with both industry and political authorities has grown in the twenty-first century, particularly in Europe (Lofstedt *et al.* 2011). This led Lofstedt and colleagues to argue that the risk-management paradigm has shifted over the last few decades to a new 'post-trust' framework of disseminating knowledge about risk and arriving at consensus. They claim it has emerged in response to a changing political landscape involving increasingly influential non-government organisations, consumer watchdogs and media hype, which in turn has heightened the need for governments to develop new ways of maintaining legitimacy with the sceptical, distrusting lay public. According to Lofstedt and colleagues, the new public risk-management paradigm has three main features:

- It aims to be more inclusive than exclusive, encouraging greater public and stakeholder participation in the policy-making process.
- It calls for regulatory strategies to be completely open and transparent and for regulators to be accountable for any policy they propose.
- The role of science is less important, as scientists are seen as just one of many stakeholders (2011: 410).

These researchers are critical of the shortcomings so far demonstrated in this suppposed new, open and transparent model of managing public knowledge about risk. They examine three case studies, including: the BSE crisis; the social hysteria surrounding aspartame (artificial sweetener) poisoning; and the concern about the safety of a cervical cancer vaccine. This latter product was taken off the market after two recipients were hospitalized for an illness that was later deemed (probably) unrelated to the vaccine (Lofstedt et al. 2011). From these case studies, they argue that open access to the wrong kind of information at the wrong time enables the media and vested stakeholders to misuse scientific uncertainty and magnify risks about commercial products unnecessarily. They are concerned that the increased participation of stakeholders, coupled with the devalued role of scientific peer-review, can lead to unscientific and unwarranted knee-jerk reactions by decision-makers in order to quell public concern. The problem, they believe, is that such reactions can needlessly restrict the market, and jeopardize patient safety by removing access to therapeutic products or enabling the sale of 'more risky replacement products' (2011: 420).

In some respects, the Kylanta case study outlined in Chapter 3 of this volume confirms that mobilized, media-savvy groups of workers and community members can – even when their experiential knowledge remains scientifically uncertain – foster social concern about corporate risk and force officials to act upon their claims. However, unlike the case studies examined by Lofstedt et al., the Kylanta workers and community members in my research were not able to activate any knee-jerk institutional response: their calls for precaution and requests for remedy went unheeded for five years before any meaningful action was taken. While 'open communication', 'transparency' and 'stakeholder participation' were frequently mentioned in the rhetoric of Kylanta management and governmental authorities, much of the negotiations regarding regulation continued to happen behind closed doors. Even when the media seemed to suggest a looming crisis, when government departments eventually leapt into action, and when compensation was paid to the workers, the long-term outcome of the controversy allowed the corporation to continue its expansion and framed the workers' allegations of environmental illness as controversial, at best. Thus, in this case, the societal response to scientific uncertainty looked very similar to the traditional, consensual model of risk-management, which subjugates workers' experiential knowledge, legitimates politico-economic growth, and is weighted against change.

This pattern is further evidenced when we examine the governance of knowledge about asbestos risks in Western Australia from a longitudinal perspective. I use this example in the discussion below to illustrate the ways in which neoliberal values continue to shape society's ongoing response to knowledge of corporate harm.

The Australian Blue Asbestos Company, started by mining magnate Lang Hancock in 1938, began mining asbestos in Wittenoom, Western Australia in the 1940s. Since asbestos is a necessary fire-proofing agent used in the sugar refining process, Hancock brokered a deal with the sugar refinery, CSR Limited, to build a mine in Wittenoom in 1943, and soon afterwards lucratively sold back his share of the company.

Even though wages at the Wittenoom mine were relatively high in a bid to attract workers, conditions were often hot and humid, and there was consequently a high employee turnover (Hills 1989). To fill the gap in recruitment and retention in the 1950s, CSR requested the help of the State Department of Immigration to contract immigrants to work in the mine. Since the political ethos at the time was 'populate or perish' – and specifically white European immigration was highly sought after – the department obliged. It facilitated contracts for over 1000 Italian immigrants – contracted by a CSR recruiter who advertised the position in their local towns, neglecting to mention the weather or the asbestos – which dictated that they would stay and work at the site until they paid off their fare (Hills 1989: 30).

Knowledge that inhalation of blue asbestos can lead to death was beginning to become public before the mine was built (see Merewether and Price 1930). In fact, as Ben Hills notes in his 1989 chronicle of the Wittenoom Disaster (titled, somewhat hyperbolically, *Blue Murder*), the risks associated with asbestos had already been well established in the insurance industry. After a report on the health impacts of asbestos produced by a statistician at an American insurance company in 1918, many insurance companies were increasing their liability insurance premiums for asbestos companies by 50 per cent while others were refusing to insure them at all (1989: 15).

[Thus, a noteworthy aside here is how knowledge of a new disease can be advanced and granted urgency by insurance companies as they seek to understand the workplace in an actuarial sense – in terms of risk and probability. Moreover, this is a prime example of how insurance acts as a form of regulation (Ericson, Doyle and Barry 2003). By refusing to insure offending companies, insurers could potentially enforce workplace safety and control the risks of new technologies. In turn, this suggests that the competitive, de-regulated market could conceivably respond to public health crises more effectively than a slow bureaucratic apparatus – not through humanitarianism, necessarily, but because of a financial bottom line. However, this potential is thwarted by the trend where large companies (like Kylanta) self-insure in order to bypass insurers' constraints. Furthermore, it would only work if the actuarial information used by insurers about emergent diseases were transparent and widely disseminated. Instead, the fact that the impact of asbestos on workers' health was common knowledge amongst insurers by the early 1920s would not become public for another half century, and asbestos companies continued to deny knowledge of toxicity throughout the following decades (Hills 1989: 15).]

The Wittenoom workers and community were kept ignorant of the dangers of asbestos and were thus laissez-fare with exposure: safety masks were non-existent and children unwittingly played on piles of asbestos-laden waste. Fast forward to today, and, so far, more than 2500 Wittenoom workers and residents have died from asbestos-related diseases (Gribbin 2013). While most of these deaths have befallen the workers, increasing numbers of their wives and children have been diagnosed with asbestos-related diseases. Given asbestos conditions can lie latent for many years after exposure, it is further estimated that up to 1500 more victims will die in the years to come (Gribbin 2013).

From a macro perspective, the collective reaction to the Wittenoom tragedy speaks volumes about how knowledge of risk is governed in Australian society – when new knowledge about risk is heeded, and who is allowed to expose others to known risks. In particular, neoliberal values shape the medico-legal response to such knowledge. In 1988, when CSR appealed a landmark decision in favour of one of the Wittenoom workers, three Victorian Supreme Court judges dismissed the appeal and found the company to be reckless with the safety of its workers given its longstanding knowledge of the dangers of asbestos. Indeed, the company was found to have 'continuing, conscious and contumelious' disregard for the rights of its workers to be free of asbestos-related disease and death. Despite this precedent, similar to the case in the United States and the United Kingdom (Durkin and Felstiner 1994; Waldman 2011), there were many shortfalls in the legal apparatus set up for dealing with asbestos litigation thereafter. The compensation was often (and continues to be) inadequate and too late for the afflicted to enjoy a quality of life before their early deaths. Moreover, many workers who received an initial small payout were unable to apply for more adequate compensation when they developed more severe asbestos-related conditions, although a recent bill has been introduced in Western Australia to overturn this problem.

There are several ways in which the law in general – and the workers' compensation apparatus specifically – has limited jurisdiction to respond to uncertain knowledge about corporate risks. The first relates to the legal status of the corporation. Paddy Ireland (2010) traces the historical process through which the corporation came to be valued as the most economically efficient and rational– the most 'natural' and logical – structure for doing business in industrializing nations (2010: 838). The corporation is based not on an 'ordinary' partnership, where a company is owned and managed by a specific group of people, but on the concept of a joint stock company, which is a 'capital fund composed of freely transferable shares owned by a large and fluctuating body of company members' (2010: 838). Over time, the legal framework has supported this business structure and consistently removed impediments to its formation and success. Joint stock companies are necessarily given corporate status so that the company has a separate legal existence from its constantly changing set of shareholder-owners. Moreover, legal liability is limited so as not to deter investors who will not have an active management role (2010: 838).

Indeed, the courts and legislature over time redefined the role of shareholders such that liability was not merely limited, but essentially removed altogether (Ireland 2010). Up until the mid-nineteenth century, corporations were largely subject to the laws of ordinary business partnerships; they were connected to their shareholder membership, and were referred to as 'theys'. Yet, they gradually came to be reified as 'its' – in other words, legal personalities in their own right – and as separate entities from their shareholders (Ireland 2010: 845). This endowed shareholders with the right to profit from a corporation's activity without *any* obligations or liability for what it does. Moreover, this situation facilitated the construction of 'strings of parent, subsidiary, sub-subsidiary and associated companies' (2010: 848). Each of these is a separate legal 'person', and its directors and shareholders (which may simply be another company or combination of companies within the chain) benefit from the freedom of no liability (2010: 848). Ireland's concern is that this lack of liability extends the invitation for corporations to engage in opportunistic behaviour, which further normalizes corporate 'irresponsibility'. (There is, though, another argument that shareholders with a collective interest in social justice can enforce corporate accountability – see Dhir 2006.)

Given the chain of ownership, corporations can be slippery when claimants, law-firms and the judiciary seek to pinpoint who is responsible for knowingly causing environmental damage or human ill-health. It is, for example, particularly difficult for medico-legal systems in host countries to hold multinational corporations to account for toxic contamination via tort litigation. As in the case of Union Carbide and the Bhopal disaster, difficult legal (and economic) questions arise regarding whether the parent company, the subsidiary or the shareholders should be held responsible; and whether the trial should be heard in the host country where the victims reside, or if the company should be tried by the more established legal system where its headquarters lie (Das 2000).

Furthermore, asbestos lawsuits in Australia and overseas have shown how defendant companies can respond to litigation by deliberately bankrupting subsidiaries and shielding company assets in order to insulate them from compensation payouts (Durkin and Felstiner 1994). It is possible for judicial decision-makers to 'pierce the veil' of corporate ownership in a court of law, and hold shareholders (including directors) liable for the behaviour of a company. However, this tends to only happen in rare instances where a company is found to have been set up fraudulently, or in the interests of evading a legal or financial responsibility (Ramsay and Noakes 2001). In Australia, it has only been used in decisions regarding smaller, privately held corporations with a small number of shareholders. It is rarely activated when it comes to publically traded corporations, partly because there are too many shareholders, and too many protective mechanisms. Courts are, furthermore, more likely to pierce the veil in the context of contractual breaches than in tort law (Ramsay and Noakes 2001).

The legal lag in responding to asbestos risk also calls into relief the concept of privacy, which is embedded in the division between criminal law and civil litigation. Criminal prosecution occurs when state law enforcers deem a crime to warrant punishment, and the criminal sentence is designed to publicly denounce that crime and deter future wrongdoing. Civil litigation, on the other hand, is an avenue for individuals to seek redress for injury or property damage. While the defendant may be forced to pay recompense and can be punished for misconduct through having to pay exemplary damages, they will not be dealt with punitively as a matter of course; their wrongdoing is not usually framed as a criminal act, and thus not perceived as so abhorrent to society or the legal system. In turn, this permits corporations more freedom than if they were under criminal investigation. Corporate lawyer Harry Glasbeek (2002) has emphasized the way in which private property ownership lies at the heart of the neoliberal order. Since corporations are inextricably linked to that order – indeed, crucial to upholding it – they enjoy a privileged position within it. From one perspective, this means they can circumvent the principles of democracy, such as the values of transparency and accountability in the spirit of the law (Glasbeek 2002). From another angle, corporations are less likely to be punished for breaching laws in the neoliberal status quo, because they have historically had significant influence in defining and sustaining these standards in the first place (Ireland 2010; Whyte 2012).

Courts are thus limited in finding a corporation criminally liable. When businesses *are* found to be culpable for exposing workers or neighbours to known risks, the consequences they face can lack substantive meaning, and can even provide an incentive (or, at least, not provide a *dis*incentive) to take the same risks in the future. This is perhaps best illustrated by the outcome of the Wittenoom tragedy in Australia. At the 1988 trial, a subsidiary of CSR (which was, conveniently, now a hollow-shell of a company) was ordered to pay a quarter of a million dollars for exemplary (punitive) damages. A trust fund set up by CSR to cover compensation for its diseased and dying workers (most of whom did not see any of this money), was invested. It made over AU$200,000 on the stock exchange, which the company kept as profit (Hills 1989: 85). Moreover, the compensation and damages paid by the company pale in comparison to the parent company's gross annual profit. In fact, it is not unreasonable to suggest that the managers involved have, despite small costs, ultimately benefited from the risks that were taken with workers' health many years ago. Gina Rinehart – daughter and heiress of Lang Hancock, the original owner of Blue Asbestos Company – is now Australia's richest woman and fourth richest in the world. Meanwhile, the net profit of CSR Sugar in 2012, for example, was AU$ 90.7million.

There were, furthermore, no legal ramifications for other parties who suppressed knowledge about the emergent risks of asbestos-related disease in Wittenoom. The Immigration Department enabled CSR to recruit European immigrants to work on the deadly Wittenoom mines for a long time after asbestos was known to be a health risk. The Health Department continued to do little when a small number of concerned medical practitioners were predicting a public health crisis (Hills 1989). However, none of these departments or the individuals involved met with formal consequences for failing to meet a duty of care, or being reckless with the lives of citizens. This too aligns with a wider limitation of legal processes to hold institutional powers to account. In analyzing deaths in custody, Sim (2010) discusses the ability of state actors to frame the popular and political debate about what is normal behaviour on the one hand, and what is pathological or deviant on the other. For example, regular individuals who act violently usually meet with harsh punishments, while the force used by state servants such as police officers are, by contrast, constructed as legitimate and unavoidable (which is a kind of 'pious hypocrisy' – Bourdieu 1994). Often, governmental representatives offer sincere, ritualistic apologies to grieving widows of people who died due to negligence, which allows them to appear empathic while, at the same time, restricting access to information about the event and closing down further debate about their own role in the loss of life (Sim 2010: 7). There are other avenues that ostensibly offer potential for identifying and reforming institutional negligence, such as judicial review, coronial inquests, parliamentary inquiries and royal commissions. However, relative to the criminal justice system, these processes rarely lead to prosecutions, which is consistent with a broader 'culture of immunity and impunity covering state servants' (Sim 2010; see also Hooper 2008). At this end of society, juridical governance is weak, surveillance mechanisms are lacking, and the penal apparatus tends to be non-intrusive.

In essence, while Lofstedt *et al.* (2011) focus on some cases of impulsive, overly precautionary regulation, a swift and sustained response to corporate risk remains the exception rather than the norm. On the whole, the legal apparatus tends to be cumbersome, ineffective and slow to recognize emergent knowledges about toxicity. Moreover, a broader neoliberal constellation restricts when and what type of knowledge comes before the courts, and limits the toolkit that legal decision-makers have available to them for responding to it.

Risk management and the governance of risky individuals

And yet, in the name of 'security', there are numerous recent examples where knowledge about other emergent risks has been swiftly legitimated and catalysed dramatic, systemic change. To explain this, it is first necessary to discuss what security is and how it relates to risk-management. 'Security' defines a form of governance targeted at the population (Gordon 1991). It is achieved through the 'identification of common risks and the provision of shared solutions' (Bull 2010: 56). In other words, it is a consensus-based framework – like that described above – for managing the risky behaviour of individuals. As outlined in Chapter 2, institutions once sought to rehabilitate offending individuals back to 'normal', but the modern focus on risk places individuals into categories – whether they are risky to others, or 'at risk' themselves. The goal, then, is to insure society against potential harms by managing these categories of individuals through actuarial principles, rather than reforming each individual (Bull 2010: 56).

Going further, some theorists have argued that risk-management of criminal behaviour has been superseded by risk control (Rose 2000; 2007). Risk management accepts that a level of risk will always exist but seeks to mitigate its impact as far as possible. So, in the context of criminality, this allows for offender education, rehabilitation and post-release supervision, while recognizing that a small risk to the community remains unavoidable (Bull 2010: 57). By contrast, in a regime of risk *control*, the group that poses the risk must be eliminated, which means the priority becomes one of socially excluding offenders, rather than managing them within the community (Rose 2000). In fact, Garland (2002) is concerned that in Anglo-American countries there is now a *culture* of control. This is where welfarist approaches to criminality (in which structural inequalities are deemed partly to blame for criminality and therefore alleviating disparity is seen as central to the solution) are replaced by prevention and punishment.

Below I outline two examples of risk control, where a low threshold of danger has been used to justify a high level of precaution, regulation and control. Knowledge about risk in these contexts is also emergent, uncertain and contested, and yet the politico-legal response to these claims is very different to the risk-management of industry above.

The first example takes us to an inner-city suburb of Perth, known for its nightclubs, restaurants and cafés. Once a somewhat rundown part of the city, Northbridge was gentrified in the early 2000s, as it was seen as playing a pivotal role in making Perth a more attractive place for locals to live and for tourists to experience the nightlife on offer. In 2003, the government responded to lobbying from local business vendors to institute a curfew for youth under the age of 18, who were seen to be causing trouble and frightening off potential patrons (Koch 2003). The curfew allowed police the power to remove youth who were deemed to be '"at risk" of physical or moral danger' and place them under police detention until 'an appropriate adult collects them' (*Child Welfare Act 1947*; Koch 2003: 7). The new law was instituted after media headlines had claimed an upsurge in youth offences (despite the fact that youth crime had reduced in the area in the 12 months prior, and at least 70 per cent of crime in the area was found to be committed by adults rather than juveniles – Koch 2003). As is often the case, the law and order crackdown on youth was celebrated by tabloid newspapers and talk-back radio commentary (Rayner 2003; see also Gibson 2000).

Crucially, of 450 children that were removed and detained from Northbridge over a 12-week period, 400 of them were Aboriginal (Rayner 2003). The curfew policy did not mention race, unlike the blatantly discriminatory policies that once explicitly banned Aborigines from certain public spaces. However, in practice it unassailably had a disproportionate impact on the Aboriginal community. Commentators decried the curfew as in contravention of international laws on the rights of people not to be racially discriminated against (Koch 2003), and Australia's *Equal Opportunity Act 1984* (Rayner 2003). It seemed to be an example of systemic racism, which is where – even if individual policy makers and law enforcers are not necessarily (consciously) prejudiced – a particular legal scheme totals a racist outcome (Cunneen 2005). As Koch (2003: 7) mentions, there are deep structural inequalities – poverty, homelessness and family breakdown – that lead many Aboriginal children to the 'bright city lights' of Northbridge, and some of them engage in anti-social behaviour. However, rather than addressing the vulnerability of 'at-risk' youth – which would require a solution involving health and welfare agencies (Koch 2003) – the problem instead was framed as a law and order one because of the threat that the youth were deemed to pose to the safety and sightliness of the area. Some youth were removed from the streets even when they were outside the curfew area, and others were taken into detention when returning home from a movie outing (Koch 2003).The outcome of this policy was to widen the net for Aboriginal youth to become entangled in a criminal justice cycle, in which they are already devastatingly over represented (Gibson 2000).

The knowledge about the risk they posed was rapidly granted legitimacy and, as per the risk control discussed by Garland and Rose above, the 'shared' solution became a punitive approach, whereby the risky category of individuals was removed and 'order' could thus be reinstated.

The second example of risk control begins on the 11th of September, 2001, when two planes hijacked by terrorists crashed into the New York twin towers. It was, of course, highly newsworthy; the unusual events were splashed across the news, and the victims' stories prompted insecurity (Greer 2007). The retaliatory response, championed by the US government, was to embark on a 'war on terror', the international military campaign targeted at eliminating militant (Islamic) terrorist organizations. To tighten national security, the Australian government hastily followed America's lead in instituting its own version of a 'PATRIOT Act'; a set of counter-terrorism laws to control the threat of terrorism on its own soil. Some of these involved tightening airport security measures, and making more explicit reference to the illegality of explosive devices. However, other amendments heightened police surveillance and search powers, expanded the definition of terrorist acts to include associating with suspected organizations, and empowered the state with greater authority to preventatively detain people suspected of terrorism (Renwick 2007). The provisions were tested in several incidents – most infamously the case of Dr Mohamed Haneef – where an innocent suspect was searched and detained, and eventually released because there was insufficient evidence for a charge to ever have been laid in the first place (see Law Council of Australia 2008).

In an unprecedented way, as Bull (2010) notes, these new laws were designed to *pre-empt* criminality; authorities can detain people before an act has been committed and even before a definite plan has been formulated (Lynch and Williams 2006). In fact, Lynch and Williams (2006: 19) argue that counter-terrorism laws are increasingly following the precautionary principle. In other words, the burden of proof is switched, and, unlike the usual order of criminal proceedings, the defendant is required to prove they had no intention to commit a criminal act even before the prosecution mounts their case and establishes such an intention ever existed.

Many commentators denounced these new counter-terrorism laws as an assault on the foundational principles of a liberal democratic nation, and specifically the rule of law, which theoretically curtail arbitrary intrusions of the state, and provide for a person's right to be informed of their charges and experience a fair trial (cf. Roberts 2005). Yet the government also pre-emptively passed an amendment to certify that the counter-terrorism legislation was within their constitutional powers (Renwick 2007). This governmental reaction to the risk of terrorism – to pass laws hastily, remove the rights of suspected individuals and suspend safeguards against overly intrusive state powers – is not new. As Sir Robert Thompson stated in regard to communist insurgency in Malaysia in 1966 (cited in Roberts 2005:

110) there is a 'strong temptation for governmental forces to act outside of the law' in this context. Thompson noted that these measures are usually rationalized by the logic that provisions for individual rights were not created with insurgents in mind, and terrorists 'deserve to be treated as outlaws anyway'. Such moral behaviouralism justifies the state making a trade-off: to control the risk of terrorism while running the very real (indeed, realized) risks of detaining the wrong person, or abusing the rights of detainees. Moreover, the immense economic costs of controlling these 'risky' individuals (surveillance operations, military campaigns, police personnel, court costs, prison beds) are not considered important when matched against the danger they are deemed to pose. Perhaps most interestingly here, authorities often rationalize circumventing safeguards because 'the processes of law are too cumbersome' (Thompson 1966; cited in Roberts 2005: 110).

So, similar to the Northbridge curfew designed to eradicate offensive behaviour by Aboriginal youth, the counter-terror laws control risk categories by removing them pre-emptively. What is similar between the response to terrorism and corporate crime is that in both contexts, the usual risk-management framework (and particularly the legal apparatus) is criticized for being slow and unwieldy in responding to emergent concerns about socio-technological changes. However – unlike alleged corporate crime – when it comes to the threat of terrorism, the usual cumbersome legal process for weighing up the debate over new and uncertain 'proof' is overridden. Moreover, the credibility accorded to knowledge about the risks of terrorism is not proportionate to the physical threat it poses; people are, for example, far more likely to be injured or killed by corporate negligence than in a terrorist attack (Slapper and Tombs 1999). But, the threat of 'terrorism' seems to quickly catalyze a 'consensus' (at least by those in control) that the acceptable level of danger has been exceeded, and that the system must be amended to control the risk. And there is a cyclical effect: when there is a swift institutional response – the risk-*control* approach, where cumbersome bureaucratic processes are bypassed and rapid, precautionary action is taken – this rhetorically removes uncertainty about that knowledge and casts moral judgment and legal suspicion over the category of people who pose that risk. By contrast, a slow ineffectual system of risk management – like the approach to Kylanta's emissions – has the opposite effect: it paints allegations of risk as controversial, and the source of the risk remains relatively unscrutinized.

Conclusion: neoliberal logic and scepticism about emergent disease

So, the two bodies of literature above suggest that the way in which neoliberal logic dictates the management of different risks has epistemological consequences. It opens the space for some new forms of knowledge and concern to quickly take root, and forecloses or slows down the debate about others. The ethnographic data on the MCS controversy in this project offers a unique perspective on how this shapes decision-making over scientific controversies in the medico-legal field.

In this story, when corporate managers, union leaders, sceptical health practitioners, and judges decided *not* to intervene when theories of toxic risk emerged, it was usually expressed in epistemological terms. It was 'unscientific', there was a 'lack of data', there was 'insufficient proof'. Consider again the following decisions: The judicial officer in Ian's case acknowledged that – while she was convinced that Ian was sick and admitted that his condition may later be proven to be toxogenic – she was constrained in finding that he was chemically injured due to 'insufficient evidence'. The union manager, speaking for his constituents, cautioned the parliamentary inquiry not to impede Kylanta's expansion – and the job opportunities and local business spin-offs it would entail – in the name of an illness that 'is not supported by scientific fact'. The company's executives were 'waiting for the science' before they instituted more expensive safety measures. The risk-assessment expert was 'left with no alternative but to come to the conclusion that there was no evidence' of toxicity.

As Chapter 6 highlights, being sympathetic to controversial science can be damaging to one's professional credibility when it goes against mainstream scientific and legal custom. However, in looking more closely at these actors' reasoning, they were each acknowledging uncertainty, but, in having to be decisive, they were making the most logical, common-sense decision within neoliberal constraints. They were discouraged from prematurely recognizing a theory that could conceivably foster social hysteria, compensate undeserving claimants, erroneously restrict industry, and enforce hasty reform in an uncertain area of science. Put simply, neoliberal logic normalizes scepticism towards environmental risk and emergent conditions, and dictates that a different type and greater amount of proof is required before a novel disease can reach the required level of scientificity to be recognized at the medico-legal interface.

Conclusion

Environmental illness and the role of the law

The people fighting for recognition of MCS in this story – injured workers, their families, and sympathetic experts – all placed some faith in the law as a tool for change. Some mentioned a desire for transformation on a grand scale – a scientific paradigm shift towards the recognition of environmental illness, greater workers' rights and stricter industrial regulation – while others sought change at a more personal level, such as a definitive legal judgment that validated their claims to injury, one that provided adequate economic assistance to get on with their lives. Sociologist Steve Kroll-Smith believes that a landmark legal decision will be the catalyst to MCS recognition:

> What will happen is, there will be a successful court case in which environmental illness gets put on the books as a diagnosis. It is not going to be the medical profession that does it. The legal profession will push the medical profession into recognizing it. That is the model for creating disease in this society.
>
> (2001: 260)

Certainly in rhetoric, the WorkCover insurance apparatus and common law litigation do allow workers an avenue to fight for better occupational safety and to receive recognition, compensation and redress if they are injured. Moreover, the medico-legal nexus seems the most appropriate space for the nature and cause of a new occupational condition to be debated, and ideally would act as an alarm when new allegations of environmental risk emerge. However, the experiences of people with MCS in this research place into stark relief the difficulties facing sufferers of new and uncertain conditions when seeking legitimacy in the law.

Epistemological constraints in the medico-legal field

While uncertainty continues to shroud MCS – there has been no moment of truth, no definitive proof, no closure on its cause – the default position taken by most decision-makers is that it is *probably not* a legitimate, toxogenic condition. The first question I asked at the outset of this ethnography was, what are the barriers that prevent and delay new epistemologies from being recognized at the medico-legal interface? The MCS story has shown that there are two layers of constraint.

On the first layer, there are the ways in which truth-claims are assessed and conflicts over new forms of knowledge are resolved in the fields of medical science, the law and the insurance sector. These intersect and reinforce each other at the medico-legal interface to restrict epistemological possibilities. To start with, there are historically entrenched assumptions that underpin the way medical science measures the body and that dictate the scientific standards of what counts as evidence. Novel diseases and causal explanations remain, essentially, non-existent and invalid until they exceed the threshold for 'proof'. Insurance schemes also shape and constrain that which is medically possible: the workers' compensation apparatus reifies injuries into categories, and treats them in actuarial terms of risk and probability, percentages of impairment and need. This has the effect of making medico-scientific facts about injury static, which, in turn, makes the framework inflexible and restricts the debate about novel, unorthodox conditions. Moreover, the politics of the medico-scientific community – and the way in which funding and credibility is allocated to professionals – mean that those experts who specialize in controversial conditions can be marginalized and 'bankrupted' in terms of scientific credit and reward. Consequently, many begin to self-govern to conform to mainstream knowledge and practice, which can dilute their epistemic challenge to scientific orthodoxy. Finally, there is an inter-dependence between the legal and medical systems that further constrains debate. On the one hand, the context of adversarial litigation – where sympathetic and sceptical experts are pitted against one another – widens the perceived incommensurability between their theories, clouding visibility and shutting down the potential for any consensus. On the other hand, legal decision-makers arbitrating over complex scientific controversies are encouraged to fall back on mainstream paradigmatic assumptions in the face of uncertainty. Novel diseases that are only supported by experiential knowledge and a nominal field of science usually do not overcome the burden of proving probability. So, insurance, medical and legal ways of knowing the body all interact at the medico-legal interface, and have the effect of reinforcing a conservative approach to the recognition of novel conditions.

Tellingly, however, there is not always a cautious response to emergent scientific theories and their probability in the courts. As presented in Chapter 2, DNA profiling was a controversial theory that emerged out of a field of inquiry once considered pseudo-science (Lynch *et al.* 2010). Yet, in the Anglo-American world, elements of uncertainty surrounding the legal, scientific and administrative legitimacy of the DNA technique were eventually deemed 'fixed', not necessarily because new 'proof' had arisen or the technique had progressed, but rather because the controversy was socially declared closed through a range of measures (Lynch *et al.* 2010). What is interesting about the treatment of DNA profiling science – when compared to the official response to theories about MCS or asbestos-related disease – is how quickly momentum built around its legitimization and how (relatively) few barriers were put up against its widespread recognition and use. As Cole (2002) demonstrates, particularly in the North American context, there is a strong political impetus behind its legitimization: DNA profiling is part of a criminal identification toolbox nurtured by the governments with law and order agendas to control and restrict the mobility of ethnically and racially diverse populations, which are already considered suspect and risky.

This leads to the second, more powerful, layer of constraint to the recognition of new epistemologies at the interface of law and medical science. There is a neoliberal pattern to the management of different risks in our society: a politico-economic order that dictates when emergent social concerns become visible and when they are deemed urgent. The corporation is politically, legally and culturally embedded as the most natural way of doing business (Ireland 2010). Neoliberal commonsense thus dictates that the onus of proof is on complainants to secure a critical mass of public concern and a favourable scientific consensus before substantive changes to a corporation will be enforced. The legal system in this context is cumbersome because, it is deemed, there must be an unhurried weighing-up of risks before a novel concern about workers' health is considered a credible reason for precautionary restrictions to be imposed upon industry. Thus, politically protected corporate forces demarcate the bounds of epistemological possibility surrounding industrial emissions and alleged environmental illnesses. In the MCS story, health inspectors often had a collegial relationship with corporate managers, rarely heeded the workers' experiences of toxicity, and tended to be lenient and delayed in their monitoring of safety compliance. Corporations accused of emitting toxins capitalized on medico-legal evidence requirements – and the burden of proof that fell in their favour – by magnifying uncertainty about the toxicity of their operations and fostering doubts about the trustworthiness of workers and their alleged injuries. Insurance companies were permitted to engage in illegal surveillance tactics in order to gain footage that emphasized workers' abilities, which further framed their claims to disability as controversial. And, in each case, the immense gap in power and resources between the worker and their solicitor on the one hand, and the employer and insurer's legal team on the other, made the lengthy and expensive struggle over knowledge unequal and imbalanced. This inequality heightened the likelihood of workers abandoning the case before its completion or taking early, confidential settlements. When cases did reach completion, more often than not, it was deemed that there was insufficient proof to compensate the workers, to change industrial processes, and to limit the expansion of allegedly toxic operations.

Thus, the neoliberal climate of the current workers' compensation scheme has a significant impact on this society's response to emergent risks and potential illnesses. In this study, neoliberalism manifested as both a set of ideas that influenced policy reforms and a form of governmentality that shaped people's thoughts and behavior (cf. Larner 2000). Concepts of economic efficiency, corporate freedom and entrepreneurialism constrain the way decisions are made about new environmental concerns, irrespective of what causes them: scepticism is encouraged and a sympathetic, precautionary response is disincentivized. Furthermore, as the values of economic efficiency and diminished state intervention are normalized and rolled into government and insurance policies, they change social life in the workplace, the clinic and the courtroom. Although these normative ideas are recognized and questioned by many, it is clear that neoliberal values deeply penetrate how experts do science and practice law, and how workers ascribe meaning to their injuries and try to cope thereafter.

So, essentially, the potential for paradigm shift in the medico-scientific community, and the law's ability to catalyze epistemological change, is limited by a broader neoliberal constellation. This leads to the second question I posed at the outset of this research: to what extent is the law, and the workers' compensation apparatus more specifically, a tool for the environmental health movement to fight for recognition and advance its social struggle? To foreground my conclusions, it is useful to revisit the extent to which the law has precipitated social change for other social movements.

The transformative potential of the law

Social scientists have long wondered whether marginalized social movements (including the feminist, labour, civil rights, Indigenous, and gay and lesbian movements) can better effect change when their rights are enshrined in law and can be defended via litigation. The rhetoric of rights is attractive; their goal to protect difference and equality is a worthy one and across the political spectrum few people would 'rationally oppose them as desirable elements in a civilized society' (Burnside 2009). However, critical scholars have continually expressed scepticism about the potential of such legal innovation to lead to social equality, a debate that offers useful insight into the role that law can (or cannot) play when emergent diseases are struggling to be recognized.[1]

On the one hand, critics question activists' preoccupation with, and dependency on, law as a solution. At a pragmatic level, as the MCS case has shown, litigation is costly and time-consuming, which some suggest may detract social movements and individual activists from more promising (non-legal) forms of political organization (Fudge and Glasbeek 1992: 56). Moreover, legalizing an issue can *de*politicize it. Waldman argued that the reason South Africa responded to asbestos more effectively and therapeutically was because it became a highly politicized issue, partly through fortuitous historical events such as the transition from apartheid. To some extent this allowed activists to circumvent the narrow scientific and legal framings of their disease; the political arena allowed them more freedom to express their understanding and experience in different ways (2011: 183).

Part of the problem is that when progressive movements work within the law, their claims must often be deradicalized to achieve legal legitimacy, which – similar to the effect of scientific hegemony on sympathetic specialists in Chapter 6 – diminishes the revolutionary nature of their demands and makes substantive reform unlikely (cf. Smart 1989). As a consequence of deradicalization in the law, social movements can gradually lower their standards in terms of what constitutes justice. Fudge and Glasbeek (1992), for example, suggest that activists once calling for fundamental social transformation eventually celebrate a victory when the courts merely permit them to *retain* rights that were fought and won on the political stage long ago. (They draw upon the example of a US movement that sought to elevate a homeless person's right to beg as a constitutional right, rather than demanding more crucial changes in terms of economic equality and the need for more adequate welfare – Hershkoff and Cohen 1991).[2]

Moreover, any landmark, symbolic legal decisions that are achieved via legal mechanisms may not necessarily lead to better lives for claimants. An example is the wax and wane of the social progress made regarding the standing of Indigenous people in Australia. Damien Short (2008), for example, highlights a paradox that despite ostensible victories for Aboriginal and Torres Strait Islander people in terms of rights and recognition (through the reconciliation paradigm and the installation of the Native Title Tribunal), the *actual* quality of life for many Indigenous people has arguably decreased over time. Suicide is endemic in many Indigenous communities, as is the eye disease trachoma which was essentially eradicated in the developed world decades ago (and has been largely eliminated in Africa – Short 2008: 3).

Perhaps most importantly, critics argue that by concentrating on litigation, social movements have ignored, or shifted the struggle away from, the economic problems of neoliberalism, which they believe remain a crucial source of inequality (Brown 1995; Fudge and Glasbeek 1992; Povinelli 2002). This perspective suggests that profound economic transformation to the current politico-economic order is required if there will ever be substantive social change.[3] Wendy Brown (1995), for example, critiques the contemporary liberal preoccupation with individual freedom and autonomy. For Brown, a preoccupation with individual rights allows people to erroneously believe that a subjective, *personal* sense of empowerment is the same as more profound freedom and equality for their marginalized group. Brown believes an individualistic focus veils the continuing economic subordination of minorities. This is because they *ostensibly* have equal 'rights', and have access to legal processes by which they can *theoretically* defend those rights, which takes away their ability to articulate how inequality remains:

> it may be that the withdrawal that rights offer, the unmarking and destigmatising they promise, has as its cost the loss of a language to describe the character of domination, violation or exploitation that configures such needs [...]
>
> (1995: 126)

These risks are inherent in the no-fault workers' compensation apparatus as well. It frames each case as an individualized struggle over one worker's disability and right to compensation. This specific focus can detract attention away from greater problems regarding what constitutes toxic production, and the contamination of public space, workplaces and homes (Gibson 2010).

There is, moreover, an important consideration as to whether legal innovations such as workers' compensation laws, which purport to offer avenues for recognition and redress, can have a hoodwinking effect. Povinelli (1998: 591) argues that legal tools such as the Native Title apparatus are even more insidious than the blatantly racist, outright violent colonial regimes of the past, because they are cunningly disguised by progressive rhetoric.

> [They allow] subjects to feel engaged in a social process labeled 'justice' and to feel that such mass subject projections like the nation, the public, and the state are equally engaged.
>
> (2002: 16)

For Povinelli, new forms of social life arise out of these politico-legal regimes, as subjects engage creatively with the structures they are presented with. However, she sees these new social formations as risky, rather than productive. For her, such regimes 're-subordinate', or continue to colonize, Indigenous people because they are forced to conform and to deradicalize, to be recognized by legal decision-makers and the state, which disallows any *genuine* difference.[4]

In essence, these theorists caution that the very existence of mechanisms for litigation – in this case, a workers' compensation apparatus – can provide a semblance of equality while masking the reality of ongoing oppression. Notably, though, other scholars take issue with several aspects of this critique of rights, liberalism and the limited role of law (Flear and Vakulenko 2010; Herman 1993; Moses 2011). First, the requirement that social change must be sweeping and revolutionary overlooks the incremental ways in which marginalized communities *have* received more equal treatment over time by working within legal frameworks, appropriating legal language, and pushing out discourses that explicitly deny them rights (Herman 1993). For example, in the context of the environmental health movement, it is important to keep in mind the role that unions and social movements have played – utilizing the discourse of rights and fighting legal battles – in gradually improving labour laws and workplace safety. This is particularly pertinent in the context of the storage, production and use of chemicals, which Pearce and Tombs (2000) – though cynical overall – concede is 'infinitely safer' than it was thirty years ago when the Bhopal disaster was enabled. (However, this acknowledgement should not preclude questioning why these safety precautions took so long, and how many workers suffered before problems in occupational safety were addressed.)

Moreover, social change cannot merely be measured by legal outcomes: activists who are cynical about the limitations of the law can nonetheless use litigation as a platform from which to politicize their cause (Herman 1993), and as a tool to mobilize people and spur on further political organization (Bartholomew and Hunt 1990). Flear and Vakulenko (2010) – who write about citizen engagement with science – argue that despite the limitations of legally defensible 'rights', the concept can nonetheless be empowering because it invites people to be conscious and critical of current deficits in the way governments regulate scientific and technological development. For these theorists, elevating civic participation to a 'human right', which can be defended through litigation, may not be a silver bullet, but it spurs the public to critically engage with their social geography.

As well as the spin-off effects of litigation, the suggestion that social activists are blinded by the promise of rights, compensation and legal liberation negates their agency, and their ability to be discerning and pragmatic. Herman (1993) argues that, at least with regard to her study of the gay and lesbian movement, activists are also cynical of the emancipatory potential of litigation, and rather use it selectively and strategically. For example, one woman who fought to have her non-heterosexual household declared a legal 'family' did so not as an attempt at revolution, or in the name of 'gay rights', but in order to receive medical and dental benefits (1993: 33). For litigants, success may not need to be sweeping but could instead be measured more in terms of practical, everyday improvements.

And while academics may denounce state-based, legal processes for offering recognition and decry the lack of more substantive transformation, what to make of the very real sense of affirmation and empowerment that claimants may feel after smaller, symbolic legal victories? Dirk Moses (2011: 155), for example, argues that Povinelli's dismissal of the national apology to Aboriginal and Torres Strait Islander people as a mere continuation of colonial repression 'misses the point that most Indigenous people thought the terms of their national inclusion had changed significantly'. Thus, these

theorists highlight that in a meta-analysis of the law's limitations, it is important not to ignore the voices of the litigants – their feelings of hope,
cynicism, victory and disappointment – because these, too, reflect and
affect social and epistemological change (or the lack thereof) on a more
micro level.

So, what does the MCS case study add to this conversation about the
law's transformative potential? What possibilities were opened up and
closed off by litigation as a form of governance of new epistemologies? And
to what extent did the lawsuits I studied further the quest of the environmental health movement, locally or globally?

Given their adverse experiences in the medico-legal field, most of the
chemically sensitive and sympathetic informants in this research have given
up altogether on the quest for official MCS recognition through the courts.
From their perspective, the legal process was, decidedly, unsuccessful,
untherapeutic and unjust. Experts and lay people alike all retain anger to
varying levels about the way they were treated in their medico-legal interactions (an experience that left Ian, for example, feeling 'like a bowstring,
just near the point of snapping'). Most of the chemically sensitive participants have moved to rural areas or the coast where they are less likely to
be exposed to daily chemicals. Some of the professionals have closed or
adjusted their businesses such that chemical injuries are no longer their
principal line of work. Others continue to treat or act on behalf of chemically sensitive people, but with less emotional investment than they once
had, since they are now weary of the personal consequences. At face value,
these circumstances illustrate a loss in momentum and might suggest a
hegemonic acceptance of the status quo, which continually delegitimizes
sufferers and sympathizers of environmental illness.

However, an interesting trend bears mention here. Although they have lost
faith in the medico-legal field as an avenue through which to seek recognition
and healing, a number of MCS litigants and their supporters have turned to
different (non-legal and non-scientific) avenues to have their voices heard.
Consider, for example, the following excerpts of life after an occupational
MCS dispute. Hayley, who worked at Kylanta for a number of years, was once
friendly with the supervisors in her team. This was the case until she
expressed her concern to them that she was becoming ill from the chimneystack emissions. Her managers then treated her at various times with
scrutiny, indifference and disbelief. Eventually, Hayley quit her position at
Kylanta. She never sought compensation for her MCS diagnosis but she
assisted her former Kylanta colleagues with their medico-legal battle. Years
later, she started a postgraduate research project in business studies. Her topic,
inspired by her ordeal, was how high-level executives compromise personal
'authenticity' when they are representing the interests of their company.

Clyde, an engineer who claimed to have contracted MCS when his office
was sprayed with insecticide, wrote a book about the difficulties faced by

victims of chemical trauma. The foreword was written by a reputable physician and the monograph was reviewed by an international humanitarian activist. No publishing houses that Clyde approached, however, accepted the manuscript for publication.

Fiona, who believes she contracted MCS as a result of her employer's toxic emissions and blatant disregard for worker safety, started a film production company with her husband. The aim, Fiona said, is to build up a reputation in the film industry, which will assist in the casting, production, marketing and distribution of their pièce de resistance: a movie about a toxic conspiracy.

Most of the litigants I interviewed have embarked upon similar adventures. Kylanta worker Evan told me he wants to write a book that educates children about the dangers of chemicals, because he thinks the new generation is a good place to start a regime change with regards to environmental risk. Ian and Jeff have written to a renowned feature columnist in a Sunday newspaper of Western Australia, who tentatively agreed to write about Ian's experiences (but so far has not). Hugh Porter, the Green's politician in the Kylanta case study, asked me to look after his box of documents relating to the dispute with care, because he 'will probably write a book about it someday'.

These where-are-they-now epilogues demonstrate that failure in the medico-legal field – and in politicizing the issue thus far – does not prevent actors from engaging in other forms of activism; indeed, following Povinelli, their discontent does produce new forms of social activity, as it inspires creativity and resourcefulness. Their epistemic challenge to medical and legal orthodoxy has not been deradicalized, necessarily; it has just shifted to a different domain. This ties in with a pattern identified by Couch and Kroll-Smith (2000) who sought to understand how social movements engage with mainstream science:

> Non-scientific movements and organizations are appropriating and using scientific and medical knowledge, dislodging this knowledge from its institutional structures and relocating it within different organizational spheres.
>
> (401)

MCS litigants, too, are analyzing their delegitimation at the interface of medical science, law and industry, harnessing their experiences and the information they have obtained, and 'relocating' it within other social forums that have exhibited more listening promise. For them, the hope is that through these alternative media, a groundswell of social support for a chemical explanation of MCS will eventually catalyze the condition's medico-scientific and legal recognition, and ameliorate their quality of life.

However, their experiences caution against an overly optimistic outlook in terms of what can be achieved, and how quickly, without legitimacy in the legal and medico-scientific realm. Certainly the media, the arts and academia might, over time, heighten social consciousness surrounding emergent disease such as MCS and may even eventually facilitate a land-mark legal decision, a (specifically physiological) label in the diagnostic manual, and a code in the workers' compensation insurance guide. But in the meantime, a *lack* of recognition of their epistemological claims remains a pivotal source of hardship in the everyday lives of chemically sensitive people. While community action and investigative journalism created momentum around MCS after the Kylanta controversy, this was not sustained and was ultimately silenced by a conservative backlash. As shown in Denmark, Germany and Canada, where there have been varying levels of legitimacy granted to MCS in terms of health provision and medical labelling, this has not necessarily improved the lives of those with MCS in terms of social acceptance and economic security (see Chapter 7). Irrespective of the gains made through alternative avenues, juridical silence continues to powerfully deny legitimacy and resources to alternative knowledges and cast its claimants as untrustworthy and undeserved. Thus, irrespective of its inherent barriers and limitations, law continues to be crucial to litigants in the quest for change.

Removing barriers to balanced debate about emergent concerns

As new emergent illnesses such as electro-sensitivity and wind turbine syndrome burgeon as health concerns with some striking parallels to MCS, they too will present similar challenges for the medico-legal system in its governance of uncertainty in Australia and around the globe. The MCS case is therefore a timely opportunity to learn from mistakes, continue with successful initiatives, and imagine better ways of governing emergent concerns. Several sites for reform became apparent in this ethnography.

In this research, when experts and lay people interacted meaningfully and at length outside of the adversarial environment – beyond agonistic scientific correspondence and courtroom battles – the narratives provided by the chemically sensitive usually led experts to better understand the link between exposures and suffering. When supportive and sceptical experts were able to deliberate together with independent facilitators, perceived differences were diminished and compromises were reached to varying levels. There is, therefore, a strong argument for more deliberative events such as medical consensus meetings, which bring together workers, employers and plaintiff and defence experts, *before* a bitter debate unfolds in the adversarial legal arena. As discussed in Chapter 7, consensus meetings have their own critics, in that these events can privilege main-stream beliefs and further alienate marginalized voices. However, since narratives are one of the only tools with which to understand elusive conditions like MCS, (Kroll-Smith and Floyd 1997: 19) events that allow meaningful listening to those stories can only contribute to further understanding, and make way for areas of agreement and potential solutions.

Furthermore, there needs to be a careful examination of the extent to which an exact physiological causal mechanism must be identified before a condition is considered compensable. Almost all of the informants in this research – on both sides of the debate over chemical sensitivity – acknowledged that the condition entailed a complex interaction between physiological, emotional and psychological mechanisms and that it can be debilitating. If it were officially determined that MCS involved both physiological *and* psychological elements – or that the details of cause were not fundamental to legitimacy and deservedness – this would allow the chemically sensitive a form of validation that would enable them to live the life of a person in the sick role and have the benefits that this entails. This multi-factorial causal explanation would not preclude their rights to financial assistance, which could help them cope with their condition and even, if possible, return to chemically-free social activities and workplaces. Such a support framework for injured workers could be government-managed and funded through a corporate tax scheme. Admittedly, however, this nuanced approach to cause and compensability is unlikely to be politically popular or financially sponsored when the current ethos surrounding both welfare and insurance is a neoliberal one where the goal is economic growth and, thus, the reduction of claims (Ericson and Doyle 2004; Wacquant 2009).

Careful attention also needs to be paid to the role of corporate interests in obscuring and refracting scientific debate over environmental risks, emergent conditions and the need for regulation. Legal decision-makers and town planners need to be better equipped to identify and manage delay tactics, withholding of data, intimidation, invasive surveillance techniques and the production of biased, corporate-funded science. As the stories in this book have emphasized, these strategies currently delay a timely response to environmental threats and obscure important information for understanding novel conditions.

Ultimately, though, the unfolding case of MCS (and the history of asbestos-related disease) reiterate that the jurisdiction of the medico-legal system – its epistemological possibilities, its power to intervene, its usefulness as a catalyst for change – is itself shaped, constrained, and sometimes overridden by a broader neoliberal tide. Radical transformation to the socio-legal process for recognizing and responding to emergent diseases is thus unlikely to be realized unless in conjunction with fundamental politico-economic reform.

Notes

1 Introducing the disease of uncertainty

1   While MCS was only labelled in 1987, there are earlier records of similar afflictions. In his 1839 text, *The Fall of the House of Usher*, Edgar Allen Poe describes an unnamed disease affecting the character Roderick Usher, who 'suffered from a morbid acuteness of the senses' which included an intolerance to many foods, textures and odours. Poe also hints that the cause was 'a pestilent and mystic vapor or gas, dull sluggish, faintly discernible, and leaden-hued.' Donnay (1999) suggests that this prose probably describes a highly toxic, illuminating gas, which was manufactured from coal in the early 1800s, and contained a number of volatile organic compounds.

2   Furthermore, as this book emphasizes, litigation can be a form of public education (Jasanoff 1995: 20) about an emergent condition. People in lower-income countries tend to have less access to established legal avenues for bringing complaints to the legal stage, particularly when it relates to corporate negligence (Al-humdani 2014). This may, in turn, impinge upon the dissemination of information about a potential new disease.

3   Medical writer, Fry (1985: 28) went on to call sceptics of RSI – who wilfully ignored 'known evidence' – the 'flat-earth society', drawing comparisons with the politically embedded naysayers of Galileo's time.

4   Most scientists believe that popular paranoia about carcinogens is leading people to generate symptoms and blame technology through the power of suggestion. Control studies, which expose electrosensitive volunteers to real and sham EMF, suggest that volunteers react just as readily to fake exposures (Rubin *et al.* 2007).

5   In a statutory workers' compensation claim, the worker is called the 'applicant' and in common law he or she is titled 'the plaintiff.' For ease and consistency, however, I refer to chemically sensitive litigants as 'workers' when talking about them as individuals or 'plaintiffs' when addressing their role in legal disputes.

6   There could be both biological and social reasons why men and women respond differently to toxicity (Arbuckle 2006). Biologically, they may have different ways of absorbing, metabolizing, storing and excreting chemicals after exposure. With regard to social context, men and women can undertake different occupational tasks, use different equipment and behave differently in the workplace.

2 Knowledge and power at the medico-legal interface

1   DNA typing involves the analysis of biological samples obtained from an

individual, which, when processed, produce a 'profile', which proponents claim is essentially unique to that individual.

2 Saks and Koehler (2005) qualify that the legitimization of DNA profiling does not constitute a paradigm shift in the traditional Kuhnian sense of the term. The technique did not overturn an entire worldview. Rather than rising above normal science, it rose *to* the status of normal, as it increased in credibility (see Lynch *et al.* 2010: 4).

3 One scientific duo predicted that this case would 'feature the most detailed course in molecular genetics ever taught to the US people' (Lander and Budowle 1994: 735).

4 This is partly because the society was largely pioneered by convicts, who inevitably had negative associations with the British legal system that banished them, often for trivial offences (Weisbrot 1990).

5 The authority of the medical and legal fields is accentuated by several trends in training and practice: the majority of students who study medicine and the law tend to hail from upper socio-economic backgrounds (Weisbrot 1990); the valued education they obtain to reach their level of expertise further demarcates them as part of the social elite (Bourdieu and Passeron 1990); and the extensive fees they often charge for their exclusive services means they continue to accumulate privilege throughout their careers (Weisbrot 1990).

6 See also Graham and Wiener (1995) who describe how interventions to reduce risks to the public can deliberately or inadvertently produce countervailing risks.

7 Critics of formal equality argue that treating disadvantaged people as though they have equal opportunities and equal access will only further entrench inequality until it becomes systemic (see for example Thornton 1990). The alternative solution is substantive equality models, which posit that meaningful equality and true fairness can only be measured by *outcomes.*

3 Risk entrepreneurialism: the social construction of toxicity and disease

1 A typical disparity between employers' and employees' conceptions of safety is that the company situates workers' complaints within a discourse of 'individual susceptibility' which removes the focus from hazardous working conditions (Draper 2000).

2 Although Jim frequently received letters threatening litigation to any employee who defamed the company, Jim maintained his employment. A number of participants believe this was due to the company's fears of a mutiny that might occur if Jim's position was terminated.

3 Professor James steadfastly refused to be paid by any party – including the state government – in the interests of maintaining strict independence.

4 The Kylanta worker who, upon advice from his solicitor, felt the offer was inadequate and did not accept the payment, continued to fight Kylanta and never received compensation.

5 Notably, however, the workers I spoke to nonetheless wished to contribute to research anonymously.

4 The medico-legal illness narratives

1 Ross River virus is an Australian virus, transmitted by mosquitoes, characterized by chronic fatigue and muscle pain, which was particularly virulent in Western Australia at about the time Ian's symptoms became obvious.

2   See Chapter 8 for cases in which the burden of proof is placed upon the accused in criminal law. Likewise, in a few exceptional cases in personal injury law, both under the statutory workers' compensation scheme and in common law avenues, the onus of proof can be reversed, such that the employer is required to establish that the condition is not work related.

5 Medical, legal and insurance reasoning in the governance of uncertainty

1   Table 5.1 indexes the 'second-schedule entitlement', which is added to the amount of lost wages the worker has sustained. If the worker proves he is 'totally and permanently' incapacitated for work, he is also entitled to an extension of the prescribed amount.

6 The deviance of sympathetic experts

1   For an insightful discussion about the difference in science between a 'puzzle' and a 'problem', see Godfrey-Smith (2003: 82) and about the difference between a 'puzzle' and a 'mystery', see Kroll-Smith and Floyd (1997: 34).
2   The Review officer conflated the extent of Ian's disability with the issue of causality, the latter of which the barrister argued was technically not part of her jurisdiction.

7 Non-legal governance and epistemological possibilities

1   That is unless there is a ruling for party/party costs, where one side may be ordered to pay the costs of the other side.
2   Western Australia is renowned in the international community for conducting such deliberative processes. While it can overcome disagreement, see Dryzek (2002) for critiques of its ability to reach true consensus.

8 Neoliberalism, scepticism and toxic knowledge

1   Ironically in this case, supermarkets communicated about the dangers of eating beef more effectively than trusted government advisors, which, for Jasanoff, 'suggested democracy [or, democratic accountability] was functioning more effectively in the marketplace than in politics' – 1997: 230.

Conclusion: environmental illness and the role of the law

1   See, for example, Bakan 1997; Fudge and Glasbeek 1992; Segal 1991; Short 2008; Stychin 2008.
2   Interestingly, 15 years after her co-authored paper with Glasbeek, Judy Fudge (2007) was pleasantly surprised at a Canadian Supreme Court decision, which, unlike her pessimistic prediction, elevated workers' collective bargaining to the status of a constitutional right. However, given the strength of the 'economic and political tide' that had, until then, consistently disenfranchised workers and benefited employers, she remained sceptical that defending this right in court would actually translate to job security and improved wages for working people.
3   This argument can be traced back to Marx's (1843) cynicism regarding the emancipatory potential of liberalism for the Jewish community.
4   For a more detailed discussion about the repression of radical alterity in Australian 'multiculturalism', see Hage (1998).

References

Afari, N. and Buchwald, D. (2003) 'Chronic Fatigue Syndrome: A review', *American Journal of Psychiatry*, 160: 221–236.

Al-humdani, M. (2014) 'Commentary: the global tobacco litigation initiative: an effort to protect developing countries from big tobacco', *Journal of Public Health Policy*, 35(2): 162–170.

American College of Government and Industrial Hygienists (ACGIH) (1942) *Report of the Subcommittee on Threshold Limits*, Transactions of the 5th Annual Meeting of the National Conference of Government Industrial Hygienists.

American College of Occupational and Environmental Medicine (ACOEM) (1999) *Position Statement: Multiple Chemical Sensitivities: Idiopathic Environmental Intolerance*. Medem Medical Library. Available online at: www.medem.com/medlib/article/ZZZ3099XAIC (accessed 23 March 2006).

Amsterdam Kliniek (1997) Available online at: www.amsterdamkliniek.com/treatments.html (accessed 4 July 2013)

Ankeny, R. (2003) *Analysis of Chronic Fatigue Syndrome (CFS) Clinical Practice Guideline Development in Australia*. Available online at: www.uow.edu.au/arts/research/bigpicturebioethics/reports/cfsreport.pdf (accessed 27 June 2009).

Arbuckle, T. E. (2006) 'Are there sex and gender differences in acute exposure to chemicals in the same setting?' *Environmental Research,* 101: 195–204.

Aronowitz, R. A. (1998) *Making Sense of Illness: Science, society and disease*, Cambridge: Cambridge University Press.

Ashford, N. A. and Miller, C. S. (1998) *Chemical Exposures: Low levels and high stakes*, 1st edn, New York: Van Nostrand Reinhold.

Australian Department of Health and Ageing, Office of Chemical Safety and Environmental Health (2010) *Scientific Review Report: Multiple Chemical Sensitivity: Identifying Key Research Needs*, Canberra.

Awerbuch, M. (1985) 'RSI, or 'Kangaroo Paw'', *Medical Journal of Australia,* 142: 237–238.

Bakan, J. (1997) *Just Words: Constitutional Rights and Social Wrongs*, Toronto: University of Toronto Press.

Balint, J. (2012) *Genocide, State Crime and the Law: In the Name of the State*, London: Routledge-Cavendish.

Bammer, G. and Martin, B. (1992) 'Repetition Strain Injury: Medical knowledge, social movement and de facto partisanship', *Social Problems*, 39(3): 219–237.

Banks, J. and Prior, L. (2001) 'Doing Things with Illness: The micro-politics of the CFS clinic', *Social Science and Medicine*, 52: 11–23.

Barnes, B. (2009) *Scientific Knowledge and Sociological Theory* Abingdon: Routledge.

Bartha, L., Baumzweiger, W., Buscher, D. S., Callender, T., Dahl, K. A. and Davidoff, A. (1999) 'Multiple Chemical Sensitivity: A Consensus', *Archives of Environmental Health* 54: 147–149.

Bartholomew, A. and Hunt, A. (1990) 'What's Wrong with Rights', *Law and Inequality*, 9: 1–58.

Beck, E. R., Souhami, R. L., Hanna, M. G. and Holdright, D. R. (2003) *Tutorials in Differential Diagnosis*, Fourth edn, Edinburgh.: Churchill Livingstone.

Beck, U. (1992) *Risk Society*, London: Sage Publications.

—— (1994) 'The Re-invention of Politics: Towards a theory of reflexive modernisation', in U. Beck, A. Giddens and S. Lash (eds) *Reflexive Modernisation*, Cambridge: Polity Press.

—— (1995) *Ecological Politics in an Age of Risk*, Cambridge: Polity Press.

—— (1996) 'Risk Society and the Provident State', in S. Lash, B. Szersynski and B. Wynne (eds) *Risk, Environment and Modernity*, London: Sage Publications.

Beder, S. (1998a) 'Manipulating Public Knowledge', *Metascience*, 7(1): 132–139.

—— (1998b) 'Public Relations' Role in Manufacturing Artificial Grass-roots Coalitions', *Public Relations Quarterly*, 43(2): 21–23.

Bell, I., Miller, C. and Schwartz, G. (1992) 'An Olfactory-Limbic Model of Multiple Chemical Sensitivity Syndrome: Possible relationship to kindling and affective spectrum disorders', *Biological Psychiatry*, 32: 218–242.

Bell, I., Schwartz, G., Peterson, J., Amend, D. and Stini, W. (1993) 'Self-Reported Illness From Chemical Odors in Young Adults Without Clinical Syndromes or Occupational Exposures', *Archives of Environmental Health*, 48(5): 315–327.

Berman, D. (1978) *Death on the Job*, New York: Monthly Review Press.

Bessant, J. (2000) 'Civil Conscription or Reciprocal Obligation: The Ethics of 'Work for the Dole'', *The Australian Journal of Social Issues* 35(1): 15–33.

Best, R. K. (2012) 'Disease Politics and Medical Research Funding: Three Ways Advocacy Shapes Policy', *American Sociological Review*, 77: 780.

Bourdieu, P. (1975) 'The specificity of the scientific field and the social conditions of the progress of reason', *Sociology of Science*, 14(6): 19–47.

—— (1994) 'Rethinking the State: On the genesis and structure of the Bureaucratic Field', *Sociological Theory*, 12(1): 1–19.

Bourdieu, P. and Passeron, J. (1990) *Reproduction in Education, Society and Culture*, London: Sage Publications.

Bradley, A. S., Ford, B. and Bansal A. S. (2013) 'Altered functional B-cell subset populations in patients with chronic fatigue syndrome compared to healthy controls', *Clinical and Experimental Immunology*, 172: 73–80.

Brodeur, P. (1974) *Expendable Americans*, New York: Viking.

Brown, P. (1992) 'Toxic Waste Contamination and Popular Epidemiology: Lay and professional ways of knowing', *Journal of Health and Social Behavior*, 33: 267–281.

—— (2007) *Toxic Exposures: Contested Illnesses and the Environmental Health Movement*, New York: Columbia University Press.

Brown, P. and Mikkelson, E. (1997) *No Safe Place: Toxic waste, leukemia and community action*, California: University of California Press.

Brown, P., Kroll-Smith, S. and Gunter, V. J. (2000) 'Knowledge, Citizens and Organisations: An overview of environments, diseases and social conflict', in S. Kroll-Smith, V. J. Gunter and P. Brown (eds) *Illness and the Environment: A reader in contested medicine*, New York: New York University Press.

Brown, W. (1995) *States of Injury: Power and Freedom in Late Modernity*, Princeton, NJ: Princeton University Press.

Bull, M. (2010) *Punishment and Sentencing: Risk, rehabilitation and restitution*, Oxford: Oxford University Press.

Burnside, J. (2009) 'A Charter of Rights for Australia', *Perspectives*. Future leaders: 48–62. Available online at: www.futureleaders.com.au/book_chapters/pdf/Perspectives/Julian_Burnside.pdf (accessed 20 May 2014).

Bury, M. (1991) 'Chronic Illness as Biographical Disruption', *Sociology of Health and Illness*, 4(2): 167–182.

Butler, L. (2003) 'Modifying publication practices in response to funding formulas', *Research Evaluations*, 12(1): 39–46.

Canadian Human Rights Commission. (2007) *Policy on Environmental Sensitivities*, Ottawa.

Canguilhem, G. (1989) *The Normal and the Pathological*, New York: Zone Press.

Caress S. M. and Steinemann A. C. (2003) 'A review of a two-phase population study of multiple chemical sensitivities', *Environmental Health Perspective*, 111: 1490–1497.

Carson, R. (1962) *Silent Spring*, New York: Houghton Mifflin.

Castleman, B. I. and Ziem, G. E. (1988) 'Corporate Influence on Threshold Limit Values', *American Industrial Hygiene Association Journal*, 13: 531–559.

Chemical Sensitivity Network. (2010). Available online at: www.csn-deutschland.de (accessed 7 July 2010).

Chubin, D. E. and Hackett, E. J. (1990) *Peerless Science: Peer Review and U.S. Science Policy*, Albany, NY: State University of New York Press.

Clarke, J. N. and James, S. (2003) 'The Radicalised Self: The impact on the self of the contested nature of the diagnosis of chronic fatigue syndrome', *Social Science and Medicine*, 57(8): 1387–1395.

Colborne, T., Myers, J. P. and Dumanoski, D. (1996) *Our Stolen Future: How Man-made chemicals are threatening our fertility, intelligence and survival*, London: Little, Brown and Company.

Cole, S. A. (2002) *Suspect Identities: A History of Fingerprinting and Criminal Identification*, Boston, MA: Harvard University Press.

Collins, H. M. (1975) 'The Seven Sexes: A Study in the Sociology of a Phenomenon, or the Replication of Experiments in Physics', *Sociology*, 9: 205–224.

—— (2004) *Gravity's Shadow: The search for gravitational waves*, Chicago, IL: University of Chicago Press.

Comcare, Australian Commonwealth Government. (2000) *The Management of Occupational Health and Safety in Commonwealth Agencies: Establishing an OHS Management System*. Available online at: www.comcare.gov.au/publications/OHS_17/index.html (accessed 18 May 2007).

Cook, W. A. (1945) 'Maximum Allowable Concentrations of Industrial Atmospheric Contaminants', *Industrial Medicine*, 11: 936–946.

Couch, S. and Kroll-Smith, S. (2000) 'Environmental Movements and Expert Knowledge', in S. Kroll-Smith, P. Brown and V. J. Gunter (eds) *Illness and the*

Environment: A reader in contested medicine, New York: New York University Press.

Cullen, M. R. (1987) 'The worker with Multiple Chemical Sensitivities: An overview', *Occupational Medicine*, 2: 655–661.

Cunneen, C. (2005) 'Racism, Discrimination and the Over-Representation of Indigenous People in the Criminal Justice System: Some Conceptual and Explanatory Issues', *Current Issues in Criminal Justice*, 17: 329–346.

Daniel, A. (1990) *Medicine and the State*, Sydney: Allen & Unwin.

—— (1998) *Scapegoats for a Profession: Uncovering procedural injustice*, Sydney: Harwood Academic Publishers.

Danish Environmental Protection Agency and Danish Ministry of the Environment (Danish EPA) (2005) *Multiple Chemical Sensitivity, MCS* Environmental project no. 988. Available online at: www2.mst.dk/common/Udgivramme/Frame.asp? http://www2.mst.dk/Udgiv/publications/2005/87-7614-548-4/html/ helepubl_eng.htm (accessed 5 February 2013).

Das, V. (2000) 'Suffering, Legitimacy and Healing', in S. Kroll-Smith, P. Brown and V. J. Gunter (eds) *Illness and the Environment: A reader in contested medicine*, New York: New York University Press, 270–286.

Daubert v. Merrell Dow Pharmaceuticals Inc. (1993) no. 509. US Supreme Court.

De Graff, M. B. and Bröer, C. (2012) 'We are the Canary in the Coal Mine': Establishing a disease category and a new health risk', *Health, Risk and Society*, 14.2: 129–147.

Deutsche Institut für Medizinische Dokumentation und Information (DIMDI) (2008) *Letter to Chemical Sensitivity Network.* Available online at: www.csn-deutschland.de/dimdi_icd-schreiben.pdf.

Deyo, R. and Psaty, B. (1997) 'The Messenger Under Attack: Intimidation of researchers by special interest groups', *New England Journal of Medicine*, 336: 1176–1180.

Dhir, A. A. (2006) 'Realigning the Corporate Building Blocks: Shareholder Proposals as a Vehicle for Achieving Corporate Social and Human Rights Accountability', *American Business Law Journal*, 43(2): 365–412.

Donnay, A. (1998) *Overlapping Disorders: Chronic fatigue syndrome, fibromyalgia syndrome, multiple chemical sensitivity and Gulf War syndrome*, Baltimore, MD: MCS Referral and Resources.

—— (1999) *Poisoned Poe: Evidence that Poe may have suffered from Neurasthenia (aka MCS and CFS) as a result of exposure to illuminating Gas.* Paper presented at the Edgar Allen Poe Conference Richmond, VA.

Donohoe, M. (2005) *MCS – A Medical Perspective.* Available online at: www.members.ozemail.com.au/~actall/A%20Medical%20Perspective.htm (accessed 5 September 2006).

Donohoe, M. and Cullen, M. R. (2007) 'Air Emissions from Wagerup Alumina Refinery', *Journal of Occupational and Environmental Medicine*, 49(9): 1027–1039.

Draper, E. (1991) *Risky Business: Genetic Testing and Exclusionary Practices in The Hazardous Workplace,* Cambridge: Cambridge University Press.

—— (2000) 'Competing Conceptions of Safety: High-risk workers or high-risk work?' in S. Kroll-Smith, N. Brown and V. J. Gunter (eds) *Illness and the Environment: A reader in contested medicine*, New York: New York University Press, 193–214.

Dryzek, J. S. (2002) *Deliberative Democracy and Beyond: Liberals, critics, contestations*, Oxford: Oxford University Press.

Dumit, J. (2006) 'Illnesses You Have to Fight to Get: Facts as forces uncertain, emergent illnesses', *Social Science and Medicine*, 62(3): 577–590.

Durkin, T. and Felstiner, W.L. (1994) 'Bad Arithmetic: Disaster Litigation as Less Than the Sum of Its Parts', in S. Jasanoff (ed.) *Learning From Disaster: Risk management after Bhopal*, Philadelphia, PA: University of Pennsylvania Press, 158–179.

Ecks, S. (2008) 'Three Propositions for an Evidence-Based Medical Anthropology', *Journal of the Royal Anthropology Institute*, S77–S92.

Edmond, G. and Mercer, D. (2004) 'Daubert and the Exclusionary Ethos: The convergence of corporate and judicial attitudes towards the admissibility of expert evidence in tort litigation', *Law and Policy*, 26(2): 231–257.

Ehrlich, P. R. and Ehrlich, A. H. (1996) *Betrayal of Science and Reason: How anti-environmental rhetoric threatens our future*, Covelo, CA: Sheerwater Books.

Einarsson, N. (1993) 'All Animals Are Equal But Some Are Cetaceans: Conservation and culture conflict', in K. Milton (ed.) *Environmentalism: The view from anthropology*, London: Routledge, 18–30.

Eisenberg, L. (1977) 'Disease and Illness: Distinctions between professional and popular ideas of sickness', *Culture, Medicine and Psychiatry*, 1(1): 9–23.

Eltiti, S., Wallace, D., Zougkou, K., Russo, R., Joseph, S., Rasor, P. and Fox, E. (2007) 'Development and evaluation of the electromagnetic hypersensitivity questionnaire', *Bioelectromagnetics*, 28(2): 137–151.

Engel, C. C., Adkins, J. A. and Cowan, D. N. (2002) 'Caring for Medically Unexplained Physical Symptoms After Toxic Environmental Exposures: Effects of contested causation', *Environmental Health Perspectives*, 110: 641–647.

Epstein, R. A. (1982) 'The Historical Origins and Economic Structure of Workers' Compensation Law', *Georgia Law Review*, 16: 775–820.

Epstein, S. (1995) 'The Construction of Lay Expertise: AIDS Activism and the Forging of Credibility in the Reform of Clinical Trials', *Science, Technology, and Human Values*, 20(4): 408–437.

—— (1997) 'AIDS Activism and the Retreat from the 'Genocide' Frame', *Social Identities*, 3(3): 415–438.

Ericson, R. and Doyle, A. (2004) *Uncertain Business: Risk, Insurance, and the Limits of Knowledge*, Toronto: University of Toronto Press.

Ericson, R., Doyle, A. and Barry, D. (2003) *Insurance as Governance*, Toronto: University of Toronto Press.

Erin Brockovich (2000) USA, directed by Steven Soderbergh, written by Susannah Grant.

Evans, G. W. and Kantrowitz, E. (2002) 'Socioeconomic status and health: The potential role of environmental risk exposure', *Annual Review of Public Health*, 23: 303–331.

Farboud, A., Crunkhorn, R. and Trinidad, A. (2013) 'Wind turbine syndrome: fact or fiction?' *The Journal of Laryngology and Otology*, 1 of 5. Available online at: www.docs.wind-watch.org/WTS-fact-or-fiction-JLO.pdf (accessed 1 July 2013).

Fisher, J. (2008) *Medical Research for Hire: The Political Economy of Pharmaceutical Clinical Trials*, New Brunswick, NJ: Rutgers University Press.

Flear, M. L. and Vakulenko, A. (2010) 'Human Rights Perspective on Citizen Participation in the EU's Governance of New Technologies', *Human Rights Law Review*, 10(4): 661–688.

Fleming, N. (2007) 'Warning on Wi-Fi health risk to children' *The Telegraph*, 24 April 2007. Available online at: www.telegraph.co.uk/news/uknews/1549944/Warning-on-wi-fi-health-risk-to-children.html (accessed 9 July 2013).

Floyd, H. H. (1999) 'Seeking Legitimacy: The Pilgrimage of Those Claiming to Have Multiple Chemical Sensitivity', in K. N. Anchor and T. C. Felicetti (eds) *Disability Analysis in Practice: Fundamental tools for an interdisciplinary science*, Kendall: Hunt Publishing.

Fortun, K. (2001) *Advocacy after Bhopal: Environmentalism, disaster, new global orders*, Chicago: University of Chicago Press.

Foucault, M. (1973) *Birth of the Clinic*, London: Tavistock.

—— (1976) 'Two Lectures', in C. Gordon (ed.) (1980) *Power/Knowledge: Interviews and Other writings 1972–1977 by Michel Foucault*, New York: Pantheon Books, 79–108.

—— (1977) *Discipline and Punish: The Birth of the Prison*, New York: Random House.

—— (1980) 'The eye of power', in C. Gordon (ed.) *Power/Knowledge: Selected Interviews and Other Writings 1972–1977 by Michel Foucault*, Sussex: Harvester Press, 146–165.

—— (1991) 'Governmentality', trans. Rosi Braidotti and revised by C. Gordon, in G. Burchell, C. Gordon and P. Miller (eds) *The Foucault Effect: Studies in Governmentality*, Chicago, IL: University of Chicago Press, 87–104.

Fox, R. C. (1959) *Experiment Perilous: Physicians and patients facing the unknown*, Glencoe, IL: Free Press.

—— (2000) 'Medical Uncertainty Revisited', in G. L. Albrecht, R. Fitzpatrick and S. C. Scrimshaw (eds) *The Handbook of Social Studies in Health and Medicine*, London: Sage Publications, 409–425.

Frank, A. (1995) *The Wounded Storyteller: Body, Illness and Ethics*, Chicago, IL: University of Chicago Press.

Frank, J. (1974) 'The Judging Process and the Judge's Personality', in J. J. Bonsignore, E. Katsh, P. d'Errico, R. M. Pipkin and S. Arons (eds) *Before the Law: An introduction to the Legal Process*, Atlanta, GA: Houghton Mifflin Company, 70–77.

Friedman, M. (1999) *Reconsidering Logical Positivism*, New York: Cambridge University Press.

Freidson, E. (1970) *Profession of Medicine*, New York: Dodd Mead.

—— (1986) *Professional Powers: A study of the institutionalisation of formal knowledge*, London: University of Chicago Press.

Fry, H. J. H. (1985) 'Over-use Injury (or RSI) – it's been around since Shakespeare's day', *Australian Law News*, 20: 28–33.

Fudge, J. (2007) 'Eating Crow: The Emergence of a Charter Right for Workers and Unions to Engage in Collective Activities', *The Court (Blog Archive)*. Available online at: www.thecourt.ca/2007/06/20/my-court/ (accessed 5 May 2013).

Fudge, J. and Glasbeek, H. (1992) 'The Politics of Rights: a politics with little class', *Social and Legal Studies*, 1: 45–70.

Gadiel, D. and Sammut, J. (2012) 'How the NSW Government Should Govern Health: Strategies for micro-economic reform' *Papers in Health and Aging*.

Available online at: www.cis.org.au/images/stories/policy-monographs/pm-128.pdf (accessed 20 June, 2014).

Galanter, M. (1994) 'The Transnational Traffic in Legal Remedies', in S. Jasanoff (ed.) *Learning From Disaster: Risk Management After Bhopal*, Philadelphia, PA: University of Pennsylvania Press, 133–157.

Gandjour, A. and Lauterbach, K. W. (2003) 'Inductive Reasoning in Medicine: Lessons from Carl Gustav Hempel's 'inductive-statistical' model', *Journal of Evaluation in Clinical Practice*, 9(2): 161–169.

Garland, D. (2002) *The Culture of Control: Crime and social order in contemporary society*, Oxford: Oxford University Press.

Gaskins, R. H. (1989) *Environmental Accidents: Personal Injury and Public Responsibility*, Philadelphia, PA: Temple University Press.

—— (1992) *Burdens of Proof in Modern Discourse*, Binghampton, NY: Vail-Ballou Press.

Genn, H. (1987) *Hard Bargaining: Out of court settlement in personal injury actions*, Oxford: Clarendon Press.

Gibson, D. (2000) 'Mandatory madness: the true story of the Northern Territory's mandatory sentencing laws', *Alternative Law Journal*, 25(3): 103–107.

Gibson, P. R. (1997) 'Culture and Delegitimization: A feminist analysis', *Feminism and Psychology*, 4(4): 475–493.

—— (2010) 'Of the World But Not In It: Barriers to Community Access and Education for Persons with Environmental Sensitivities.' *Health Care for Women International*, 31: 3–16.

Giddens, A. (1990) *The Consequences of Modernity*, Cambridge: Polity Press.

Glasbeek, H. (2002) *Wealth by Stealth: Corporate Crime, Corporate Law and the perversion of democracy*, Toronto: Between the Lines.

Godfrey-Smith, P. (2003) *Theory and Reality: An Introduction to the Philosophy of Science*, Chicago, IL: University of Chicago Press.

Goklany, I. M. (2001) *The Precautionary Principle: A critical appraisal of environmental risk assessment*, Washington DC: Cato Institute.

Good, A. (2008) 'Cultural Evidence in Courts of Law', *Journal of the Royal Anthropological Institute*, 14.S1: S47–S60.

Gordon C. (ed.) (1980) *Power/Knowledge: Selected Interviews and Other Writings 1972–1977 by Michel Foucault.* Sussex: Harvester Press, 146–165.

—— (1991) 'Governmental rationality: an introduction.' *The Foucault effect: Studies in governmentality*, 1: 52.

Gordon, D. (1988) 'The Tenacious Assumptions of Modern Medicine', in M. Lock and D. Gordon (eds) *Biomedicine Examined*, Boston, MA: Kluwer Academic Publishers, 19–56.

Gordon, R. L. (1998) 'No Balm in Gilead: Why workers' compensation fails workers in a toxic age ', in B. L. Matthews (ed.) *Defining Multiple Chemical Sensitivity*, Jefferson, NC: McFarland & Company Inc. Publishers.

Graham, J. D. and Weiner, J. B. (1995) *Risk vs. risk tradeoffs in protecting public health and the environment*, Cambridge: Harvard University Press.

Grant, G. M. and Studdert, D. M. (2013) 'The Injury Brokers: An empirical profile of medical expert witnesses in personal injury litigation', *Melbourne University Law Review*, 36: 831–870.

Grant, G. M., O'Donnell, M., Spittal, M. J., Creamer, M. and Studdert, D. M. (2014) 'Relationship Between Stressfulness of Claiming for Injury Compensation and Long-term Recovery: A prospective cohort study', *JAMA Psychiatry*, 71(4): 446–453.

Greer, C. (2007) 'News Media, Victims and Crime', in P. Davies, P. Francis and C. Greer (eds) *Victims, Crime and Society*, Sage Publications: London, 21–25.

Greer, J. and Bruno, K. (1996) *Greenwash: The reality behind corporate environmentalism*, Penang: Third World Network.

Gribbin, C. (2013) 'New Bill Introduced in WA for Asbestos Victims', Available online at: www.abc.net.au/worldtoday/content/2013/s3882002.htm (accessed 9 April, 2014).

Grossman, E. (2006) *High Tech Trash: Digital Devices, Hidden Toxics, and Human Health*, Washington DC: Island Press.

Hage, G. (1998) *White Nation*, London: Pluto.

Halton, D. M. (1988) 'A Comparison of the Concepts used to Develop and Apply Occupational Exposure Limits and Ionizing Radiation and Hazardous Chemical Substances', *RegulToxicolPharmacol*, 8: 343–355.

Hamilton, J. (1995) 'Testing for environmental racism: Prejudice, profits, political power?' *Journal of Policy Analysis and Management*, 14(1): 107–132.

Hanrahan v. Merck, Sharp And Dohme (1988) Supreme Court of Ireland, ILRM 629.

Harr, J. (1996) *A Civil Action*, New York: Vintage.

Hausteiner, C., Mergeay, A., Bornschein, S., Zilker, T. and Forstl, H. (2006) 'New Aspects of Psychiatric Morbidity in Idiopathic Environmental Intolerances', *Journal of Occupational and Environmental Medicine*, 48(1): 76–82.

Hempel, S. (2007) *The Strange Case of the Broad Street Pump: John Snow and the Mystery of Cholera*, Berkeley, CA: University of California Press.

Henry, N. (2013) 'Memory of an Injustice: The "comfort women" and the legacy of the Tokyo trial, *Asian Studies Review*: 1–19.

Herman, D. (1993) 'Beyond the Rights Debate', *Social and Legal Studies*, 2: 25–43.

Hershkoff, H. and Cohen, A. S. (1991) 'Begging to Differ: The First Amendment and the Right to Beg', *Harvard Law Review*, 104: 896–916.

Hess, D. J. (2005) 'Medical Modernisation, Scientific Research Fields and the Epistemic Politics of Health Social Movements', in P. Brown and S. Zavestoski (eds) *Social Movements in Health*, Malden: Blackwell Publishing, 17–30.

Hillert, L., Berglind, N., Arnetz, B. B., and Bellander, T. (2002) 'Prevalence of self-reported hypersensitivity to electric or magnetic fields in a population-based questionnaire survey', *Scandinavian Journal of Work and Environmental Health*, 28(1): 33–41.

Hills, B. (1989) *Blue Murder: The shocking truth behind Wittenoom's deadly dust*, Sydney: Sun Books.

Hojo, S., Kumano, H., Yoshino, H., Kakuta, K. and Ishikawa, S. (2003) 'Application of Quick Environment Exposure Sensitivity Inventory (QEESI) for Japanese population: study of reliability and validity of the questionnaire', *Toxicology and Industrial Health*, 19(2)–6: 41–49.

Hood, C. C. (1996) 'Where extremes meet: "SPRAT" versus "SHARK" in public risk management', in C. Hood and D. K. C. Jones (eds) *Accident and Design: Contemporary debates in risk management*, London: UCL Press, 208–228.

Hooper, C. (2008) *The Tall Man: Death and Life on Palm Island*, Sydney: Penguin.

Horwitz, A. V. and Wakefield, J. C. (2007) *The Loss of Sadness: How psychiatry transformed normal sorrow into depressive disorder*, Oxford: Oxford University Press.

Huber, P. W. (1991) *Galileo's Revenge: Junk Science in the Courtroom*, New York, NY: Basic Books.

Huibers, M. J. H. and Wessley, S. (2006) 'The Act of Diagnosis: Pros and cons of labelling chronic fatigue syndrome', *Psychological Medicine*, 36: 895–900.

Ireland, P. (2010) 'Limited liability, shareholder rights and corporate irresponsibility' *Cambridge Journal of Economics*, 34(5): 837–856.

Jasanoff, S. (1995) *Science at the Bar: Law, science and technology in America*, Massachusetts: Harvard University Press.

—— (1997) 'Civilization and madness: the great BSE scare of 1996', *Public Understanding of Science*, 6: 221–232.

Joffres, M. R., Williams, T., Sabo, B. and Fox, R. A. (2001) 'Environmental sensitivities: prevalence of major symptoms in a referral center: the Nova Scotia environmental sensitivities research center study', *Environmental Health Perspectives*, 109(2): 161–165. Available online at: www.ncbi.nlm.nih.gov/pmc/articles/PMC1240637/ pdf/ehp0109-000161.pdf (accessed 26 June 2013).

Johansson, O. (2006) *Electrosensitivity recognized in Sweden* Available online at: www.weepinitiative.org/LINKEDDOCS/World%20commentary/emf-hypersensitivity_recognized_in_Sweden_0906.pdf (accessed 22 March 2013).

Johnson v. Harper and Ors t/as Allambie Pastoral Company (1997) no. R400074/93, Supreme Court of New South Wales.

Karmel, P. E. (2008) 'Toxic Torts: The threshold limit values controversy ', *The New York Law Journal*, 3 January 2008. Available online at: www.bryancave.com/files/Publication/a8aaf076-474e-47bd-8a69-426333fb4de0/Presentation/PublicationAttachment/43b87c11-6094-4af6-995f-44af2ece1ec6/ToxicTorts-1-3-08.pdf (accessed 6 August 2009).

Katz, J. (1984) *The Silent World of Doctor and Patient*, New York: Free Press.

King, M., Freiberg, A., Bagatol, B. and Hyams, R. (2009) *Non-adversarial Justice*, Canberra: Federation Press.

Kirby, M. (2008) 'Expert Evidence: Causation, proof and presentation: Law in the world of science and technology', *Judicial Review*, 2008. 8 February 2008. Available online at: www.hcourt.gov.au/speeches/kirbyj/kirbyj_expert.htm (accessed 8 February 2008).

Klawiter, M. (2005) 'Breast Cancer in Two Regimes: The impact of social movements on illness experience', in P. Brown and S. Zavestoski (eds) *Social Movements in Health*, Malden: Blackwell Publishing, 161–189.

Kleinman, A. (1980) *Patients and Healers in the Context of Culture: An exploration of the borderland between anthropology, medicine and psychiatry*, Berkeley, CA: University of California Press.

—— (1983) 'The Cultural Meanings and Social Uses of Illness', *Journal of Family Practice*, 16(3): 539–545.

—— (1995) *Writing at the Margin: Discourse between Anthropology and Medicine*, London: University of California Press.

Koch, T. (2003) 'Curfews: Aboriginal Legal Service of Western Australia', *Indigenous Law Bulletin*, 54.

Kroll-Smith, S. (2001) 'Appendix A: A sociologist's view', in G. McCormick (ed.) *Living with Multiple Chemical Sensitivity: Narratives of coping*, Jefferson, NC: McFarland & Co., 260–261.

Kroll-Smith, S. and Floyd, H. (1997) *Bodies in Protest: Environmental illness and the struggle over medical knowledge*, New York: New York University Press.

Krygier, M. (1980) 'Law in Society: Anthropological Approaches', in E. Kamenka and A. Erh-Soon Tay (eds) *Law and Social Control*, London: Edward Arnold.

Kuhn, T. (1962) *The Structure of Scientific Revolutions*, Chicago, IL: University of Chicago Press.

Lakatos, I. (1976) *Proofs and Refutations*, Cambridge: Cambridge University Press.

Lander, E. S. and Budowle, B. (1994) 'DNA Fingerprinting Dispute Laid to Rest', *Nature*, 371: 735–738.

Larkin, M. (1998) 'Elaine Showalter: hysteria's historian' *The Lancet*, 351.9116: 1638.

Larner, W. (2000) 'Neo-liberalism: Policy, ideology, governmentality.' *Studies in Political Economy*, 63, 5–26.

—— (2006) 'Review of A Brief History of Neoliberalism', *Economic Geography*, 82: 449–451.

Latour, B. and Woolgar, S. (1979) *Laboratory Life: The social construction of scientific fact*, Beverley Hills, CA: Sage Publications.

Laudel, G. (2006) 'The art of getting funded: how scientists adapt to their funding conditions', *Science and Public Policy*, 33(7): 489–504.

Law Council of Australia (2008) 'Submission to Clark Inquiry into the case of Dr Mohamed Haneef', *Law Council of Australia*, Available online at: www.lawcouncil.asn.au/lawcouncil/images/LCA-PDF/a-z-docs/LawCouncilSubmissiontoHaneefInquiry-Final.pdf (accessed 20 April 2012).

Lea, T. (2008) *Bureaucrats and Bleeding Hearts: Indigenous Health and Northern Australia*, Sydney: UNSW Press.

Lean, G. (2007) 'Germany warns citizens to avoid using Wi-Fi' *The Independent*, 9 September 2007. Available online at: www.independent.co.uk/environment/green-living/germany-warns-citizens-to-avoid-using-wifi-401845.html (accessed 1 July 2013).

Lewontin, R. C. and Hartl, D. L. (1991) 'Population genetics in forensic DNA typing', *Science*, 254.5039: 1745–1750.

Lipson, J. G. (2001) 'We are the canaries: Self-care in multiple chemical sensitivity sufferers', *Qualitative Health Research*, 11(1): 103–116.

—— (2004) 'Multiple Chemical Sensitivities: Stigma and Social Experiences', *Medical Anthropology Quarterly*, 18(2): 200–213.

Lofstedt, R., Bouderb, F., Wardmanc, J. and Chakrabortyd, S. (2011) 'The changing nature of communication and regulation of risk in Europe', *Journal of Risk Research*, 14(4): 409–429.

Lumb, R. D. (1993) 'The Mabo Case – Public Law Aspects', in M.A. Stephenson and S. Ratnapala (eds) *Mabo: A Judiciul Revolution*, Brisbane: University of Queensland Press.

Lupton, D. (1994) *Medicine as Culture: Illness, disease and the body in Western society*, London: Sage Publications.

—— (1995) *The Imperative of Health: Public Health and the Regulated Body*, London: Sage Publications.

Lynch, A. and Williams, G. (2006) *What Price Security?: Taking Stock of Australia's Anti-Terror Laws*, Kensington: University of New South Wales Press.

Lynch, M., Cole, S. A., McNally, R. and Jordan, K. (2010) *Truth Machine: The contentious history of DNA fingerprinting*, Chicago, IL: University of Chicago Press.

Marshall, B. J. (2005) *Barry J. Marshall: Biographical.* Available online at: www.nobelprize.org/nobel_prizes/medicine/laureates/2005/marshall-bio.html.

McCluskey, M. T. (1997) 'The Illusion of Efficiency in Workers' Compensation "Reform"', *Rutgers Law Review*, 50: 657–942.

McCormick, S. (2009) *Mobilizing Science: Movements, participation and the remaking of knowledge*, Philadelphia, PA: Temple University Press.

McCoy, D., Chand, S. and Sridhar, D. (2009) 'Global health funding: how much, where it comes from and where it goes', *Health Policy and Planning*, 24(6): 407–417.

McKenzie, Johnson and Tiedemann v. Harper and Ors T/as Allambie Pastoral Company (1997) no. R400073/93, Supreme Court of New South Wales.

MacLachlan, J. (1997) *Galileo Galilei: First Physicist*, Oxford: Oxford University Press.

Marx, K. (1843) 'On the Jewish Question', *Deutsch-Französische Jahrbücher*.

Melnick, R. M. (2005) 'A Daubert Motion: A legal strategy to exclude essential scientific evidence in toxic tort litigation', *American Journal of Public Health*, 95.S1: S30–S34.

Mendelson, D. (1998) *The Interfaces of Medicine and the Law: The history of liability for negligently caused psychiatric injury (nervous shock)*, Aldershot: Ashgate.

Merewether, E. R. A. and Price, C. W. (1930) *Report on Effects of Asbestos Dust on the Lung*, United Kingdom: H.M. Stationery Office.

Merlan, F. (1995) 'The Regimentation of Customary Practice: From Northern Territory land claims to Mabo', *The Australian Journal of Anthropology*, 6(1–2): 64–82.

Michaels, D. (2005) 'Doubt is Their Product', *Scientific American*, 292(6): 96–101.

Michaels, D. and Monforton, C. (2005) 'Manufacturing Uncertainty: Contested science and the protection of the public's health and environment', *American Journal of Public Health*, 95: S39–S48.

Moore, S. F. (1973) 'Law and Social Change: The semi-autonomous social field as an appropriate subject of study', *Law and Society Review*, 7(4): 719–746.

Monshipouri, M., Welch, C. E., and Kennedy, E. T. (2003) 'Multinational Corporations and the Ethics of Global Responsibility: Problems and Possibilities', *Human Rights Quarterly*, 25(4): 965–989.

Moses, A. D. (2011) 'Official apologies, reconciliation, and settler colonialism: Australian indigenous alterity and political agency', *Citizenship Studies*, 15(2): 145–159.

Muehlebach, A. (2012) *The Moral Neoliberal: Welfare and Citizenship in Italy*, Chicago, IL: University of Chicago Press.

Murphy, M. (2006) *Sick Building Syndrome and the Problem of Uncertainty: Environmental Politics, Technoscience, and Women Workers*, Durham: Duke University Press.

Nadeau, G. and Lippel, K. (2014) 'From individual coping strategies to illness codification: What place for a gender lens in the social study of Multiple Chemical

Sensitivities (MCS)? A literature review', *International Journal of Equity in Health* 13(78). Available online at: www.equityhealthj.com/content/13/1/78#ack (accessed 17 October, 2014).

Niemeyer, L. O. (1991) 'Social Labelling, Stereotyping, and Observer Bias in Worker's Compensation: The impact of provider-patient interaction on outcome', *Journal of Occupational Rehabilitation*, 1(4): 251–269.

Osborne, D. (2009) 'Pathways into bullying'. *Asia Pacific Conference on Educational Integrity* (4APCEI).

Pakulski, J. and Crook, S. (1998) 'Introduction', *Ebbing of the Green Tide: Environmentalism, public opinion and the media in Australia'* eds J. Pakulski and S. Crook, Hobart: School of Sociology and Social Work, 1–20.

Pall, M. L. (2007) *Explaining 'Unexplained Illnesses': Disease Paradigm for Chronic Fatigue Syndrome, Multiple Chemical Sensitivity, Fibromyalgia, Post-Traumatic Stress Disorder, and Gulf War Syndrome,* Binghamton, NY: Harrington Park Press.

Parker, C. (2004) 'A Critical Morality for Lawyers: Four approaches to lawyer's ethics', *Monash University Law Review*, 30(1): 49–74.

Parsons, T. (1951) *The Social System*, Chicago, IL: Free Press.

Pearce, F. and Tombs, S. (1998) *Toxic Capitalism: Corporate Crime and the Chemical Industry*, Aldershot: Ashgate.

—— (2000) 'Questions of risk and regulation: Hegemony, governance and the US chemical industry', in E. Coles, D. Smith and S. Tombs (eds) *Risk Management and Society*, London: Kluwer Academic Publishers, 165–187.

Pearson, S. D. (2000) 'Caring and Cost: The challenge for physician advocacy', *Annals of Internal Medicine*, 133(2): 149–153.

Peck, J. and Tickell, A. (2002) 'Neoliberalizing Space' *Antipode*, 34: 380–404.

Pols, J. (2013) 'Knowing Patients: Turning Patient Knowledge into Science', *Science, Technology and Human Values*.

Popper, K. (1963) *Conjectures and Refutations*, London: Routledge and Keagan Paul.

Porter, T. M. (1995) *Trust in Numbers: The Pursuit of Objectivity in Science and Social Life*.

Povinelli, E. (1998) 'The state of shame: Australian multiculturalism and the crisis of indigenous citizenship', *Critical Inquiry*, 24: 575–610.

—— (2002) *The Cunning of Recognition: Indigenous Alterities and the Making of Australian Multiculturalism*, Durham: Duke University Press.

Prior, L. (2003) 'Belief, Knowledge and Expertise: The emergence of the lay expert in medical sociology', *Sociology of Health and Illness*, 25(3): 41–57.

Radetsky, P. and Phillips, B. (1997) *Allergic to the Twentieth Century: The explosion of environmental allergies: from sick buildings to multiple chemical sensitivity*, New York: Little Brown and Company.

Raffensperger, C. and Tickner, J. (1999) *Protecting Public Health and the Environment: Implementing The Precautionary Principle*, Washington DC: Island Press.

Ramsay, I. and Noakes, D. B. (2001) 'Piercing the Corporate Veil in Australia', *Company and Securities Law Journal*, 19: 250–271.

Rayner, M. (2003) 'Northbridge Curfew', *Indigenous Law Bulletin*, 56.

Reid, J. and Reynolds, L. (1990) 'Requiem for RSI: The explanation and control of an occupational epidemic', *Medical Anthropology Quarterly*, 4(2): 162–190.

Reid, J., Ewan, C. and Lowy, E. (1991) 'Pilgrimage of Pain: The illness experiences of women with repetition strain injury and the search for credibility', *Social Science and Medicine*, 32(5): 601–612.

Renwick, J. (2007) 'Counter Terrorism and Australian Law', *Security Challenges*, 3.3: 67–77.

Roberts, A. (2005) 'The "war on terror" in historical perspective', *Survival*, 47(2): 101–130.

Romanucci-Ross, L. and Moerman, D. E. (1991) 'The Extraneous Factor in Western Medicine', in L. Romanucci-Ross, D. E. Moerman and L. R. Tancredi (eds) *The Anthropology of Medicine: From culture to method*, New York: Bergin and Garvey, 351–369.

Romanucci-Ross, L. and Tancredi, L. R. (2007) *When Law and Medicine Meet: A cultural view*, New York: Springer Science.

Rose, N. (1996a) 'Psychiatry as a political science: advanced liberalism and the administration of risk', *History of the Human Sciences*, 9(2): 1–23.

—— (1996b) 'Governing "Advanced" Liberal Democracies', in A. Barry, T. Osborne and N. Rose (eds) *Foucault and Political Reason: Liberalism, Neoliberalism, and Rationalities of Government*, Chicago, IL: University of Chicago Press.

—— (2000) 'Government and Control' in D. Garland and R. Sparks (eds) *Criminology and Social Theory*, Oxford: Oxford University Press, 183–208.

—— (2007) *The politics of life itself: Biomedicine, power and subjectivity in the twenty-first century*. Woodstock, NJ.: Princeton University Press.

Rosenberg, C. E. (1992) 'Framing Disease: Illness, society and history', in C. E. Rosenberg and J. L. Golden (eds) *Framing Disease: Studies in cultural history*, New Brunswick, NJ: Rutgers University Press, xiii-1.

Saks, M. J. and Koehler, J. J. (2005) 'The Coming Paradigm Shift in Forensic Identification Science', *Science*, 309(5736): 892–895.

Satterfield, T. (2002) *Anatomy of a Conflict: Identity, knowledge and emotion in old-growth forests*, Vancouver: UBC Press.

Scheppele, K. L. (1995) 'Manners of Imagining the Real', *Law and Social Inquiry*, 995–1022.

—— (2010) 'Liberalism against neoliberalism: resistance to structural adjustment and the fragmentation of the state in Russia and Hungary', in C.J. Greenhouse (ed.) *Ethnographies of Neoliberalism*, Philadelphia, PA: University of Pennsylvania Press.

Schuck, P. H. (1987) *Agent Orange on Trial: Mass toxic disasters in the courts*, Cambridge: Harvard University Press.

Schofield, T. (2012) 'Gender, Health, Research and Public Policy' In *Designing and Conducting Gender, Sex and Health Research*. Edited by Oliffe, J. L. and Greaves, L. London: Sage Publications, 203–214.

Sears, M. E. (2007) *The Medical Perspective on Environmental Sensitivities*. Ottawa: Canadian Human Rights Commission.

Segal, L. (1991) 'Feminism and the Future', *New Left Review*, 185: 81–91.

Shapiro, B. (1991) *'Beyond Reasonable Doubt' and 'Probable Cause'*, Berkeley, CA: University of California Press.

Sharpe, M. and Carson, A. (2001) '"Unexplained" Somatic Symptoms, Functional Syndromes, and Somatization: Do we need a paradigm shift?' *Annals of Internal Medicine*, 134.9 (Part 2) Supplement: 926–930.

Shearer, C. (2011) *Kivalina: A Climate Change Story*, Chicago, IL: Haymarket Books.

Short, D. (2008) *Reconciliation and Colonial Power: Indigenous Rights in Australia,* Aldershot: Ashgate.

Showalter, E. (1997) *Hystories: Hysterical epidemics and the modern media,* New York: Columbia University Press.

Shrivastava, P. (1987) *Bhopal: Anatomy of a crisis,* Cambridge: Ballinger.

Sim, J. (2010) 'Thinking about state violence', *Criminal Justice Matters,* 82(1): 6–7.

Slapper, G and Tombs, S. (1999) *Corporate Crime,* London: Longman.

Smart, C. (1989) *Feminism and the Power of Law,* London: Routledge.

Smallman, C. (2000) 'Challenging the Orthodoxy in Risk Management: The need for a paradigm shift?' in E. Coles, D. Smith and S. Tombs (eds) *Risk Management and Society,* London: Kluwer Academic Publishers, 53–80.

Snell, C. R., Stevens, S. R., Davenport, T. E. and Van Ness, J. M. (2013) 'Discriminative Validity of Metabolic and Workload Measurements for Identifying People with Chronic Fatigue Syndrome', *Physical Therapy,* 93: 1484–1492.

South Australian Health Department (SA Health) (2010). *Guidelines for South Australian Hospitals: Multiple Chemical Sensitivity.* Available online at: www.sahealth.sa.gov.au/wps/wcm/connect/a7da1b004754557a8a71fa2e504170d4/MultipleChemicalSensitivity-PHCS-1107.pdf?MOD=AJPERES&CACHEID=a7da1b004754557a8a71fa2e504170d4 (accessed 1 July 2013).

Stauber, J. and Rampton, S. (1995) *Toxic Sludge is Good for You!: Lies damn lies and the public relations industry,* Monroe, ME: Common Courage Press.

Staudenmayer, H. (1999) *Environmental Illness: Myth and reality,* Boca Raton, FL: Lewis Publishers.

Strang, V. (2004) 'Raising the Dead: Reflections on native title process', in S. Toussaint (ed.) *Crossing Boundaries: Cultural, legal, historical and practice issues in native title,* Melbourne: Melbourne University Press, 9–23.

Stychin, C. F. (2008) 'Faith in Rights: the struggle over same- sex adoption in the United Kingdom', *Constitutional Forum Constitutionelle,* 17.1: 7–15.

Sunstein, C. R. (2005) *Laws of Fear: Beyond The Precautionary Principle,* Cambridge: Cambridge University Press.

Thornton, M. (1990) *The Liberal Promise: Anti-discrimination legislation in Australia,* New York: Oxford University Press.

Tiedemann v. Harper and Ors t/as Allambie Pastoral Company (1997) no. R400074/93, Supreme Court of New South Wales.

Timmermans, S. and Berg, M. (2003) *The Gold Standard: The challenge of evidence-based medicine and standardization in health-care* Philadelphia, PA: Temple University Press.

Tishelman, C. and Sachs, L. (1998) 'The diagnostic process and the boundaries of normal', *Qualitative Health Research,* 8(1): 48–60.

Travis, G. D. L. and Collins, H. M. (1991) 'New light on old boys: cognitive and institutional particularism in the peer review system', *Science, Technology and Human Values,* 16(3): 322–341.

Trimble, M. R. (1981) *Post-traumatic neurosis: from railway spine to the whiplash,* Chichester; New York: Wiley.

Trundle, C. (2011) 'Biopolitical endpoints: diagnosing a deserving British nuclear test veteran', *Social Science and Medicine,* 73(6): 882–888.

Vakas, N. (2007) 'Interests and the Shaping of an Occupational Health and Safety Controversy: The BAe 146 case', PhD Thesis, University of Woollongong. Research Available online at: www.ro.uow.edu.au/theses/76.

Van Den Bergh, O., Devriese, S., Winters, W., Veulemans, H., Nemery, B., Eelen, P. and VandeWoestijne, K. P. (2001) 'Acquiring Symptoms in Response to Odors: A learning perspective on multiple chemical sensitivity', *Annals of the New York Academy of Sciences*, 933: 278–290.

Van Diest, I., De Peuter, S., Piedfort, K., Bresseleers, J., Devriese, S., Van de Woestijne, K. P. and Van den Bergh, O. (2006) 'Acquired Lightheadedness in Response to Odors after Hyperventilation', *Psychosomatic Medicine*, 68: 340-347.

Wacquant, L. (2009) *Punishing the Poor: The Neoliberal Government of Social Insecurity* Durham: Duke University Press

Waldman, L. (2011) *The Politics of Asbestos: Understandings of Risk, Disease and Protest*, London: Earthscan.

Walmsley, H. (2009) 'Biobanking, Public Consultation and the Discursive Logics of Deliberation: Five lessons from British Columbia', *Public Understanding of Science*, 1–17.

Ware, N. C. (1992) 'Suffering and the Social Construction of Illness: The deligitimation of illness experience in Chronic Fatigue Syndrome', *Medical Anthropology Quarterly*, 6(4): 347–361.

Weiner, J. (2003) 'The Law of the Land: A review article', *The Australian Journal of Anthropology*, 14(1): 97–110.

Weisbrot, D. (1990) *Australian Lawyers*, Melbourne: Longman Professional.

Wessely, S., M. Hotopf, and M. Sharpe. (1998) *Chronic fatigue and its syndromes*, Oxford: Oxford University Press.

Westra, L. and Lawson, B. (2001) *Faces of Environmental Racism: Confronting issues of global justice*, Lanham, MD: Rowman and Littlefield Publishers.

Whyte, D. (2012) 'Victims of Corporate Crime' in *Handbook of Victims and Victimology*, S. Walklate, (ed.) Hobokken: Taylor and Francis: 446–463.

Widener, P. (2000) 'Lead Contamination in the 1990s and Beyond: A follow-up', in S. Kroll-Smith, P. Brown and V. J. Gunter (eds) *Illness and the Environment: A reader in contested medicine*, New York: New York University Press, 258–269.

Williams, D. D. R. and Garner, J. (2002) 'The Case against the 'Evidence'', *British Journal of Psychiatry*, 180: 8–12.

Willis, E. (1994) *Illness and Social Relations*, St Leonards, NSW: Allen & Unwin.

Willis, E. and Coulter, I. (2004) 'The Rise and Rise of Complementary and Alternative Medicine: A sociological perspective', *Medical Journal of Australia*, 180(11): 587–589.

Wignall v. State of New South Wales (Department of Education) (no. No 21198 of 1995)

Willis, E. and White, K. (2004) 'The Challenge of Evidence Based Medicine', in P. Tovey, J. Adams and G. Easthope (eds) *The Mainstreaming of Complementary and Alternative Medicine*, London: Routledge, 49–63.

Winder, C. (2002) 'Mechanisms of Multiple Chemical Sensitivity', *Toxicology Letters*, 128: 85–97.

Wing, S. (2000) 'Limits of Epidemiology', in S. Kroll-Smith, P. Brown and V. J. Gunter (eds) *Illness and the Environment: A reader in contested medicine*, New York: New York University Press, 29–45.

Winters, W., Devriese, S., Van Diest, I., Nemery, B., Veulemans, H., Eelen, P., Van de Woestijne, K. P., Van den Bergh, O. and Devriese, S. (2003) 'Media Warnings about Environmental Pollution Facilitate the Acquisition of Symptoms in Response to Chemical Substances', *Psychosomatic Medicine*, 65: 332–338.

Woelert, P. (2013) 'The "Economy of Memory": Publications, Citations, and the Paradox of Effective Research Governance', *Minerva*, 51: 341–362.

Wolfe, P. (1999) *Settler Colonialism and the Transformation of Anthropology*, London: Cassell.

WorkCover Western Australia (2001) *Stress, Compensation and the General Practitioner*. Available online at: www.workcover.wa.gov.au/NR/rdonlyres/ 2565A9BF-F39D-4C1F-B034-16AB94046BC3/0/Stress_Compensation_and_ the_GP_0307.pdf (accessed 13 November 2009).

—— (2007) Scheme Development Branch, *Report on Common Law Proceedings in Western Australia*. Available online at: www.workcover.wa.gov.au/NR/ rdonlyres/3B32BD59-4440-4BA8-854A-608F369479E6/0/Common_Law_Proc_ WA_0406.pdf (accessed 10 August 2009).

—— (2008) *Guides for the Evaluation of Permanent Impairment*. Available online at: www.workcover.wa.gov.au/NR/rdonlyres/640A12F8-6531-4515-9AD5- 4994E2B5F989/0/IRBWorkCoverWAGuidesfortheEvaluationofPermenantImpairm ent.pdf (accessed 10 August 2009).

—— (2014) *Welcome to WorkCover WA Website*. Available online at: www.workcover.wa.gov.au/Default.htm (accessed 13 August 2014).

WorkSafe Australia (1995) *Exposure Standards for Atmospheric Contaminants in the Occupational Environment: National exposure standards*. National Occupational Health and Safety Commission.

Wynne, B. (1996) 'May the Sheep Safely Graze?' in S. Lash, B. Szersynski and B. Wynne (eds) *Risk, Environment and Modernity*, London: Sage Publications.

Zavestoski, S., Brown, P., McCormick, S., Mayer, B., D'Ottavi, M. and Lucove, J. C. (2004a) 'Patient Activism and the Struggle for Diagnosis: Gulf War illness and other medically unexplained physical symptoms in the US', *Social Science and Medicine*, 58: 161–175.

Zavestoski, S., Morello-Frosch, R., Brown, P., Mayer, B. and McCormick, S. and Gasior, R. (2004b) 'Embodied Health Movements and Challenges to the Dominant Epidemiological Paradigm', *Research in Social Movements, Conflict and Change*, 25: 253–278.

Ziem, G. E. and Castleman, B. I. (2000) 'Threshold Limit Values: Historical perspectives and current practice', in S. Kroll-Smith, N. Brown and V. J. Gunter (eds) *Illness and the Environment: A reader in contested medicine*, New York: New York University Press: 120–134.

Index

Aboriginal and Torres Strait Islanders
32, 95, 154, 163, 165, 171–3
American College of Occupational and
Environmental Medicine 5
Ansett Australia 17
Australian Blue Asbestos Company
157–8, 161
Australian Chemical Trauma Alliance
133–4
accountability 5, 40, 41, 43, 52, 156,
159, 160, 180
activism 7–8, 9, 12, 46, 61, 148–9,
170–1, 173, 175
actuarial 37, 104–6, 108–9, 157–8, 162,
168
adversarialism 20, 80, 82–8, 97–100,
112–13, 140–5, 150–1, 168: non-
adversarial reforms 80, 146–7, 151,
176
advocacy: lay 7, 20, 67, 79; expert 120,
122, 128–34, 138–9
Agent Orange 6
asbestos companies 1, 157–8, 161
asbestos litigation 9, 39, 72, 158–61,
140, 169–71, 158
asbestos manufacturing process 1, 157
asbestos related diseases 1, 9, 13, 140,
157–61, 177
allergy 5, 11, 77, 134, 149
anxiety 3, 8, 14, 56–7, 83, 109, 127

barriers to recognition 6, 12, 13, 20–1,
47, 74, 99–100, 119, 130–4, 138–9,
142–4, 166, 167-9
Beck, U. 35, 153
Bhopal 6, 46, 155, 159, 173
biomedicine see medicine
black-box 111

breast cancer 7, 12, 46
Brown, P. 12, 35, 46, 51, 59, 61, 102,
132
Brown, W. 171–2
Brockovich, E. 7, 65, 128
bovine spongiform encephalopathy
(BSE) see mad cow disease
burden of proof 33, 37, 89–92, 93, 99,
164, 169, 180
burn-out 136–8

capitalism 19, 38, 39, 152, 155
Carson, R. 7
causation: lay explanations 59, 61, 117;
in the law 9, 12, 89, 93, 112–14,
115–18, 126, 180; in medical science
4–5, 27, 46, 52–5, 62, 101–3, 106,
126, 130, 141, 168, 177
change agent 27, 39, 61
chronic fatigue syndrome 4, 11–12, 18,
54, 86, 105, 121, 123, 142, 145–6,
148
class see socio-economic disparities
climate change 8, 29
clinical ecology 4–5, 121, 131, 134
closure: of scientific controversy 24, 26,
30–1, 46, 74; of personal conflict
70–1
Cole, S. 104, 169
Collins, H. M. 24, 31, 120, 132
common law 16, 82, 88, 89, 109–10,
112, 114–19, 137, 167, 178, 180
compensation: in asbestos litigation 1,
9, 140, 158, 160, 161; for Bhopal
victims 6, 159–60; for chemical
injuries xii, xiv, 3, 7, 8, 13, 49,
69–70, 98, 115, 122
consensus: about disease 55–6, 74, 90,

115, 118, 125, 127, 142, 168–9; about
risk 55–6, 74, 146, 154, 162, 165,
176, 180; consensus-reaching
strategies 145, 146, 150–1, 176, 180;
in a scientific paradigm 22–4, 26,
122–3, 125, 127, 168–9
corporate: accountability 5, 40, 41, 43,
52, 156, 159, 160, 180; deregulation
/freedom 38–9, 40, 43 177; influence
38, 40, 46, 99–100, 129, 159–61, 177;
social responsibility 47, 156, 159–60;
science 49–58, 74, 177
credibility: of lay activists 58, 60, 74; of
experts 35, 44, 63, 134, 136, 166,
168; of science and technology 24,
30, 35, 52, 134, 136, 165, 179
Cullen, M. 2, 5, 87, 125
Cultural shift 7, 36, 102; see also social
change

Danish Environmental Protection
Agency 5, 149–50
Daubert standard 113–14, 118
depression xii, 14, 83, 85, 90, 92, 97–9,
127
decision-making: judicial 13, 29, 30–1,
32–7, 42, 62, 91–2, 113, 114–19, 158;
medico-scientific 24, 28–9, 44, 62,
105, 109, 122–7, 128–30, 141–4;
neoliberal 41, 44, 154–6, 165–6;
regarding risk 37–8, 154–6, 165–6
delegitimation 19, 34, 140, 151, 174,
176
depoliticization 9, 140, 147–8, 170–1
deliberation 145–7, 150–1, 176, 180
Department of Industry and Resources,
Western Australia 66–7, 69, 72
Department of Health, South Australia
147
Department of Health, Western
Australia 16, 54, 63–4, 66–9, 145,
147, 161
deradicalization 120, 171–2
deservedness 2, 14, 39, 48, 129, 148,
176, 177
deviance 40, 122–7, 130–1, 134, 138
diagnosing MCS xiii, 1–5, 8, 11–12, 34,
48, 54–5, 70, 77–8, 81–4, 87, 91, 99,
104–6, 123–7, 167, 176
diagnostic process 26, 27, 34–5, 36,
103–6, 108, 111, 144
dichlorodiphenyl-trichloroethane
(DDT) 37

disability: 12, 49, 69–70, 114, 169, 179
disease: classification 26, 149;
difference with illness 24; see also
MCS
DNA profiling 29–31, 44, 104, 113, 144,
168–9, 178–9
Dumit, J. 11, 12, 34, 80, 86

economic efficiency 38–9, 105–6,
109–11, 155
electro-sensitivity 10, 176, 178
environmental health movement 7, 12,
34, 35, 43, 46–7, 65, 168, 171, 173–5
environmental illness see multiple
chemical sensitivity
environmental racism 154
environmentalism 7, 37, 56–8
epidemiology 12, 27, 59, 62, 103
epistemological conflict 24, 29–31, 44,
46–7, 80–4, 86–8, 100, 144, 146,
150–1, 166–9
epistemological change see paradigm
shift
equality 39, 44, 171–2, 179
ethics, 47, 129, 143–4
evidence-based medicine 104–5
experiential knowledge 34, 115, 119,
126, 133, 146, 151 156
expert witness xiii, 81–4, 121–2, 140–4,
146–7, 168

Floyd, H. 11, 12, 19, 84, 103, 114, 177,
180
Foucault, M. 32, 36, 41–3, 101–2, 104,
105 see also governmentality
Frank, A. 76
Frank, J. 92
Fudge, J. 170–1, 180

Garland, D. 40, 162, 164
gender 19, 153, 178
Germany: recognition of environmental
illnesses 5, 10, 149–50; research
infrastructure 28
Gibson, P. 75, 148, 172
governance 31: 176–7; of emergent
illness 44, 97, 106, 150–1, 157–8,
168–9, 176–7; of individuals 35–6;
41–2, 97, 138–9; of corporations 9,
37, 38, 43, 49, 50–2, 56–7, 67–8,
155–7, 158, 161–2, 177
governmentality 41–3, 95–7, 120, 138,
152, 170

greenwash 56–8
Gulf War Syndrome 4, 7, 18, 46, 114

Hanrahan v. Merck, Sharp And Dohme
    118
hegemony 42, 154, 171, 174
herbicide 6
Herman, D. 172–3
hospital policy 32, 38, 102, 147–8, 151
hysteria 3, 8, 13, 18, 19, 156, 166

iatrogenesis 8, 54, 81, 86
illness narratives 75–80, 99–100
Immigration Department of Western
    Australia 157, 161
incommensurability 11, 23, 102, 150, 168
Indigenous community *see* Aboriginal
    and Torres Strait Islanders
inequality 40–1, 65, 74, 92–3, 97,
    99–100, 147, 153–4, 162–3, 169, 171
injury management schemes 15, 80–1,
    106–10, 119, 146–7, 168, 170
insurance companies xiii, 8, 11, 13, 39,
    49, 54, 75, 82, 92–3, 169
insurance industry 13, 37, 39, 81, 168,
    177
insurance inspectors 19, 81, 86–7, 94–7
insurance as regulation 37, 47, 128,
    157–8
International Classification of Diseases
    (ICD) 5, 26, 149

Jasanoff, S. 25, 29, 71, 89, 117–18, 134,
    178, 180
junk science 5, 121

Kirby, M. 92, 113
knowledge and power 32–5, 44, 74,
    101–4, 112–13, 119, 132, 138–9,
    168–9
Kroll-Smith, S. 11, 12, 19, 84, 103, 114,
    167, 175, 180
Kuhn, T. 23, 26–7, 122, 124, 179

landmark decisions 1, 9, 15, 17, 32,
    118, 140, 158, 167, 171, 176
land rights *see* native title
Latour, B. 23–4, 27, 31, 111, 132
law: and social change 177; criminal
    versus civil 44, 89, 112, 160, 161;
    history 15, 33, 80, 112–13;
    relationship with medicine 35;
    relationship with science 29–31

lay knowledge/expertise 7, 35, 46,
    59–62, 74, 112, 115, 117–18, 119,
    155, 176
lead poisoning xii, 77
legal costs 9, 69, 89, 180
legal versus non-legal avenues 43,
    150–1, 170–3, 175–6
legal profession 12, 13, 33–5, 36,
    134–8, 167
legitimacy: of disease 2–3, 6, 12–14, 26,
    32, 34, 63–6, 70–2, 88, 111, 167–9,
    175–6; scientific legitimacy *see*
    credibility; corporate legitimacy 47,
    156
leukaemia 6–7, 59
litigation 8–9; chemical injury 69–72,
    114–18, 140–4, 150–1, 167–8, 174;
    asbestos 9, 72, 158–61, 169–71, 158;
    rights 42–3, 170–3
Lofstedt R. 66, 155–6
Love Canal 132
lung cancer caused by cigarettes 1, 4
Lynch, M. 30–1, 104, 111, 144, 168

Mabo decision 32–3
mad cow disease 155–6
Marshall, B. 28
*McKenzie, Johnson and Tiedemann v
    Harper and Ors T/as Allambie
    Pastoral Company* 115–16
media 4, 7, 35, 47, 63–6, 72–4, 156,
    175–6
medical profession xiii, 5, 20, 25–6,
    27–8, 31, 34, 120, 130–4, 138–9, 168
medical orthodoxy 5, 11, 12, 28, 44,
    121, 122, 133–4, 138, 168
medicine: relationship to science 25,
    117; relationship with law 35, 112,
    116–17, 140–4, 168
mesothelioma *see* asbestos-related
    diseases
miasma 27
moral behaviouralism 40, 42, 163–5
moral reasoning 28, 39, 40, 52, 92,
    97–8, 128–30, 155, 163–5
multiple chemical sensitivity: causal
    theories 2–5, 48–9, 52–5, 77, 81–4,
    122–7; in the developing world 3–4;
    diagnosis 3, 81–4, 122–7; history 2,
    178; litigation 69–72, 114–18, 140–4,
    150–1, 167–8, 174; onset 47–9, 76–7;
    prevalence 2; stigma 72, 78–9, 86–7,
    133, 149; symptoms 2, 48, 76–7

multinational corporations 40, 49, 56–8, 74, 92, 154, 159–61
Murphy, M. 8, 19
myalgic encephalomyelitis *see* chronic fatigue syndrome

native title 32–3, 42, 95–6, 171, 172
negligence 15–16, 62, 70, 87, 89, 109, 112–13, 142, 161, 177, 178
neoliberal 38–41, 44, 169–70, 177: logic 13, 41, 44, 154–6, 165–6, 169, 170; effects on insurance 39, 81, 147; deregulation 38–9, 155; governmentality 43–4, 152, 165–6, 170; privatization 38–9; versus welfare 38–40, 80–1, 162, 177
nuclear test veterans 6
no-fault scheme *see* workers compensation statutory scheme
normalization 41–3, 95–7, 138, 159, 166, 170
Northbridge 163, 165

objectivity 34, 60, 103, 105, 125–6, 127, 128
out-of-court settlement xii, 16, 69–72, 118
over-use syndrome *see* repetitive strain injury

paradigm: in science 23, 26–9, 122; of disease 26, 101–4, 124–5
paradigm shift 26–9, 30–1, 32–3; regarding MCS 11, 20–1, 122–3, 170
paranoia xii, 3, 7–8, 95, 178
Parsons, T. 34
Pearce, F. 19, 153, 155, 173
Perth 17
pesticides 7, 37
Poe, E.A. 178
poisoning xii, xiii, 78, 86
political economy 28, 38–40, 44, 81, 104, 119, 74, 152–3, 169, 171, 177
polarization 84, 140–5, 150–1
politicization 62–3, 74, 170–1, 173
Popper, K. 23
positivism 13, 22, 101–4, 116, 118, 119, 125–6
post-traumatic stress disorder 95
Povinelli, E. 172, 173
power: corporate 46, 99–100, 129, 159–61; juridical/legal 32–5, 112, 116–17,; medical 34–5, 101–4, 119,

132–4, 138–9
precautionary principle 37, 164–5, 169
probability 30, 36–7, 92, 109, 112–19, 123, 126, 167–9
problem-solving *see* decision-making
professions 25–6, 32, 33–5, 120, 130–6, 138, 168
psychosomatic xiii, 3, 13, 87–8, 95, 106, 144
pulmonary fibrosis *see* asbestos related diseases

quackery 5, 134, 138

racism 163
recognition 6, 12–13, 34, 42, 70–2, 80, 98–100, 101, 119–20, 139, 147–8, 149–51, 167, 173, 177
research politics 28, 29, 70, 131
responsibility 6, 38–41, 42, 44, 47, 55, 152–3, 159
repetitive strain injury 8–9, 95, 128
regulation: of industry 9, 37, 38, 43, 50–2, 56–7, 67–8, 155–7, 162, 177; by insurers 49, 158
rights 32–3, 42–3, 95–6, 170–3
risk: environmental 13, 35–6, 46–7, 52, 56, 65, 71, 157–8 professional 138–9, 166, occupational 8–9, 13, 46–7, 71, 74, 157–8; risky individuals 40, 162–5
risk society 35, 65, 153
risk-management 36–8, 53–4, 71, 124, 152–7, 162–3, 165–6, 167–70
Rose, N. 36, 38, 153, 162, 164
Royal Brisbane Hospital 147

safety crimes 155
scapegoating 131
sceptical reasoning 3, 12–13, 122–7, 128–30, 141–4, 165–6, 167–70
science: relationship with law 29–31; relationship with medicine 25, 117
scientific authority 24, 26, 30, 34 35, 52, 134, 136, 165, 179
scientific controversy 24, 29–31, 144, 146, 151, 166, 168–9
scientific method 23, 122–7
security 162–5
self-insurance 49, 158
self-surveillance *see* governmentality
Short, D. 171
Showalter, E. 3–4, 18

sick building syndrome 8, 19
sick role 34, 54, 71, 79, 86, 177
Snow, J. 27
social change 40, 74, 170–3 *see also* cultural shift
socio-economic disparities 19, 92–3, 130, 153–4, 179
solvents 16, 78, 91
sovereignty *see* power
standard of proof 101, 104, 112, 125, 146
stigma 72, 78–9, 86–7, 133, 149
stress 8, 14, 28, 75, 77, 83, 95, 111
surveillance 40–3, 81, 93–7, 99, 130, 138, 162, 164–5, 169, 177
sympathetic reasoning 3–5, 8–9, 12–14, 44, 120–7, 128–30, 135–9, 141–4
synergism 51

terrorism 164–5
threshold limit values 50–2, 61, 154–5
Tombs, S. 19, 153, 155, 173
toxic cabin air 17, 77
toxicity 2, 55, 60–1, 63, 74 103, 123–4, 153, 158, 162, 169, 178
toxicology xiii, 25, 54, 61, 117–18, 123, 125, 129, 141, 148

tort of negligence *see* negligence
town planning 11, 27, 59–60, 155, 177

uncertainty 10, 13–14, 36–8, 46–7, 52, 55–6, 89–92, 113–14, 123–7, 144, 168–9

volatile organic compounds 48, 61, 178

Wacquant, L. 38–40, 42, 43, 44
Waldman, L. 9, 19, 39, 72, 140, 170–1
welfare 38–40, 44, 80–1, 163, 171, 177
Wignall v. State of New South Wales 116
wind turbine syndrome 10, 176
Wittenoom 157, 158, 161
Woburn, Massachusetts 7, 59, 132
Woolgar, S. 23–4, 27, 31, 111, 132
World Health Organization 5, 26, 149
WorkCover *see* workers' compensation system
workers' compensation: statutory scheme 15–16, 20–1, 39, 41, 80–1, 86, 93, 99–100, 106–9, 142, 158, 168, 172, 178; common law 16, 88–9, 109–10; in Victoria 146

For Product Safety Concerns and Information please contact our EU
representative GPSR@taylorandfrancis.com
Taylor & Francis Verlag GmbH, Kaufingerstraße 24, 80331 München, Germany

www.ingramcontent.com/pod-product-compliance
Lightning Source LLC
Chambersburg PA
CBHW070419270326
41926CB00014B/2855

9 781138 241626